"Achieving Independence and Mastery in School (AIMS) is a well-designed, evidence-based intervention that targets the executive functioning challenges most commonly experienced by autistic youth. It offers clear, practical strategies grounded in neurodiversity-affirming principles, designed to build confidence and self-advocacy around school success. This manual is an essential resource for clinicians and educators supporting autistic students in therapeutic and academic environments."

Deanna Dow, PhD, *Founder & Clinical Director, Spectrum Psych LA*

"Autistic adolescents experience significant difficulties in school because of executive functioning problems. Achieving Independence and Mastery in Schools fills a critical gap by offering the rare program developed specifically for autistic youth and rigorously tested in multiple studies. AIMS allows clinicians to support parents and autistic children in working with each other, to learn, practice, and master practical skills that are proven to help autistic students in school."

Alex Holdaway, PhD, *Research Psychologist, Children's Hospital of Philadelphia*

"Providers can deliver the AIMS curriculum with fairly little preparation, and see results. This program was built to address the organizational challenges that so often prevent autistic young people from reaching their goals. There are very few programs that are this comprehensive and clear."

Susan W. White, Ph.D., *ABPP, Doddridge Saxon Chairholder in Clinical Psychology and Director of the Center for Youth Development and Intervention, the University of Alabama*

Improving Academic Executive Functioning for Autistic Middle Schoolers

Improving Academic Executive Functioning for Autistic Middle Schoolers is an intervention manual comprised of a structured curriculum for clinicians with the primary goal of providing support and strategies to autistic adolescents and their parents/caregivers.

Achieving Independence and Mastery in School (AIMS) is an 8-week intervention that targets the development and improvement of academic executive functioning skills (e.g., problem solving, organization, planning) to facilitate positive outcomes at home and at school. AIMS consists of weekly 90-minute sessions attended by both the caregiver and their autistic adolescent in the outpatient setting. The evidence-based, manualized curriculum includes content and handouts for each session that can be easily administered by clinicians.

This book is an integral purchase for clinicians who seek to fill the gap in academic support for autistic adolescents. Not only does it provide clinicians with direct instruction on strategies targeting executive functions that are challenging to autistic teens, but it also incorporates the caregiver as a coach who can continue supporting the teen in utilizing these essential skills as they transition to high school and the adult world. The views expressed by the authors do not necessarily reflect those of Cincinnati Children's Hospital.

Amie Duncan is a clinical psychologist in the Division of Behavioral Medicine and Clinical Psychology at Cincinnati Children's Hospital and a professor of Pediatrics at the University of Cincinnati College of Medicine. She has been working with autistic children, adolescents, and young adults for over 20 years.

Leanne Tamm is a clinical psychologist in the Division of Behavioral Medicine and Clinical Psychology at Cincinnati Children's Hospital and a professor of Pediatrics at the University of Cincinnati College of Medicine. She specializes in ADHD, autism spectrum disorder, reading disorders, and children born prematurely.

Improving Academic Executive Functioning for Autistic Middle Schoolers

The Achieving Independence and Mastery in School (AIMS) Clinician Workbook

Amie Duncan and Leanne Tamm

Routledge
Taylor & Francis Group

NEW YORK AND LONDON

Designed cover image: Getty Images

First published 2026
by Routledge
605 Third Avenue, New York, NY 10158

and by Routledge
4 Park Square, Milton Park, Abingdon, Oxon, OX14 4RN

Routledge is an imprint of the Taylor & Francis Group, an informa business

© 2026 Amie Duncan and Leanne Tamm

For Product Safety Concerns and Information please contact our EU representative GPSR@taylorandfrancis.com. Taylor & Francis Verlag GmbH, Kaufingerstraße 24, 80331 München, Germany.

Trademark notice: Product or corporate names may be trademarks or registered trademarks, and are used only for identification and explanation without intent to infringe.

ISBN: 978-1-032-81413-1 (hbk)
ISBN: 978-1-032-80548-1 (pbk)
ISBN: 978-1-003-50020-9 (ebk)

DOI: 10.4324/9781003500209

Typeset in Times New Roman
by SPi Technologies India Pvt Ltd (Straive)

AIMS

ACHIEVING INDEPENDENCE
and MASTERY in SCHOOL

Academic Success is for Everyone

The AIMS Intention manual and all related materials were developed by Amie Duncan, Ph.D. & Leanne Tamm, Ph.D.

This work was partially supported by grants from the Eunice Kennedy Shriver National Institute of Child Health and Human Development (NICHD, R21HD090334-01A1 and R01HD113534-01). The content is solely the responsibility of the authors and does not necessarily represent the official views of the U.S. National Institutes of Health (NIH).

This manual is dedicated to all of the individuals – including autistic teens and their families, teachers and other school personnel, and many, many AIMS Leaders, Research Coordinators, and graduate trainees – who have helped shape AIMS over the last 10 years! We are incredibly grateful for the time and energy that so many people devoted to this intervention.

Contents

Preface

The Achieving Independence and Mastery in School (AIMS) intervention has been iteratively developed over the last 11 years since 2014 through a series of research studies focused on its development, evaluation, and refinement. AIMS was inspired by the evidence-based groups targeting executive functions developed for youth with attention-deficit/hyperactivity disorder (ADHD) and the observation that autistic middle schoolers shared similar challenges. These include challenges such as forgetting to complete or losing homework assignments, difficulties planning for the completion of long-term projects and studying for tests, and problems keeping class materials organized. We pulled together a small group of caregivers and autistic middle schoolers and administered the academic success intervention developed for middle schoolers with ADHD. We soon realized that while the ADHD intervention was helpful, it would need to be modified because autistic youth learn differently than those with ADHD. We took what we know about how to teach autistic youth and developed AIMS with funding support from the Eunice Kennedy Shriver National Institute of Child Health and Human Development (NICHD; Grant #: R21HD090334-01A1). This also included focus groups with teens, parents, and teachers to learn more about the specific needs of autistic youth and how to best address their skills deficits with AIMS. We iteratively tested various AIMS versions in the outpatient clinic setting to optimize uptake. Results have been promising and with additional funding from the NICHD (Grant #: 1R01HD113534-01A1), we are now testing the clinic version of AIMS in a much larger sample of autistic middle schoolers and their caregivers. We also realized that intervention in the naturalistic middle-school setting where students actually need to use AIMS skills might also be helpful. With funding from the Institute of Education Sciences (Grant #: R305A200028), we conducted additional focus groups with school personnel (e.g., administrators, teachers, special education staff, intervention specialists) and developed a school-based version of AIMS to deliver in the classroom context. While the content is similar to the clinic version of AIMS, the school-based version includes additional time for practice and some new content relevant for the school context (e.g., locker organization, social-communication skills relevant for academics such as group projects). The current clinic version of the AIMS manual has been refined after each of the above studies with significant input and feedback from autistic adolescents and their caregivers and the therapists who facilitated the intervention.

Acknowledgments

We are incredibly grateful to our team of collaborators, colleagues, and stakeholders, in helping make AIMS what it is today. We started working together knowing that middle school is a key time when expectations for independence and initiative increase and supports fade, and that autistic youth struggle academically and with executive functioning. However, we could not have developed an intervention that makes a difference without key feedback from caregivers, autistic middle schoolers, school personnel, clinicians, and other experts in autism. Too often, researchers develop treatments without consideration for future dissemination and uptake in the real-world setting. We are proud to have developed AIMS with feedback from parents and teachers who experience and observe the academic challenges of autistic teens on a daily basis, and from collaborators with expertise in the best approach for teaching autistic teens, to optimize AIMS to be delivered successfully.

We are incredibly grateful for the invaluable feedback from our team of consultants and collaborators. This includes experts in ADHD and academic executive functioning interventions, Allison Zoromski, Alex Holdaway, Aaron Vaugh, and Josh Langberg; experts in autism and interventions, Lauren Kenworthy, Kara Hume, Cathy Pratt, Janine Stichter, and David Test; experts in focus group methodology, Lori Crosby, Rhyanne McDade, and Anna Hood; and experts in biostatistics, James Peugh and Constance Mara. Our team of clinical research coordinators who invested their time, energy, and creativity into AIMS has included Meera Patel, Ellen Kneeskern, Elizabeth Freehling, Elisabeth Thoma, Allison Birnschein, Nicole Estelle, Nico Bilinski, Chaya Fershtman, and Abigail Evans. We thank Jobi Yeung, Heather Lacey, Sydney Risley, Angela Combs, Jamie Patronick, Emily Beckmann, Katherine Garr, and Melissa Liddle for their role as AIMS interventionists and coaches. An extra shout out goes to Heather Lacey and Jobi Yeung who painstakingly formatted and edited earlier versions of the AIMS materials. We also especially thank Ellen Kneeskern and Meera Patel who creatively scripted many of the animated videos used in AIMS; we are also grateful to Loring Robbins at Bouncy Fruit Animations for producing those videos and to Tommy Sheehan at TommyInk for developing our brand, including our logo and website, www.aims-ef.com.

Lastly, we want to offer our gratitude to the autistic teens and their families who have participated in our research studies and provided invaluable feedback as we refined the AIMS intervention. Our hope is that this manual can help autistic middle schoolers develop skills in organization, planning, materials management, and effective studying that will promote academic achievement and increase the likelihood of a successful transition to high school and college.

Using the AIMS Intervention Manual

The Achieving Independence and Mastery in School (AIMS) intervention manual has the following components:

- **Overview of the AIMS Intervention** – This preliminary section discusses specific components of the AIMS intervention, including purpose, roles and responsibilities of AIMS Leaders, core components of AIMS, parent/caregiver involvement, time management, and teen engagement. The final subsection includes information on the research evidence of the AIMS intervention.
- **AIMS Session Overviews 1–8** – These chapters discuss the objectives and content of each of AIMS' 8 sessions in detail, including the content needed to facilitate the groups. The handouts for each session are included within each Session Overview.

  - Specifically, the chapter will begin by describing necessary supplies and handouts that are needed. The next subsection reviews important points that are meant to increase the likelihood of the Leader(s) being prepared to facilitate a smooth and efficient session. A Get Ready Checklist includes the activities that need to be completed prior to beginning the session. The content (e.g., activities, discussion, instruction) is described in detail for the Large Group, Teen Group and Caregiver Group. The session handouts for caregivers and/or teens are provided after the content. Any videos that need to be shown to caregivers and teens are available at the AIMS website (www.aims-ef.com).

Overview of the Achieving Independence and Mastery in School (AIMS) Intervention for Leaders

Welcome to AIMS, an outpatient-based program that encourages autistic teens to aim for academic success with the support of their parent/caregiver! This overview serves as an introduction to AIMS and should be reviewed carefully by AIMS Leaders prior to the delivery of AIMS sessions. This overview will also serve as a resource if AIMS Leaders have any questions after closely reviewing each individual session. Specifically, this overview provides tips and guidance on how to deliver AIMS, which targets core academic executive function (EF) difficulties through the use and implementation of strategies at home and in the classroom to increase teens' success and independence.

Content covered in this overview includes:

- Purpose of AIMS
- Roles and Responsibilities of Key Players
- Logistics
- Using the AIMS Manual
- Core Components of AIMS
- Parent/Caregiver Involvement
- Time Management
- Teen Engagement
- Leader Materials
- Research Evidence on the AIMS Intervention.

Purpose of AIMS

The purpose of AIMS is to improve the executive functions (EFs) that are key to achieving academic success in youth who struggle with solving problems, getting started on tasks, organizing materials, managing time, planning and prioritizing, and studying effectively.

Target Population

The AIMS intervention was specifically designed for middle school-aged autistic children/teens (5th–8th grades) with co-occurring executive function deficits, including those with a diagnosis of attention-deficit/hyperactivity disorder (ADHD). While teens are not required to have medical or educational diagnoses of these disorders, this program was developed to serve the unique intersection of teens who have challenges in the areas of social communication and executive functioning. The subset of teens best served by this program are those without an intellectual disability (i.e., should have a full scale IQ greater than a standard score of 70). Teens in AIMS should be able to read and write at a third-grade level.

While AIMS is an executive functioning intervention, it does not specifically target flexibility, which is critical for planning, solving problems, and setting goals. One such program that addresses this concern for teens with autism, ADHD, and other learning challenges is *Unstuck and On Target!: An Executive Function Curriculum to Improve Flexibility, Planning, and Organization*, 2nd edition (Cannon et al., 2021). Likewise, AIMS is not primarily a social communication intervention. Teens in need of social skills training may be better served by a school-based social skills intervention such as *The PEERS Curriculum for School-Based Professionals: Social Skills Training for Adolescents with Autism Spectrum Disorder* (Laugeson, 2013). Depending on teens' most immediate needs, it may be beneficial to target these skills prior to starting AIMS.

Setting

AIMS should be delivered in an outpatient setting at a convenient day/time to a group of 4–7 teens and their caregivers. Both caregivers and teens will first meet together in a large room, then caregivers and teens will meet separately in different rooms, and then they will reunite in a large room. Thus, 2 large rooms are needed to accommodate caregivers, teens, and Leaders.

Targeted Executive Functioning Skills

Adolescents who are a good fit for AIMS typically have EF challenges that impact their ability to get started on assignments, organize their materials, plan and prioritize upcoming assignments and tests, and study effectively for tests. AIMS is designed to teach teens, with support from their caregivers, to learn and master strategies that will increase academic independence and foster learning.

These key EFs include Getting Started, Organization, Planning, Prioritizing, and Working Memory, as defined below.

- **Getting Started**: Beginning tasks without procrastinating. This means starting on a task at a set time and not avoiding work by doing other things (e.g., texting, playing video games). With schoolwork, teens may have a good sense of what to do and how to do it, but may drag their feet or avoid starting a project or assignment.
- **Organization**: Maintaining structured systems to keep things in order. Teens need to organize their belongings (e.g., binders, backpacks) and also need to utilize systems for organizing materials on a consistent and regular basis.
- **Planning**: Establishing steps to reach a goal. For example, teens need to make a plan for what assignments need to be completed for homework each day. Planning also applies to breaking down the steps for writing an essay, completing a long-term assignment, or studying for a test.

- **Prioritizing**: Arranging steps in order of importance. This skill is particularly critical for teens who need to coordinate multiple deadlines, such as assignments, tests, long-term projects, as well as extracurricular activities (e.g., band practice, soccer, etc.), and preferred activities (e.g., go to the park, draw, play video games).
- **Working Memory**: Keeping things in mind while they are needed. For example, teens need to listen when teachers give assignments and then write down the accurate and important information. This is an important skill because on most school days, teens are required to listen to classroom lectures, pay attention to instructions when assignments are given, write assignments down, and remember information that they have studied when taking tests and quizzes. Without working memory, teens are unlikely to get things to "stick" in their brains so that they remember them in both the short-term and long-term.

Roles and Responsibilities of Key Players

AIMS Leaders

AIMS is designed to be delivered by two Leaders (Caregiver and Teen) with the support of a Teen Therapist.

- The Caregiver Leader will co-lead the Large Group content with the Teen Leader and be solely responsible for facilitating the Caregiver Group portion of each session.
  - The Caregiver Leader should have experience with autistic teens and an understanding of behavior management principles and group leadership (e.g., pacing of a session, engaging participants, assessing motivation, etc.). Ideally, the Leader would be a graduate-level mental health professional, such as a Clinical Psychologist, School Psychologist, or Clinical Social Worker with experience in facilitating caregiver groups and working with autistic teens.
- The Teen Leader will co-lead the Large Group content with the Caregiver Leader and be solely responsible for facilitating the Teen Group portion of each session.
  - The Teen Leader should have experience with autistic teens and an understanding of behavior management principles and group leadership. Ideally, the Leader would be a graduate-level mental health professional, such as a Clinical Psychologist, School Psychologist, or Clinical Social Worker with experience working with autistic teens.
  - If the Caregiver Leader is absent, the Teen Leader should fill in for them and facilitate the Caregiver Group session. The Teen Therapist (see below) can then facilitate the Teen Group session.

The AIMS Leaders are expected to deliver the majority of the intervention (i.e., should not miss more than two sessions) in order to maintain the integrity of the intervention. They should discuss what portions of the Large Group they will lead prior to the session so that they can adequately prepare. The Leaders should also identify who will be in charge of ensuring that all supplies are available for each session (e.g., Prize Menu and prizes, handouts, etc.) and are set up for each session. It is helpful to have a back-up Leader (e.g., a Teen Therapist) who has attended the AIMS sessions with both caregivers and teens and can fill in as needed.

AIMS Leaders can anticipate the following investment of time related to delivering AIMS:

- Deliver weekly 90-minute AIMS sessions
- Prep for AIMS a minimum of 20–30 minutes per week
- Debrief and/or attend a supervision meeting with other Leader and Teen Therapist(s) after each session
- Coordinate any absences with the AIMS Leader and Teen Therapists.

Teen Therapist

It is recommended that 1–2 Teen Therapists help facilitate the Teen Group alongside the Teen Leader.

- These individuals can be graduate students, post-doctoral fellows, or graduate-level mental health professionals and will primarily assist with providing feedback and guidance as teens practice various skills.
- The Teen Therapists may also serve as the AIMS Leader for the Teen Group session as needed so it is important that they understand how to facilitate the Teen Group.
- The Teen Therapist should assist with setting up each session (e.g., handouts, materials for AIMS binders, games/activities for Teen Group).

AIMS Teen Therapists can anticipate the following investment of time related to delivering AIMS:

- Deliver weekly 90-minute AIMS sessions
- Prep for AIMS a minimum of 15–20 minutes per week
- Debrief and/or attend a supervision meeting with other Leaders and Teen Therapist(s) after each session
- Coordinate any absences with the AIMS Leaders and other Teen Therapists.

Logistics

AIMS Training

Formal training on the AIMS intervention is optional but encouraged. The formal training includes attending a virtual training session, which will provide a broad overview of delivering the AIMS intervention (e.g., logistics, content). While this is not mandatory, it can be helpful for clinicians who want additional information above and beyond what the manual provides. See the AIMS website – www.aims-ef.com – for additional information.

Frequency and Timing of Sessions

AIMS consists of 8 sessions and is intended to be delivered weekly for 90 minutes to a group of 4–7 autistic teens and their caregivers.

Composition of Group

The group should include no more than 7 teens and their caregivers to ensure that all content can be covered, and caregivers and teens are able to discuss their progress on the weekly Real World Practice assignments each week. Multiple caregivers are welcome to attend, but typically one caregiver is sufficient.

Physical Facilities

A large room that can seat up to 24 individuals (Caregiver Leader, Teen Leader, Teen Therapist(s), caregiver and teen dyads or triads) is needed (see Figure 1). The room should have a whiteboard (or equivalent) and the capability to show videos (projector/screen or blank wall). It can be helpful to set up a camera to record sessions for supervision of clinicians (e.g., graduate students) or for research purposes (e.g., ensuring Leaders are adhering to the manual). A second room with the same supplies will also be needed each week to accommodate all teen participants and the Teen Leader and Teen Therapist(s).

For all parts of the session where caregivers and teens are together, the teens should sit at the table (on stable, non-swiveling chairs) and caregivers should sit behind them or diagonal from them (see Figure 1 for example room set-up). This will help establish the teen's role as an independent attendee with key responsibilities. Questions from the Leaders should be directed to teens first and then to caregivers – again to establish the role of the teen as taking initiative for their own participation. The Leaders should plan for snacks (e.g., chips, pretzels, bottled water) and/or meals (e.g., pizza) prior to the group if offering.

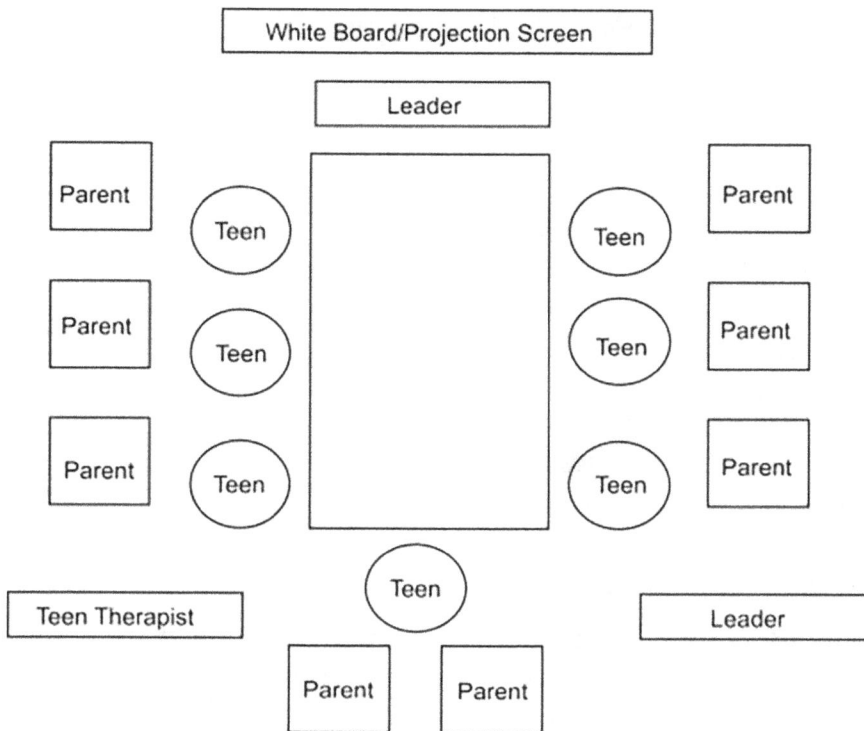

Figure 1 Example Room Configuration for AIMS Large Group.

Fidelity and Adherence

When delivering the AIMS intervention, AIMS Leaders should strive as much as possible to adhere to session structure and content in the AIMS Manual. It is important not to skip content and/or pick and choose content to cover. If an activity is optional, it will be clearly noted in the AIMS manual. To make adherence to the manual easier, the manual includes suggested language (depicted in *italics*) that AIMS Leaders should read verbatim.

Absences

When teens and caregivers are absent, AIMS Leaders should utilize the Review of the Real World Practice Assignment section and the Review of Material from Last Session section, which are at the beginning of each session, to catch the teens up on content that they missed. If time allows, Leaders can go over concepts in more detail or engage other teens to discuss the content that was taught in the previous session. It may be helpful to direct some of the review towards the teen who was absent, (e.g., "Alex wasn't here last session, so who can tell him what we learned about organization?"). AIMS Leaders can also use extra time at the beginning and end of a session to provide support to individual teens and/or caregivers who were absent. If needed, Leaders can meet with the teen and caregiver for 10–15 minutes before or after a group session to discuss any content that they missed.

Using the AIMS Manual

AIMS targets each of the five core EFs (planning, prioritizing, organization, working memory, and getting started) across 8 sessions.

AIMS Sessions

1. Understanding Executive Functioning and How it Impacts Academic Strengths and Challenges
2. ABCs of Problem Solving
3. Using a Problem Solving Plan
4. Developing a Homework System
5. Backpack and Binder Organization Systems
6. Using a Planner for Homework Assignments
7. Building Effective Study Strategies
8. Moving Forward After AIMS

Individualizing and Applying AIMS Content

While it is important to adhere to the manual, there are many opportunities to individualize AIMS content so that the material and strategies are applicable to teens. It is strongly recommended that AIMS Leaders have teens apply AIMS strategies to actual schoolwork and assignments (e.g., use school-wide planner to keep track of assignments). Other ways to individualize the AIMS intervention include identifying prizes that teens may be particularly motivated to earn (e.g., art supplies, fidget toys, specific candy or snacks). AIMS Leaders should discuss ideas about how to personalize and apply AIMS content and strategies with the team at weekly supervision meetings.

Structure of AIMS Sessions

Each AIMS session (after Session 1) is organized to include the following elements:

- Large Group (Caregivers and Teens)
    - Review Session Schedule
    - Review Group Rules and Prize Menu
    - Review Real World Practice Assignment
    - Review of Material from Last Session
    - Goals for Session
    - Instruction and Practice of New Content
- Break into separate Teen and Caregiver Groups for additional instruction, practice, and discussion
- Large Group (Caregivers and Teens)
    - Discussion of Teen Session Material
    - Take Home Points
    - Real World Practice Assignment
    - Trade in Tickets.

This structure provides consistency for teens and is also included on the <u>Session Schedule</u> handout that the teens receive at the beginning of each session. Further, exposing teens to core content in a consistent and frequent manner increases the likelihood of mastery (e.g., discussing Take Home Points, reviewing previous Real World Practice Assignments, etc.) despite possible difficulties with attention, comprehension, interest, and motivation.

Session Handouts

Specific session handouts should be passed out to caregivers and/or teens when indicated in the manual. On each handout, the session number, handout number, and page number are clearly stated in the footer for Leaders and for caregivers and teens to refer to and organize easily. Teens will have the opportunity to organize handouts in their AIMS binder and practice finding and filing handouts in each AIMS session.

Handouts and Supplies

At the beginning of each session in the manual, the **Session-Specific Supplies** section indicates additional materials needed for the current session. For example, for sessions involving a video, a projector connected to a computer will be needed.

The **General AIMS Supplies** section includes the materials needed for every session.

The **Handouts Needed** section includes all of the handouts that Leaders need to prepare and pass out to caregivers and/or teens in the session.

All of the handouts, supplies, and equipment listed will need to be prepared prior to the session by Leaders and/or the Teen Therapist(s). In particular, Leaders will need to ensure that they are refreshing the Prize Box regularly and adding in any prizes that may be motivating to the teens.

Important Points

The **Important Points** section at the beginning of each session highlights the key considerations and provides guidance and tips on how to prepare for each session. AIMS Leaders should read this section carefully because it helps Leaders effectively deliver the content to successfully implement AIMS as it is intended to be delivered.

Get Ready Checklists

The **Get Ready** section contains a checklist for the steps and tasks that need to be done to start each session. The **Get Ready** checklist should be used at the start of each session by AIMS Leaders to ensure they have all the materials needed for the session.

Leader Materials

The AIMS Leader Materials (see Appendix) are those materials that support the delivery of AIMS but are not necessarily handouts for teens. Leaders will utilize these materials during sessions (e.g., Prize Menu, Real World Practice Tracker) and there are optional materials that can be passed out to caregivers or teens (e.g., extra handouts). The Teen Leader and Teen Therapist(s) should familiarize themselves with the various games that can be played during sessions. The Leader Materials contains the following:

- Prize Menu
- Prize Menu Example
- Ticket Savings Tracker
- Real World Practice Tracker
- Blank handouts from AIMS Sessions (i.e., Problem Solving Plan, Long-Term Assignment Plan, Study Plan, 5 Ws, Star Graphic Organizer, Storyboard)
- AIMS Evaluation Form
- AIMS Trivia Game Instructions for Leaders (used in Session 8)
- AIMS Graduation Certificate
- Games for AIMS Sessions.

AIMS Website

Leaders are encouraged to use the AIMS website, www.aims-ef.com, to access materials and videos needed to facilitate AIMS sessions. Specifically, under the "About AIMS Outpatient" page, there is a button "FOR AIMS LEADERS" that provides access to the manual and all session handouts and videos. The AIMS Leaders section is password protected and the case sensitive password is "efaims". The password should not be shared with teens or caregivers. AIMS handouts and videos are available for teens, parents/caregivers, and teachers to access on the "RESOURCES FOR PARENTS & TEACHERS" page.

Core Components of AIMS

Session Schedule

At the beginning of each AIMS session, Leaders pass out a <u>Session Schedule</u> handout to teens that outlines the activities that they will be doing throughout the AIMS session. This schedule provides teens with a consistent structure and clear set of expectations around what will be completed each session. Leaders start each session by reviewing the <u>Session Schedule</u> handout for the session, which also encourages development of the EF skill of getting started (i.e., beginning tasks without procrastinating). Some teens will use the <u>Session Schedule</u> as a checklist and check off activities as they are completed during the session. Teens can choose to file their <u>Session Schedule</u> in their AIMS binder, or they can choose to recycle it.

Consistent Group Rules for AIMS

AIMS Leaders will have the teens and caregivers establish the rules of the group for all AIMS Sessions in Session 1. More details are provided in Session 1, but the list of group rules should include any rules the teens and caregivers generate and should also include the following:

- Follow instructions
- Participate
- Be respectful of one another
- No electronics or other unnecessary objects (e.g., a calculator) (unless being used for an activity)
- Raise your hand before speaking
- Wait for your turn to speak
- Stay on topic when answering questions
- Wait to have "off-topic conversations" until the end of AIMS.

The AIMS Rules Poster should be hung up at every session so that teens and caregivers can see them. It may be beneficial to have two copies of the AIMS Rules Poster so that it can be displayed in the Large Group room and the Teen Group room. Leaders should review the group rules as needed.

AIMS Binder

Each teen will receive a binder to organize their AIMS handouts. The AIMS binder is a *separate* binder from their school binder that contains materials for school subjects. The AIMS binder should be brought to each session so that teens have many opportunities to practice and receive feedback on the organization strategies taught in AIMS (e.g., filing handouts at the end of the session in the appropriate place, keeping track of Real World Practice Assignments, etc.). Caregivers can also provide support and assistance on how teens can remember to bring the binder and file the handouts during AIMS sessions. A folder will also be used to file Real World Practice assignments in a "To Do" pocket and a "Completed" pocket. AIMS Leaders should provide regular reminders to teens that they need their AIMS binders every session and should promote and reinforce teens actively using them during each session. These reminders for both bringing and utilizing the AIMS binder are included in each session. If remembering their AIMS binders is challenging for teens, Leaders may want to reward teens when they bring their AIMS binders to session. Caregivers will be given a folder to store all of their handouts.

Handouts

Handouts will be distributed throughout each session. They are used to further reinforce content that the AIMS Leaders have communicated verbally. Handouts are also used to provide additional instruction and practice around core AIMS concepts. Teens will learn how to file and find handouts using the footer at the bottom of each handout to reinforce their organization skills. Handouts should be filed behind their respective session divider in the order of the session and handout numbers. AIMS Leaders will remind teens at the end of each session to file handouts in the appropriate section of their AIMS binder. It can also be helpful for Leaders and Teen Therapists to assist teens with filing handouts throughout each session.

Problem Solving Plans

Problem Solving Plans are another AIMS tool designed to help teens understand strategies that will help them further develop their academic EF skills. Teens will use Problem Solving Plans to identify a solution to a specific academic problem and will be held accountable for implementing the solution with the support of their caregiver. Specifically, teens will create Problem Solving Plans in Sessions 3–8. All Problem Solving Plans will be filed in teens' AIMS binders in their Real World Practice folder.

Real World Practice Assignments

Real World Practice assignments allow the teens to practice skills that have been learned in AIMS sessions in the "real world." Real World Practice Assignments are an integral component of AIMS and promote content mastery and generalization to both the classroom and to home environments. The completion of Real World Practice Assignments allows teens to use and practice strategies to address EF challenges. Caregivers and teens will be encouraged to work on Real World Practice assignments together, and teens can earn a ticket (see Motivation System) if they complete it.

A Real World Practice Tracker (see Leader Materials) can also be a useful tool to keep track of completed assignments and motivate teens to complete them. This tracker may help some teens to realize that their Real World Practices are not turned in as consistently as they thought, and also allows them to compare their progress to other teens. Keep in mind that Leaders should record the completion of a Real World Practice for the session it was assigned, not returned (i.e., During Session 2, mark that the Session 1 Real World Practice was completed and returned). If teens are not consistently completing the Real World Practice assignment, it will be helpful to engage in some problem solving with both the teen and the caregiver so that the teen is able to practice the skills that they are learning in AIMS sessions.

Motivation System

AIMS Leaders will use an in-session motivation system to promote teen engagement and incentivize following rules and practicing newly learned skills and strategies. During AIMS, teens can earn tickets for appropriate behavior, which includes following the group rules, participating in session activities (e.g., practicing skills in-session, doing Real World Practice Assignments, etc.), and making positive and meaningful contributions to group discussions and activities.

The use of a ticket system provides Leaders with flexibility around which behaviors they want and need to target. For example, if targeting completion of Real World Practice assignments, the Leader may deliver extra tickets to teens who complete and then discuss their Real World Practice assignment in session. Likewise, if targeting teen behavior, the AIMS Leaders may provide tickets to teens who are paying attention, responding appropriately to questions, making comments that are relevant to the topic, or raising their hand to answer a question.

Teens should earn *at least* 3–5 tickets per session to maintain engagement. Teens who particularly struggle with participation and engagement should be rewarded for following group rules in order to engage them with the AIMS session and content.

When teens earn tickets during a session, they may keep them on the table in a pile or place them in their binder. If teens become distracted by their tickets, the AIMS Leaders may opt to put the teens' tickets in envelopes designated for each teen at the front of the room. This strategy chosen for managing earned tickets should be used for all teens in AIMS so that certain teens do not feel penalized for being distracted by their tickets.

It can be helpful to have Leaders and Teen Therapists provide tickets to teens throughout the session. For example, as one of the AIMS Leaders is reviewing the Real World Practice assignments with teens, the Teen Therapist can be providing the teens who completed the assignment with a ticket. The Leaders and Therapists may want to discuss who will be ticketing, what they will be ticketing in the Large Group and Teen Group, and when and how to label the behavior that teens are earning tickets for (e.g., "Thanks for raising your hand to answer" prior to giving a teen a ticket).

Teens can trade in their tickets at the end of each session or can save up their tickets to exchange for larger prizes at any point during AIMS. It is helpful to designate one of the Leaders or Teen Therapists to be in charge of trading in tickets each week. If teens opt to save tickets, record this on the ticket savings tracker (see Ticket Savings Tracker handout in Leader Materials) and collect all tickets at the end of each session. For teens who struggle with delaying gratification, it may be particularly beneficial for them to exchange tickets at the end of each session for smaller prizes or for the opportunity to do something (e.g., play a computer game) during any free time they may have at the end of the AIMS session.

Leaders should ensure that they have tickets to pass out prior to each session. Any ticket can be used, but it is helpful to use non-descript raffle tickets. Leaders and Teen Therapist(s) should work together to identify individualized prizes their teens may be motivated to earn. A prize box with a range of possible prizes including school supplies such as pens, pencil cases, folders, notebooks, binders, planners, art supplies, stickers, notebooks, healthy snacks or drinks, and games should be created prior to the first AIMS session. Additional prizes identified by the teens, Leaders, or Teen Therapist(s) as being motivating for teens can be added throughout the AIMS intervention. Teens also discuss their preferences for prizes during Session 1 so that the prizes can be individualized to increase teens' motivation to earn them. The majority of the prizes should be related to academics to encourage the teens to utilize the concepts discussed in the group. The value of the prizes should vary and 1 ticket should be equal to about 10-25 cents. It can be helpful to designate a specific person (e.g., Leader, Teen Therapist) to be in charge of purchasing prizes and monitoring the supply of prizes for each session.

Prize Menu

Leaders will develop a Prize Menu prior to Session 1 (see Leader Materials) to ensure the prizes will be available to be earned in the first AIMS session. The Prize Menu clearly indicates the prizes that can be earned and the number of tickets that each prize costs (e.g., 2 tickets = piece of candy, 6 tickets = 1 mechanical pencil, 10 tickets = small sketchpad, 20 tickets = pencil case, 30 tickets = set of colored pencils). Ideally, teens should be able to get a small prize (e.g., 3–5 tickets) each session, but teens should have to save up for larger prizes over the course of several sessions. The Prize Menu should be posted (e.g., near the AIMS Rules Poster) so that teens are aware of what prizes are available and how many tickets are needed to earn certain prizes. The Prize Menu should be modified whenever new prizes are added. For example, teens will brainstorm about prizes that they want to earn in Session 1, and these prizes may be added over the course of the intervention. See Figure 2 for an example of a completed Prize Menu.

Leaders may have to adjust the Prize Menu depending on how many tickets the teens in their group are earning each week. It is important that the number of tickets each teen earns drives the "prices" on the Prize Menu, and not the other way around. Specifically, Leaders should not find themselves holding back from rewarding a teen's contribution or behavior because they are concerned that they will achieve too many tickets by the end of the session. Rather, the Leaders should adjust the prices on the Prize Menu *at the next session* as needed so that teens are motivated in the short-term with tickets or small prizes and in the long-term with larger prizes. The function of the motivation system is to provide immediate rewards for appropriate behavior at each session and provide long-term rewards that will motivate teens to continue to do well.

AIMS	Prize Menu
Tickets	**Prize(s)**
2	small snack/treat eraser
6	mechanical pencil notepad
10	small sketchpad post-it notes

Figure 2 Example Prize Menu.

AIMS

	Ticket Savings Tracker							
Student	Session Number							
	1	2	3	4	5	6	7	8

Figure 3 Example Ticket Savings Tracker.

Ticket Savings Tracker

Tickets can be tracked by (1) having teens place them in their AIMS binder or on the table, (2) storing tickets in an envelope for each teen, or (3) utilizing a Ticket Savings Tracker (see Leader Materials). At the end of each session, teens should be included in the process of trading in and then recording their remaining tickets (if any) on the Ticket Savings Tracker.

Parent/Caregiver Involvement

Parents/caregivers are an integral component of the AIMS intervention. They will provide support to their teen as they work to apply the strategies that they learn in session to address their EF challenges. In the Caregiver Group session, all of the caregivers will have an opportunity to discuss how their teen is doing when applying a new solution to address problems in the areas of planning, prioritizing, organizing, getting started, and/or working memory. It will be critical for the Caregiver Leader to encourage participation from all caregivers and to create an atmosphere where caregivers feel that they can share concerns, ask questions, and provide feedback and support to others. A major goal of AIMS is to help the caregivers feel comfortable with using the Problem Solving Plan to identify solutions to problems or challenges their teen may be having and then implement specific strategies while also rewarding their teen for effort and progress.

Time Management

Each AIMS session is 90 minutes long and there are time estimates for each activity. Leaders should strive to adhere to these time estimates to ensure that all material is covered within each session. It will be important for Leaders to review the session content carefully prior to each session. Some suggestions for effectively managing time are included below:

Prepare for Each Session

Leaders should adequately prepare for each session so that they are familiar with the content and can deliver it efficiently and flexibly. Specifically, Leaders should review the Important Points for each session prior to reviewing the session in its entirety.

Read the Italicized Text Verbatim

Leaders are also encouraged to read the italicized text verbatim to ensure that all content is completely covered. While preparing for each session, Leaders can jot down notes about things that they may want to individualize when covering the content (e.g., EF strategies that may work for them).

Use Timers

A timer may be a helpful tool for Leaders to use to stay on track with time estimates and ensure all material is covered. Some ways to incorporate a timer include:

- Timers may be useful for keeping track of how much time is left for specific individual activities (e.g., teens organizing their binder) or group activities (e.g., creating a study card).
- Timers may be useful for keeping track of when the teens need to transition back to the Large Group.

Strategically Manage Participation from Teens

While it is important that teens are given the opportunity to participate and ask questions, Leaders may have to be strategic in determining how many teens can respond to questions before moving on. For example, when asking the teens questions or reviewing content, the Leader can alternate the teens called upon to provide answers.

Strategically Manage Talkative Teens and Caregivers

As teens and caregivers become more comfortable with the dynamic of the AIMS group, they may be more likely to chat with peers or provide lengthy (and sometimes off-topic) responses. Leaders should redirect talkative individuals to ensure that all material can be covered in AIMS sessions. Some helpful strategies include:

- Ask close-ended questions (e.g., yes/no questions) to decrease the likelihood of lengthy or tangential responses.
- Remind teens and caregivers at the beginning of the session that they need to remain on-topic in session. Leaders may need to give feedback to teens on the difference between on-topic and off-topic responses.
- Provide verbal praise and/or tickets to teens who do provide on-topic and appropriate responses.

- Allow for teens to chat or have free time during the last 2–3 minutes of the Teen Group or after they have chosen prizes in the Large Group.
- Encourage caregivers to ask off-topic questions with any remaining time at the end of the session. For example, a "parking lot" can be designated during the last 5 minutes of the Caregiver Group to allow caregivers to "park" any off-topic conversations. Alternatively, the Leader can encourage caregivers to discuss certain topics after the session is over (e.g., in the waiting room).

Teen Engagement

The Leaders should strive to be interactive and upbeat during sessions in order to engage teens and caregivers in the material. It will also be important for Leaders to be mindful of individual teens' challenges and how this may affect their ability to learn, master, and generalize the strategies taught in AIMS.

Use Humor

Leaders should use humor to aid in the explanation of the content and maintain engagement. It can be helpful to use funny personal stories (e.g., how you solved a problem using the ABCs of Problem Solving) or discuss relevant examples from television shows, movies, etc.

Personalize Material

Leaders should provide simple and concrete examples from the real world, including their own experiences (e.g., an EF that is challenging for them, how they use their planner to prioritize what needs to be done each day). Leaders are encouraged to get to know the teens and pull them in when discussing topics that relate to the interests that they have mentioned over the course of the group (e.g., a teen who is in a drama club probably knows some memory strategies for memorizing their script).

Adapt to Ensure Comprehension of Concepts

Leaders should pay close attention to the teens and adapt as needed to ensure that they are understanding and applying the material. If it is clear that many of the teens are not paying attention, Leaders should feel free to stop and re-energize the teens by playing a quick game (see Leader Materials) or taking a break to stretch or move around. If it is clear that teens are not comprehending a concept, Leaders are encouraged to spend additional time reviewing and practicing the concept.

Use Games or Activities

Games and brief activities that can be helpful for engaging and motivating teens during AIMS sessions include the following:

- Board games such as Connect Four, Checkers, and Jenga or card games such as Uno and Spoons may be fun for the teens to play during the Teen Group (as time allows) and can typically be played in 5–10 minutes.

- Minute-to-Win-It Games: These games require minimal supplies, take only a few minutes to play, and allow for discussion of how executive functioning skills are used (see Leader Materials). The games may be implemented to briefly re-engage teens with the AIMS material. The Minute-to-Win-It games include (1) Stack Attack, (2) Penny Stack, and (3) Suck it Up. When playing Minute-to-Win-It games, make sure teens follow the rules, and praise any observed skills or behaviors that relate to the 5 EFs of getting started, organization, planning, prioritizing, and working memory.

Guidelines to support the inclusion of these games are listed below:

- Tell teens that they are going to play a game requiring them to use their EF skills of getting started, organization, planning, prioritizing, and working memory.
- Pass out materials and the instructions handout (see Leader Materials) to teens and have them read the rules.
- Have the teens compete in the game.
- Discuss each EF as it relates to the game. Group leaders may praise the teens who demonstrated strong academic EFs during the task.

Leader Materials

This appendix section of the manual provides handouts and resources for Leaders that will likely be helpful as they deliver the AIMS intervention. Specifically, this section includes blank copies of key handouts used in the intervention (e.g., Problem Solving Plan). This section also includes handouts and activities for the final AIMS session (e.g., AIMS Trivia game instructions, AIMS Graduation Certificate). Leader Materials include the following:

- Prize Menu
- Prize Menu Example
- Ticket Savings Tracker
- Real World Practice Tracker
- Blank handouts from AIMS Sessions

  - Problem Solving Plan
  - Long-term Assignment Plan
  - Study Plan
  - 5 Ws
  - Star Graphic Organizer
  - Plot Diagram
  - Storyboard

- AIMS Evaluation Form – can be used to get feedback from teens and caregivers at the end of AIMS
- AIMS Trivia Game Instructions for Leaders
- AIMS Graduation Certificate
- Games for AIMS sessions

  - Stack Attack
  - Penny Stack
  - Suck it Up.

Research Evidence on the AIMS Intervention

Development of the clinic and school-based versions of AIMS included focus group and a review of IEPs. We found that parents and youth identified academic executive functions and learning behaviors as an area requiring intervention and that few school-based interventions targeting these behaviors are available. We also showed that learning behaviors and performance on a real-world planning measure (Weekly Calendar Planning Activity) are impaired in autistic youth and require intervention (Duncan et al., 2023; Duncan et al., 2025; Tamm et al., 2020a; Tamm et al., 2024a).

An initial trial of the AIMS clinic intervention with 3 families showed that although parents and youth with ASD benefited from the intervention designed for youth with ADHD (e.g., gains in academic EF skills), significant work was needed to adapt the intervention for the ASD population (e.g., youth with ASD reported not fully understanding EF concepts, parents reported that youth struggled with implementing skills) (Tamm et al., 2020a).

After iterative improvements, including adding evidence-based strategies to promote learning in autistic teens (e.g., use of visual supports, video models, peer support, etc.), a trial of AIMS with 21 families showed that we could feasibly deliver AIMS in the outpatient setting with high satisfaction ratings from caregivers and youth. We also showed that AIMS improved academic executive functions, particularly organization and materials management, as rated by parents and classroom teachers (Tamm et al., 2020b).

Refining AIMS for use in the classroom setting and school context was also successful. Results of the development trial in a specialized school for autism suggest high feasibility, youth satisfaction, and improved EF skills and academic behaviors by parent and teacher report. A pilot study comparing youth randomized to AIMS versus a waitlist control group showed that individuals randomized to AIMS improved from baseline to post on academic executive functioning outcome and academic functioning measures (Tamm et al., 2023; Tamm et al., 2024b).

Session Overviews

Session 1   Understanding Executive Functioning and How it Impacts Academic Strengths and Challenges

Session 1 Preparation

Session Specific Supplies

- Nametags
- AIMS binder for each teen with the following materials:

  - 8 numbered dividers
  - Real World Practice 2-pocket folder – left side should be labeled "To Do" and the right side should be labeled "Completed"

- AIMS folder for each caregiver
- Sharpie markers
- Projector/computer for video
- Mt. Executive Function video (available at www.aims-ef.com)

General AIMS Supplies

- AIMS Rules Poster
- Prize Menu and Prize Box
- Ticket Tracker and tickets
- Real World Practice Tracker
- Whiteboard and dry erase markers
- Large Post-It easel pad and markers (for AIMS Rules Poster)
- Pens/Pencils
- Game/Activity for Teen Group

Handouts Needed

- Large Group

  - Session 1 Schedule
  - Academic Strengths and Difficulties Survey
  - EF Skills Diagram
  - Overview of AIMS Sessions
  - Goals of AIMS

DOI: 10.4324/9781003500209-2

- Teen Group
  - EF Self-Assessment
- Caregiver Group
  - Understanding How to Tackle EF Challenges
  - EF Self-Assessment
- Large Group
  - Real World Practice – Session 1

Important Points for Session 1

- **Set-Up**
  - Leaders should have caregivers sit behind or slightly diagonally from the teens. This encourages the teens to take the lead in responding to questions and participating without relying on their parents. If the room and the table is large enough, caregivers can sit next to teens, but Leaders should strongly encourage teens to take the lead in responding to questions and engaging in discussions.
  - Leaders can provide a snack for teens/caregivers to eat at the beginning of the session. It is helpful to set the rule of 1 snack/drink per person and Leaders may want to help teens/caregivers get rid of any trash after they finish eating.
  - Leaders should wear nametags and should also have teens and caregivers fill out and then wear nametags when they enter the Large Group session.
  - It may be helpful for Leaders to set up a way to communicate with one another when they split into the separate teen and caregiver groups (e.g., when teens should rejoin the caregiver group).

- **General Session Notes**
  - Leaders should feel free to engage in small talk with caregivers and teens while they are arriving (e.g., how their week is going, the weather, etc.).
  - Introductions should be brief to prioritize finishing the session as Leaders will get to know the teens and caregivers over the course of the intervention.
  - While many of the questions are directed to teens, the Leader can also ask caregivers to provide their thoughts/perspectives – especially if the teens are struggling to come up with responses.
  - When asking questions, Leaders can also use polling to encourage teens and caregivers to respond (e.g., "Raise your hand if you sometimes have challenges with organizing your materials."). Easy polling methods include raising hands or thumbs up/thumbs down.
  - Leaders should NOT pass out tickets until the motivation system has been introduced.
  - Reward teens who participate by passing out tickets when they participate in session (e.g., answer questions from the video, discuss why the EFs are a strength or challenge for them, discuss results of their EF Self-Assessment, etc.).
  - At points, this session is highly didactic. Encourage active participation and regularly assess comprehension of both teens and their caregivers (e.g., "What questions do you have?").

- All Leaders should assist teens with filing and organizing handouts in their AIMS binder as needed. Leaders may need to demonstrate how to file handouts (e.g., which divider to use, how to reference the footers at the bottom of each handout) and can eventually fade back support by verbally reminding teens or subtly prompting them (e.g., pointing to binder or handout as a reminder to file it, touching or tapping the Real World Practice folder).
- During the caregiver group, Leaders should clearly state that this is the time for parents/caregivers to openly ask questions, problem solve, and discuss their thoughts and concerns each week.
- At the end of the session, Leaders are encouraged to utilize the Ticket Tracker (see Leader Materials) to track tickets, or should encourage teens to store their tickets in a safe place (e.g., pocket of their AIMS binder).

  - It can be helpful to designate the same Leader each week to use the Ticket Tracker and give out prizes to teens.

- **Prize Menu**

  - The Prize Menu should be developed according to the instructions in the Overview of the AIMS Intervention for Leaders earlier in this manual. Leaders can also refer to the Prize Menu Example (see Leader Materials).
  - Leaders should have initial prizes (e.g., candy, snacks, fidget toys, pencils, erasers, etc.) that are listed on the Prize Menu before the first session so that teens will be able to redeem tickets for prizes in the first session.
  - It is important to get an understanding of additional prizes that the teens may want to earn for future sessions. Leaders will ask the teens directly, but may also want to follow-up with them about this in the teen group and also take note of comments that teens make about things that they like (e.g., if several teens like to draw, possible prizes could be colored pencils or a sketch pad).

- **Real World Practice Assignment**

  - It is important not to refer to Real World Practice Assignments as homework in order to distinguish the AIMS intervention from classes at school.

Get Ready Checklist for Leaders

❑ Prep the handouts to be passed out
❑ Prep the AIMS binders for teens
❑ Prep the AIMS folders for parents/caregivers
❑ Hang up Prize Menu
❑ Check that Prize Box has range of several prizes to be earned
❑ Hang up Real World Practice Tracker (if used)
❑ Hang up Ticket Tracker (if used)
❑ Set up projector and/or computer
❑ Open the Mt. Executive Functioning video
❑ Get any supplies for the games to be played in the Teen Group

Session 1 Manual

Large Group – Caregivers and Teens (60 mins)

- **Introduction to AIMS (4 mins)**

  - Leaders should encourage caregivers and teens to fill out and then wear name tags.
  - Leaders should briefly introduce themselves (e.g., name, their role for the AIMS group) and can also give additional information about themselves during the Getting to Know You Activity.
  - *This group is called AIMS – which stands for Achieving Independence and Mastery in School. The goal of this group is to teach you how to build your problem solving, organization, planning and prioritizing, and homework and study skills so that you can do better at school. Another goal is to help you become more independent with homework and studying so that you have more free time to do what you want! We will talk more about the goals of AIMS later in today's session.*
  - Leader should pass out binders that already contain the dividers and the Real World Practice folder to the teens. Leaders should pass out a folder to parents/caregivers so that they can store and organize their handouts.
  - *All teens are receiving a binder that will be used for AIMS materials only and you should bring it to each AIMS session. You have 8 dividers in your binder, which represent the 8 AIMS sessions. We will discuss the folder that is in your AIMS binder at the end of today's session. You should write your name on the binder using a pen or marker so that it can be returned to you if you misplace it.*
  - *All caregivers are receiving a folder that will be used for storing and organizing AIMS handouts.*
  - *We will pass out handouts throughout each session. At the bottom of each handout, it clearly indicates the Session Number, Handout Number, and Page Number, which will help you to organize each handout in order in your AIMS binder or folder.*

- **Session Schedule (3 mins)**

  - Pass out and refer to <u>Session 1 Schedule</u> handout.
  - *Let's look at your first handout for Session 1, which is a schedule of everything we will be doing during our AIMS session so that you know what to expect. The schedule for each session will be similar in that we will usually learn a new skill, practice the newly learned skill, discuss the "take home points", and then go over the Real World Practice Assignment that will be due at the next session. You can cross off activities on your schedule as we complete them.*
  - *Each session we will start as a large group, then break into separate caregiver and teen groups, and then reunite at the end of the session in our large group.*
  - *The caregiver group provides an opportunity for caregivers to openly ask questions and discuss any issues related to AIMS content, challenges and successes at school, and the weekly Real World Practice assignments.*

- *The teen group will allow for teens to get additional practice with AIMS content while also getting to know one another and playing some fun games. Teens will also be able to openly discuss their experiences and ask any questions.*
- Briefly go over the activities that are listed on the Session 1 Schedule handout.

- **Getting to Know One Another (8 mins)**

  - *Let's spend a few minutes getting to know one another since we will be working together in AIMS sessions for the next 8 weeks.*
  - Leaders may want to write the questions that teens and caregivers will be answering on a whiteboard as they introduce themselves.
  - Leaders can also answer the questions as a way to model how to do introductions (e.g., the Leaders could answer the same questions that the caregivers answer).
  - *Let's start with each teen introducing themselves by saying the following*:

    - *Name*
    - *School*
    - *Grade in School*
    - *Favorite food or restaurant*
    - *Favorite thing to do in your spare time.*

  - *Now let's have each caregiver introduce themselves by saying the following*:

    - *Name*
    - *Favorite food or restaurant*
    - *Favorite things to do in your spare time*
    - *Favorite thing about your teen.*

- **Rules for AIMS (5 mins)**

  - *Let's brainstorm some rules or guidelines for our AIMS sessions. These rules should be similar to the ones that you follow at school. What are some rules that we should have?*

  - Have teens take the lead on generating a list of rules for AIMS sessions and then write their responses on a large Post-It.

  - After 2–3 minutes of discussion, Leaders should write down the following rules if they have not yet been mentioned by the teens or caregivers:

    - Follow instructions
    - Participate
    - Be respectful of one another
    - No electronics or other unnecessary items (e.g., a calculator) unless being used for an AIMS activity
    - Raise your hand and wait to speak
    - Stay on topic.

- *We will hang up our AIMS Rules Poster each week so that you know what rules are important to follow during each session.*

- **Reward System (5 mins)**

  - *Now that we have come up with our group rules for AIMS, Leaders will be passing out tickets when the rules are followed or when you participate in each AIMS session by answering questions. These tickets can then be traded in for prizes from the Prize Box at the end of each session. You can also save up your tickets from multiple sessions to trade them in for larger prizes.*
  - Refer to Prize Menu that has already been developed by the Leaders. This Prize Menu can be hung up or displayed next to the Prize Box.
  - *This is our initial Prize Menu.*

    - Show teens and caregivers the Prize Menu that will be hung up/displayed at each session and states how many tickets are needed to earn various prizes from the Prize Box. Leaders should also show teens the prizes in the Prize Box so that they know what they can earn for the first session.

  - *We are just starting off with this Prize Menu, and in the future we may add new prizes or adjust the number of tickets as you get better at following the group rules, participating in sessions, and using AIMS strategies.*
  - Ask: *What rewards or prizes would you like to work towards earning during AIMS sessions?*

    - Leaders should write down any prizes that the teens would like to earn (e.g., candy, snacks, drinks, school supplies, art supplies, fidget toys, etc.).

  - *We will try to add some of the prizes you requested to the Prize Menu so that you will be more motivated to work towards them by participating in sessions and also learning and applying AIMS strategies! I will start passing out tickets now for following the rules and participating in AIMS sessions!*

- **Goals for Session 1 (2 mins)**

  - *Our goals for today are the following*:

    - *Introduce you to AIMS by discussing group rules and going over the goals of AIMS.*
    - *Discuss common challenges that middle schoolers experience with schoolwork, homework, and studying for tests.*
    - *Learn about the 5 executive functions.*
    - *Think about how you use your 5 executive functions at school.*
    - *Complete a self-assessment of your executive function strengths and challenges.*

- **Teens' Perspectives on School and Homework (7 mins)**

  - *In our AIMS sessions, we will be teaching you strategies to help make schoolwork and homework easier. But first, we want to learn more about your thoughts and feelings on school and homework.*

- Ask the teens the following questions and briefly discuss responses. Leaders should poll teens (e.g., raise hands, thumbs up/thumbs down) and then choose 2–3 teens to get additional information from.

  - *Do you feel like you spend too much time doing homework?*
  - *Do you feel like you have trouble keeping your backpack or other materials for school organized? For example, do you sometimes lose, forget, or misplace things?*
  - *Do you feel like you spend too much time studying?*
  - *Do you feel like you don't have enough time to do the activities you want to do because you have to do schoolwork?*
  - *Do you feel like you are not performing as well as you would like in school?*
  - *Do you feel like your parents are often nagging you about school and homework?*
  - *Do you feel like your parents are having to remind or help you with school and homework?*

- If time allows, Leaders can also have caregivers share their thoughts and opinions, but they will have an opportunity to discuss this topic more in the separate Caregiver Group.

- **Identifying Academic Strengths and Challenges (6 mins)**

  - Pass out and refer to <u>Academic Strengths and Difficulties Survey</u> handout.
  - *With your parent or caregiver, take 2–3 minutes to complete this handout by checking whether the specific skills related to school and homework are strengths or challenges for you. It is unlikely that everything will be a strength or that everything will be a challenge. All of us have things that we are good at and things that are hard for us. It is also OK if you disagree with your parent or caregiver and it can be helpful to be open to discussing why you differ in opinion about your academic strengths and challenges.*
  - Leaders may want to set a timer for this activity.
  - *Let's have each teen share one strength and one challenge with the group.*

    - Ask each teen to volunteer one strength and one challenge that they identified and briefly discuss as needed.

- **What is EF? (9 mins)**

  - *As we just discussed, many of us have some challenges in school. However, the good news is that the main goal of this AIMS group is to teach you the strategies and tools that will make it easier to do homework, organize your school materials, and study for tests. During AIMS sessions we will learn and practice executive functioning skills such as organization, working memory, getting started, planning, and prioritizing. We are going to watch a video that goes over some of the most important executive functioning (or EF for short) skills that lead to success at home and at school.*
  - Show teens the Mt. Executive Function video (6m 19s).

    - NOTE: If the teens are having difficulty paying attention or remaining engaged, the video can be paused and the Leader can ask questions (see below) to increase the likelihood that they will understand the concepts.

- Ask the following questions (if needed) to assess teens' understanding of the concepts presented in the video:

  - *Have you ever had any trouble using your EFs to get tasks done?*
  - *What is an example of an EF skill?*
  - *What strategies were helpful for Emma?*

- *As you saw in the video, the 5 EF skills are really important to make sure that you are as successful as possible at home and school.*

- **EF Skills at School and Home (6 mins)**

  - Pass out and refer to <u>EF Skills Diagram</u> handout.
  - *Let's learn more about the 5 EF skills. We will read through the definition of each EF together and then discuss how you use each of the EFs at school or for homework and studying.*
  - Have a teen read the definition for each of the 5 EFs on the handout. Ask the following questions and briefly discuss.

    - *How do you use the EF of Planning at school or for homework and studying?*

      - Possible answer: writing down daily homework assignments in a planner.

    - *How do you use the EF of Prioritizing at school or for homework and studying?*

      - Possible answer: figuring out what homework assignments are most important each day.

    - *How do you use the EF of Organization at school or for homework and studying?*

      - Possible answer: filing handouts from each class in the appropriate folder so that you always know where they are.

    - *How do you use the EF of Working Memory at school or for homework and studying?*

      - Possible answer: remembering to grab the items you need for each class so that you are prepared.

    - *How do you use the EF of Getting Started at school or for homework and studying?*

      - Possible answer: using extra time in classes to get started on homework instead of doing other things.

  - *During AIMS sessions, we will teach you specific strategies to help with all 5 EFs that can help you to be much more successful at school and when doing homework or studying for tests at home – which can then lead to you having more free time to do the things that you want to do!*

- **What is AIMS? (5 mins)**

  - Pass out and refer to <u>Overview of AIMS Sessions</u> handout.

- *AIMS consists of 8 sessions that will focus on teaching you strategies and tools to help with organizing your backpack, organizing your classroom materials in a binder, creating a distraction free homework space, writing down assignments in a planner, prioritizing your daily assignments, and identifying effective study strategies to help you get better grades. This handout shows you what we will be focusing on during each AIMS session.*

- Pass out and refer to <u>Goals of AIMS</u> handout.

  - *As you will see from the handout, one of the major goals of AIMS is to build your EF skills.*
  - Have teens and caregivers take turns reading each of the goals from the <u>Goals of AIMS</u> handout and discuss as needed:

- Ask: *Any questions about the goals we will be targeting in AIMS?*
- *In each AIMS session, we will break into separate teen and caregiver groups to practice some skills and then we will come back together about 10 minutes before the end of the group to discuss our "take home points" and go over the Real World Practice assignment.*
- Leaders should have caregivers and teens split into separate groups.

  - Remind teens to file handouts in their AIMS binder and provide assistance as needed.

Teen Group (20 mins)

- **EF Strengths and Challenges (20 mins)**

  - Leaders can briefly go over the activities that are listed on the <u>Session 1 Schedule</u> handout for the Teen Group. State that teens can cross off activities on the schedule as they are completed.
  - Leaders may want to review the AIMS Rules Poster with the teens and remind them that they can earn tickets for following the rules, answering questions, and participating in activities.
  - *While some EF skills may be a strength and come easy to you, most of us have challenges with at least some EF skills. The good news is that we can learn strategies to increase our EF skills so that we can be more successful at school and home.*

    - NOTE: It may be helpful for the Leader to state what EF is hard for them and a strategy that they use to be successful at home or work (e.g., if working memory is challenging, strategies such as putting a sticky note on a backpack as a reminder to bring a lunchbox and water bottle to work may be helpful).

  - *You are going to fill out a questionnaire that will help you understand your EF strengths and your EF challenges. Please answer each question honestly because this will help us to understand what strategies will help you to be successful at school and at home.*
  - Pass out and refer to the <u>EF Self-Assessment</u> handout.
  - Briefly go over the directions and scoring instructions.
  - Leaders should read each question aloud and have teens answer each question. After the teens have completed the assessment, they should complete the scoring page.

- Provide assistance as needed with understanding the specific questions or scoring of the questionnaire.
- Leaders may want to walk around the room to help teens out as needed and keep them on task.

- Ask the following questions for each of the 5 EFs and have teens respond by raising their hands or using thumbs up/thumbs down:

  - *Is [Planning/Prioritizing, Organization, Working Memory, Getting Started] easy or a personal strength for you?*

    - Follow up by asking 1–2 teens: *Why is this a personal strength for you?*

  - *Is [Planning/Prioritizing, Organization, Working Memory, Getting Started] hard or a personal challenge for you?*

    - Follow up by asking 1–2 teens: *Why is this a challenge for you?*

- Discuss the following questions as a large group:

  - *How do you think your EF strengths help you at school with completing assignments, getting homework done, and getting good grades on tests and quizzes?*
  - *How do you think your EF challenges affect your ability to complete assignments, get homework done, and get good grades on tests and quizzes?*

- *When we rejoin your caregivers in the large group, we will have each of you share 1 EF strength and 1 EF challenge.*
- Remind teens to file handouts in their AIMS binder and provide assistance as needed.
- If time allows, Leaders can allow the teens to play a short game that utilizes EF skills. Possible games to play include Stack Attack, Penny Stack, Connect 4, or Uno (see Overview of the AIMS Intervention for additional information including instructions and materials needed for games).

  - Leaders may want to set a timer for this activity.

- The teens should rejoin their caregivers for the reunification with the Large Group.

Caregiver Group (20 mins)

- **Psychoeducation on EF challenges in Autistic Teens (8 mins)**

  - Pass out and refer to <u>Understanding How to Tackle EF Challenges</u> handout.
  - *We are going to talk about how to tackle EF challenges in your teen. It may be helpful to take some notes during this discussion.*
  - *During the caregiver group each week, we will review some key concepts related to EF and strategies to address EF challenges. It is also an opportunity for you to ask questions and discuss your thoughts and experiences.*
  - *As we discussed in the large group, EF includes skills such as planning, prioritizing, organization, working memory, and getting started on tasks. EF skills help us to decide what*

activities or tasks we will pay attention to and how we choose to start, stick with, and finish. These skills are critical to success not only in school but also in everyday life, but they are not directly taught to teens.

- *EF challenges are due to differences in your teen's brain and your teen is NOT purposely choosing not to plan, prioritize, organize, start, stick with, or finish tasks. Many caregivers often report that they feel like they are their teen's EF and that they are often the ones doing things or reminding their teens about school and homework.*
- *For example, it is easy to see how EF difficulties would affect a teen's ability to do their homework because they may struggle with any of the following:*

  - *Writing assignments down in a planner*
  - *Knowing what tests, quizzes, or long-term assignments need to be studied for or worked on*
  - *Bringing the correct materials home*
  - *Prioritizing homework assignments that need to be completed*
  - *Deciding to start their homework instead of doing other preferred activities*
  - *Persevering with homework assignments*
  - *Asking for help with difficult assignments*
  - *Coming back to a homework assignment after taking a break or eating dinner*
  - *Knowing how much time they should be spending on assignments or studying*
  - *Finishing homework.*

- Check-in: *I want to stop for a moment and check in to see what your reactions or thoughts are to this information.*

  - Briefly discuss any questions or comments.
  - Leaders should also be aware of the time and can let caregivers know that they may have time to discuss additional questions/comments at the end of the session or could discuss things with one another after the session is over.

- *It is also important to consider your middle schooler's developmental stage and their own profile of strengths and difficulties that may impact or exacerbate how their EF challenges affect their schoolwork. Possible issues that may impact your middle schooler include:*

  - *Increased expectations and demands: The transition from elementary school to high school often involves a significant increase in demands for teens. For example, middle school students will have demands such as switching classes, managing long-term assignments, trying to understand the expectations of multiple teachers, managing more homework, and organizing materials using a locker.*
  - *Other competing demands outside of school: Teens may also need to balance other competing demands such as extracurricular activities, chores, or household responsibilities.*
  - *Motivation: While some teens are motivated to complete homework and study, many teens are not and would prefer to engage in their preferred interests or activities.*
  - *Other challenges: Many teens may also have challenges including managing emotions such as anxiety or frustration, fine or gross motor difficulties, social-communication issues such as perspective taking, asking for help from others, or interacting with peers during group projects.*

- Ask and briefly discuss caregiver responses: *What are some challenges or issues that affect your teen's ability to do well in school or work on their homework assignments?*
- *A goal of AIMS is to teach the teens effective strategies to address EF challenges related to school and homework, while also considering their individual profile of strengths and challenges. These strategies can be used in middle school, but also in high school, college, and in the workplace.*

- **Role of Caregivers in Building Independence (7 mins)**

  - *Another factor that has a strong influence on a teen's ability to learn new strategies to address their EF challenges is for the caregiver to develop an understanding of whether they are providing the appropriate level of support to build a teen's independence so that they can succeed now, but also in high school, college, and the workplace.*
  - *When implementing strategies and supports to target academic skills, it is important to build independence whenever possible. It may be easier and faster to write down and prioritize your teen's daily assignments in their planner for them, but this does not help the teen build skills or increase their independence in knowing what they have to do for homework.*
  - Poll: *How many of you feel like you could use some support in building your teen's independence when it comes to schoolwork, homework, and studying?*

  - *Caregivers also need to assess if they are providing too much support. For example, often caregivers are heavily involved in or may complete their teen's homework. They may also check in with the teen's teacher directly about missing assignments or test grades. Although EF difficulties and other challenges may require increased involvement from the caregiver, it is important to be aware of how to identify and implement strategies and supports that will build academic independence in the teen.*
  - Poll: *How many of you feel like you sometimes provide your teen with too much support with homework or studying?*

  - *As teens become older, they will likely have to take on more and more responsibilities such as schoolwork, extracurricular activities, chores, and taking care of themselves. Taking on more responsibilities is a normal part of growing up. Teens may sometimes be reluctant to take on new responsibilities or responsibilities that their caregivers have previously completed for them. You may need to directly point out that increasing independence leads to teens being able to engage in more enjoyable activities and do more things on their own, with less involvement from parents.*
  - Ask and discuss caregiver responses: *What are your thoughts on your role in building independence for your teen by stepping back or encouraging increased independence?*

- **The AIMS Approach to Addressing Strengths and Challenges While Building Independence (5 mins)**

  - *To summarize, in the upcoming AIMS sessions, both caregivers and teens will need to be patient and devote time and effort to building effective tools and strategies that can be implemented to increase academic success, which is a primary goal of the AIMS intervention.*
  - *We want to be realistic about a teen's challenges and difficulties so that supports can be put into place to help them reach their goals. If they are struggling with turning homework in*

even when it is completed, we can problem solve to identify possible solutions including keeping all completed homework in the same folder and/or turning all homework in at the beginning of class.

- *We also want to make sure that we are implementing strategies and supports that will increase their independence, such as turning in an assignment on their own at the beginning of the class rather than a teacher checking in with them about any homework that needs to be turned in.*

- *Lastly, we want to re-emphasize that your teens are NOT purposely choosing NOT to plan, NOT to prioritize, NOT to organize, NOT to remember multi-step directions, and NOT to get started, persevere, and finish tasks. EF difficulties are a brain-based problem and they are also one of the last parts of the brain to finish developing!*

- *Your teens will be rejoining us shortly and they have just completed a self-assessment of their EF skills. The goal of this was to increase their understanding of their profile of EF strengths and challenges, but also increase their motivation for wanting to learn strategies in AIMS that will help with their EF challenges. They will share 1 EF strength and 1 EF challenge when they rejoin us, but it may be helpful for you to review the EF Self-Assessment handout with them later.*

- Pass out and refer to <u>EF Self-Assessment</u> handout.

- *You can also complete the EF Self-Assessment for yourself so that you can have a better understanding of your own profile of EF strengths and challenges.*

Reunification – Large Group (10 mins)

- **Discussion of Teen Session Material (2 mins)**

  - *In their session, the teens completed an assessment of their EF strengths and challenges. Each teen is going to share 1 EF strength and 1 EF challenge.*
  - Have each teen share 1 EF strength and 1 EF challenge with the large group.

- **Take Home Points (3 mins)**

  - *At the end of each session, I will be asking you questions about the "take home points," which are the important things that were discussed. If you answer these questions you will have the chance to earn tickets.*
  - Ask the following questions (if time allows) and discuss as needed:

    - *What does EF stand for?*

      - Executive Functioning.

    - *What are the 5 EFs that were discussed today?*

      - Organization – Maintain systems to keep things in order
      - Working Memory – Keep things in mind while you need to use them
      - Planning – Set steps to reach a goal
      - Prioritizing – Organize steps in order of importance
      - Getting Started – Begin tasks without procrastinating.

    - *What are the goals of AIMS?*

- Understand your executive functioning (EF) strengths and challenges
- Understand the EF strategies that work for you
- Solve problems related to schoolwork and homework
- Organize materials needed for classes and homework assignments
- Plan and prioritize homework assignments and studying for tests
- Study better for tests and quizzes
- Get better grades
- Spend less time doing schoolwork so you have more free time to spend on fun activities.

- **Real World Practice Assignment (4 mins)**

  - Pass out and refer to <u>Real World Practice – Session 1</u> handout.
  - *Each session you will be given a Real World Practice assignment that will help you build EF skills such as organizing your materials, planning and prioritizing your homework assignments, and studying for tests. Completing these Real World Practice assignments will help you become more successful at school! For most Real World Practice assignments, you will need to work together with your caregiver.*
  - *For your first Real World Practice assignment, you should use the EF Self-Assessment you completed in session to discuss your EF strengths and challenges with your caregiver. Together, choose one of the areas that you identified as an EF challenge and set 1 goal of how you could improve in this area at school. For example, if you identified working memory as being difficult for you, you could set a goal to start writing down your homework assignments and what materials you need to bring home in a planner.*
  - Ask: *Any questions about your Real World Practice assignment?*

  - *In your AIMS binder, you will see that there is a folder at the front that is labeled "Real World Practices." This folder will help you keep the Real World Practice assignments you will need to do after each AIMS session organized. There are two pockets inside, and the left side is labeled "To Do" and the right side is labeled "Completed." You should keep the incomplete Real World Practice assignment that you have not yet done in the "To Do" pocket. Once you have completed them, you can move the completed Real World Practice assignment to the "Completed" pocket. Take a moment to file your Real World Practice assignment now in the "To Do" side of the folder.*
  - *You should also take a moment to file all of your other handouts behind the Session 1 divider.*
  - *Also, please remember to bring your AIMS binder or folder back next week!*
  - Ask: *Any final questions before we get ready to trade in your tickets for prizes?*

- **Trade in Tickets (1 min)**

  - *At the end of each session, you will be able to trade in your tickets for prizes. You can trade them in after each session or save them up for larger prizes. You are responsible for storing your tickets from session to session, so it may be a good idea to place them in the pocket of your binder for safekeeping.*
  - The Leader should give all teens who earned a ticket an opportunity to trade them in for prizes using the Prize Menu.
  - Leaders should record the number of remaining tickets on the Ticket Tracker (if used).

Session 1 Schedule

Large Group

❏ Introduction to AIMS

❏ Session Schedule

❏ Getting to Know One Another

❏ AIMS Rules

❏ Reward System

❏ Goals for Session 1

❏ Teens' Perspectives on School and Homework

❏ Identifying Academic Strengths and Challenges

❏ What is EF?

❏ EF Skills at School and Home

❏ What is AIMS?

Teen Group

❏ EF Strengths and Challenges

Reunification – Large Group

❏ Discussion of Teen Session Material

❏ Take Home Points

❏ Real World Practice Assignment

❏ Trade in Tickets

Academic Strengths and Difficulties Survey

Directions: Indicate whether this is a strength (S) or difficulty (D) for you.

S	D	
☐	☐	Making connections between concepts (e.g., similarities or differences)
☐	☐	Using appropriate spelling, punctuation, and capitalization
☐	☐	Putting ideas into a logical sequence when writing
☐	☐	Getting started on homework or a project independently
☐	☐	Showing work for math assignments
☐	☐	Communicating ideas in an organized way
☐	☐	Summarizing material that has been read (e.g., book chapter)
☐	☐	Keeping track of assignments and tests
☐	☐	Breaking down large projects or assignments into smaller components
☐	☐	Organizing materials efficiently (e.g., backpack, locker)
☐	☐	Turning homework assignments in after completed
☐	☐	Asking for help from teachers when needed
☐	☐	Checking for mistakes before turning in assignments
☐	☐	Performing at a level that matches my potential
☐	☐	Coming prepared to class with necessary materials
☐	☐	Utilizing a range of study skills (e.g., flashcards, study guide)
☐	☐	Completing homework assignments when they are due
☐	☐	Writing a 5-paragraph essay (intro, 3 body, conclusion)
☐	☐	Understanding how to effectively study for a test
☐	☐	Prioritizing what assignments need to be completed each day
☐	☐	Breaking down studying for a test across multiple days

AIMS

EF Skills Diagram

Executive Functioning (EF) Skills Targeted during AIMS

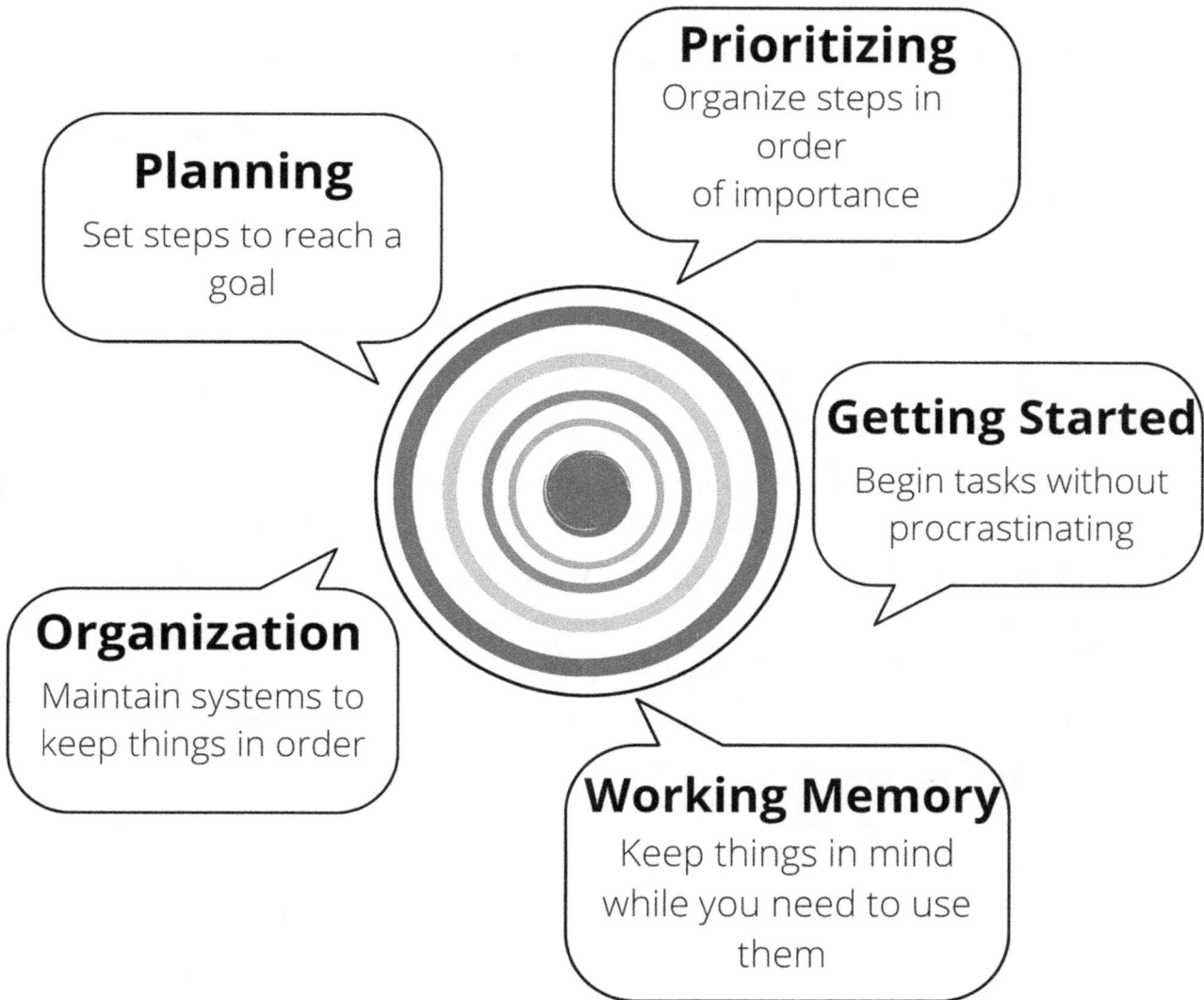

Planning
Set steps to reach a goal

Prioritizing
Organize steps in order of importance

Getting Started
Begin tasks without procrastinating

Organization
Maintain systems to keep things in order

Working Memory
Keep things in mind while you need to use them

Overview of AIMS Sessions

Date	Session
	1. Understanding Executive Functioning and How it Impacts Academic Strengths and Challenges
	2. ABCs of Problem Solving
	3. Using a Problem Solving Plan
	4. Developing a Homework System
	5. Backpack and Binder Organization Systems
	6. Using a Planner for Homework Assignments
	7. Building Effective Study Strategies
	8. Moving Forward After AIMS

Goals of AIMS

- Understand your executive functioning (EF) strengths and challenges
- Understand the EF strategies that work for you
- Solve problems related to schoolwork, homework, and studying
- Organize materials needed for classes and homework assignments
- Plan and prioritize homework assignments and studying for tests
- Study better for tests and quizzes
- Get better grades
- Spend less time doing schoolwork so you have more free time to spend on fun activities

Executive Functioning (EF) Self-Assessment

Directions: This assessment will help you to understand which executive functioning (EF) skills are a strength or challenge for you related to school, doing homework, and studying for tests. Read each item and choose the answer that describes you best. Then add up the score from the 3 items in each item set. Use the **Key** on the last page to determine your executive functioning strengths and challenges.

1. **I forget to do things that I said I would do (e.g., turn in a permission slip, start my homework, etc.).**

    Most of the time   Some of the time   Rarely or Never
    1   2   3

2. **I forget to do or turn in homework assignments and/or forget to bring home materials I need to do homework or study for tests.**

    Most of the time   Some of the time   Rarely or Never
    1   2   3

3. **I lose or misplace belongings such as papers, notebooks, water bottles, etc.**

    Most of the time   Some of the time   Rarely or Never
    1   2   3

Working Memory Score
(add up the score for items 1 – 3)

4. **I put off doing homework, working on projects, or studying for tests/quizzes until the last minute.**

    Most of the time   Some of the time   Rarely or Never
    1   2   3

5. **It's hard for me to put aside fun activities (i.e., things I want to do) to start homework or study for tests (i.e., things I have to do).**

    Most of the time   Some of the time   Rarely or Never
    1   2   3

6. **I need reminders to start my homework.**

    Most of the time   Some of the time   Rarely or Never
    1   2   3

Getting Started Score
(add up the score for items 4 – 6)

7. **I have trouble breaking down the steps for big projects or long-term assignments.**

Most of the time	Some of the time	Rarely or Never
1	2	3

8. **It's hard for me to figure out how to prioritize my homework when I have many things to do (e.g., figuring out what to do first, what to do second, etc.).**

Most of the time	Some of the time	Rarely or Never
1	2	3

9. **I struggle with using a planner or assignment notebook to write down homework assignments, tests/quizzes, or projects.**

Most of the time	Some of the time	Rarely or Never
1	2	

Planning and Prioritizing Score
(items 7 – 9)

10. **I have trouble keeping my backpack organized (e.g., cannot find things).**

Most of the time	Some of the time	Rarely or Never
1	2	3

11. **My desk or homework space at home is messy and/or cluttered.**

Most of the time	Some of the time	Rarely or Never
1	2	3

12. **I have trouble keeping my papers, notebooks, folders, and binders organized at school (e.g., may lose papers, cannot find things).**

Most of the time	Some of the time	Rarely or Never
1	2	3

Organizing Materials Score
(items 10 – 12)

EF Self-Assessment – KEY

After you have added up your score for each of the 4 item sets, check the appropriate boxes based on your scores:

- **Strength** = Scores of 8–9
- **Doing OK** = Scores of 5–7
- **Challenge** = Scores of 3–4

Items	Executive Functioning Skill	Strength (8–9)	Doing OK (5–7)	Challenge (3–4)
1 – 3	Working Memory			
4 – 6	Getting Started			
7 – 9	Planning/Prioritizing			
10 – 12	Organizing Materials			

Understanding How to Tackle EF Challenges

- Executive Functioning (EF) skills include planning, prioritizing, organization, working memory, and getting started on tasks.

  - Due to differences and changes in brain development, teens are not purposely choosing NOT to plan, prioritize, organize, start, stick with, or finish tasks.

- EF challenges may affect a teen's ability to do HW in the following ways:

  - Writing assignments down in a planner
  - Knowing what tests or quizzes need to be studied for
  - Breaking down a long-term assignment or project
  - Bringing the correct materials home
  - Prioritizing homework assignments that need to be completed
  - Deciding to start their homework
  - Persevering with homework assignments
  - Asking for help with difficult assignments
  - Coming back to a homework assignment after taking a break
  - Knowing how much time they should be spending on assignments
  - Finishing homework.

- It is important to consider the following when deciding how to address EF challenges in your teen:

  - Profile of strengths and challenges
  - Increased expectations and demands in middle school
  - Competing demands outside of school
  - Motivation
  - Other challenges (e.g., emotion regulation, motor skills, social-communication skills, sensory issues).

- Caregivers also need to assess their role in addressing EF challenges with their teen:

  - Actively encouraging independence
  - Fading back support over time
  - Identifying strategies that help them to be successful.

Real World Practice – Session 1

Choose one of the areas that you identified as an EF challenge from the EF Self-Assessment. Set 1 goal of how you could improve in this area at school.

Example

EF challenge:
Working memory

Goal to improve EF challenge:
Start writing down my homework assignments and what materials I need to bring home in a planner

EF challenge:

_____

Goal to improve EF challenge:

_____

_____

_____

Session 2   ABCs of Problem Solving

Session 2 Preparation

Session Specific Supplies

- Projector/computer for video
- ABCs of Problem Solving video (available at www.aims-ef.com)

General AIMS Supplies

- AIMS Rules Poster
- Prize Menu and Prize Box
- Ticket Tracker and tickets
- Real World Practice Tracker
- Whiteboard and dry erase markers OR large Post-It easel pad and markers
- Pens/Pencils
- Game/Activity for Teen Group

Handouts Needed

- Large Group

  - Session 2 Schedule
  - ABCs of Problem Solving Infographic
  - Problem Solving Practice – Messy Room

- Teen Group

  - Problem Solving Practice – Math Class

- Caregiver Group

  - Tips for Helping Teens with the ABCs of Problem Solving

- Large Group

  - Real World Practice – Session 2

DOI: 10.4324/9781003500209-3

Important Points for Session 2

- **General Session Notes**

  - If there are any new teens or caregivers joining the group, the Leaders should do a brief round of introductions.
  - This session is highly didactic and teens are more likely to understand the steps of problem solving the more they actively participate.

    - While many of the questions are directed to teens, the Leader can also ask caregivers to provide their thoughts/perspectives – especially if the teens are struggling to come up with responses.
    - When asking questions, Leaders can also use polling to encourage teens and caregivers to respond (e.g., "Raise your hand if you sometimes have challenges with organizing your materials."). Easy polling methods include raising hands or thumbs up/ thumbs down.
    - Leaders may want to use timers or make a note of when they need to be done with a certain activity to help with managing time during the session.
    - Leaders may want to use the whiteboard or a large post-it to write down teen and caregiver responses during various activities (e.g., Review of Real World Practice Assignment, 5 Ws, etc.). This may increase the attention and focus of teens.

  - One Leader should be in charge of completing the Real World Practice Tracker each week, which can be completed by marking off which teens completed their assignment. The Leader may need to walk around the room to check that it was completed.

    - It can be helpful to incentivize individual teens to complete their Real World Practice assignment. For example, teens can earn an extra 8 tickets at Session 8 if they complete all of their Real World Practice assignments.
    - Leaders can also incentivize the whole group to complete Real World Practice assignments. For example, all teens can earn an extra 2 tickets if every teen completes the Real World Practice assignment each week.

  - Leaders should also verbally praise teens who complete the Real World Practice assessment – either individually or as a group (e.g., "I just want to say it is really impressive that all of you did your Real Word Practice assignments! We know that teens who practice the things we talk about in our sessions have more success in solving problems and meeting goals!").

  - Consider rewarding teens who participate by passing out tickets when they:

    - Discuss how they solve problems
    - Answer questions from the ABCs of Problem Solving video
    - Answer the 5 Ws, generate solutions, and identify pros and cons for the Messy Room Activity
    - Participate during the teen session

- Answer questions during the Take Home Points
- File handouts in their AIMS binder.

- Leaders can also reward teens by giving them specific jobs during the session (e.g., count up tickets at the end as teens trade them in for prizes, pass out handouts, write concepts on the whiteboard, etc.).

- Leaders should display the new Prize Menu and can allow teens to ask questions about the new prizes that they are able to earn.
- Leaders should continue to regularly remind teens to file handouts throughout the session.
- At the end of the session, Leaders are encouraged to utilize the Ticket Tracker (see Leader Materials) to track tickets or should encourage teens to store their tickets in a safe place (e.g., pocket of their AIMS binder).

  - It can be helpful to designate the same Leader each week to use the Ticket Tracker and give out prizes to teens.

- **Practice – Brainstorming Solutions**

  - In general, the goal is to come up with as many solutions as possible, even solutions that are unrealistic or humorous. Feel free to let teens be creative with this process. Leaders should ultimately emphasize that even though not all of the solutions that were generated were good solutions, the process of coming up with a wide range of solutions will help us figure out how to best handle the problem.

    - Caregivers can also participate in brainstorming solutions.

- **Teen Group**

  - It can be helpful to remind teens that the harder that they work and the more focused they are during activities and discussions, the more time they may have to play games or to talk at the end of the teen group.
  - Leaders may choose to do a "brain break" to refocus or re-energize teens so that they are able to focus and pay attention to the content being presented. For example, games such as Stack Attack and Penny Stack (see Leader Materials) only take 1–2 minutes, but can serve to get teens back on track.
  - Leaders want to balance the importance of presenting and practicing new skills that are taught in AIMS with also having fun and building rapport with the teens.

- **Caregiver Group**

  - Leaders are encouraged to utilize the script to ensure that they cover all of the key concepts for this session. Leaders can individualize session content by incorporating examples or checking in more frequently (e.g., "Any questions so far?").

- It is important to have caregivers focus on solving academic problems. While teens may also struggle in other areas (e.g., building friendships, getting along with siblings, doing chores), the Leader should actively bring discussions back to academic challenges.
- This session has a lot of content and the Leader will have to balance presenting the content with any caregiver discussions. The Leader may need to remind caregivers about the importance of covering all material so that they are ready to start implementing strategies in the next several weeks.

    - The Leader can also set up a "parking lot" at the end of the caregiver session or after the AIMS session for any topics that are not able to be discussed. For example, if caregivers want to talk about specific summer camps or extracurricular activities, the Leader could write this on the whiteboard and then remind caregivers that they can discuss it at the end of the caregiver session or in the waiting room after the AIMS session ends.

- If the Leader is not able to cover all of the content, they can cover it at the start of the next session during the caregiver group.

Get Ready Checklist for Leaders

❑ Prep the handouts to be passed out
❑ Hang up AIMS Rules Poster
❑ Hang up Prize Menu
❑ Check that Prize Box has range of prizes to be earned
❑ Hang up the Real World Practice Assignment Tracker (if used)
❑ Hang up Ticket Tracker (if used)
❑ Set up projector and/or computer
❑ Open the ABCs of Problem Solving video
❑ Get any supplies for the games to be played in the Teen Group

Session 2 Manual

Large Group – Caregivers and Teens (50 mins)

- **Session Schedule (1 min)**

  - Pass out and refer to <u>Session 2 Schedule</u> handout.
  - *Let's make sure to get started the right way so that we can fully focus on what you will be learning today. Put all materials away except for your AIMS binder and a pen or pencil.*
  - Briefly go over the activities that are listed on the <u>Session 2 Schedule</u> handout. State that teens can cross off activities on the schedule as they are completed.

- **Review Group Rules and Prize Menu (2 mins)**

  - Refer to the AIMS Rules Poster and briefly review each of the rules.
  - Remind teens that they will earn tickets that can be traded in for prizes at the end of each session when they:

    - Follow the group rules
    - Participate in the session
    - Complete activities in session
    - Complete Real World Practice Assignments
    - File handouts.

  - Briefly review that the Prize Menu shows how many tickets are needed to earn various prizes.

- **Review Real World Practice Assignment (6 mins)**

  - Instruct teens to get out their Real World Practice Assignment from the Real World Practice folder in their AIMS binder.
  - Ask: *Who completed the Real World Practice Assignment?*

    - If utilizing the Real World Practice Assignment Tracker, Leaders should indicate which teens completed their Real World Practice Assignment.
    - Check that teens filed their Real World Practice Assignment in the "Completed" section of their Real World Practice folder in their AIMS binder.

  - *Your Real World Practice from the last session was to choose one of the areas that you identified as an EF challenge and set 1 goal of how you could improve in this area at school. For example, if you identified working memory as being difficult for you, you could set a goal to start writing down your homework assignments and what materials you need to bring home in a planner. You can earn a ticket for completing your Real World Practice.*

    - Ask teens to share the EF challenge and goal that they identified.

      - It may not be possible to have all teens share. Leaders should make sure that they rotate what teens are able to share the progress on their Real World Practice assignment each week.

- If teens did not complete the Real World Practice assignment, the Leader should briefly troubleshoot with them about how to make sure that they complete it next week (e.g., add a reminder, set aside a day/time to work on it with their caregiver).
- Remind teens to file their completed Real World Practice Assignment in their folder.
- If teens completed Real World Practice Assignment, they should be rewarded with 1 ticket.

- **Review of Material from Last Session (2 mins)**

  - Ask the following questions (if time allows) and discuss as needed:

    - *What does EF stand for?*

      - Executive Functioning.

    - *What are the 5 EFs?*

      - Organization – Maintain systems to keep things in order
      - Working Memory – Keep things in mind while you need to use them
      - Planning – Set steps to reach a goal
      - Prioritizing – Organize steps in order of importance
      - Getting Started – Begin tasks without procrastinating.

    - *What are the goals of AIMS?*

      - Understand your executive functioning (EF) strengths and challenges
      - Understand the EF strategies that work for you
      - Solve problems related to schoolwork and homework
      - Organize materials needed for classes and homework assignments
      - Plan and prioritize homework assignments and studying for tests
      - Study better for tests and quizzes
      - Get better grades
      - Spend less time doing schoolwork so you have more free time to spend on fun activities.

- **Goals for Session 2 (1 min)**

  - *Our goals for today are the following:*

    - *Learn how to solve problems at home and school using the ABCs of Problem Solving.*
    - *Learn the first 3 steps of the ABCs of Problem Solving: Aim – Identify the Problem, Brainstorm Solutions, and Choose the Best Solution.*

- **How Do You Solve Problems? (10 mins)**

  - *In order to be successful at school and in life, you need to become skilled at solving problems. It is also important to become an expert at solving the problems that may be due to your EF challenges.*
  - Ask the teens the following questions and discuss their responses as a group:

- *What problems at school do you have to solve?*

  - Leaders should emphasize that everyone has problems that need to be solved.

- *Whose responsibility is it to solve your problems?*

  - Leaders should emphasize that it is teens' responsibility to take steps to solve their problems. While caregivers and teachers can support and help, teens should become more independent over time.

- *How many solutions to a problem are there?*

  - Leaders should emphasize that there are many, many solutions for problems, even if it might not seem like it, but it can take time to determine which solution is the best solution.

- *We are now going to watch a video about the ABCs of Problem Solving. When you are watching the video, I want you to keep these questions in mind.*

  - *What is the teen's problem?*
  - *What solutions does he brainstorm?*
  - *What solutions does he end up trying?*
  - *How does his solution help to solve his problem?*

- Show the ABCs of Problem Solving video (4m 14s).
- Ask teens the following questions to assess what they learned and remembered from the video:

  - *What is the name of the character in the video?* Michael.
  - *What is his problem?* Michael was failing English. He does not hand in homework and gets zeros on these assignments.
  - *What solutions does he brainstorm?*

    - Keep a planner for his assignments
    - Do English first every night and put it in his backpack
    - Hire someone to do his homework
    - Do English during study time
    - Talk to the teacher and get ideas.

  - *What solutions does he end up trying?* He combined some of his initial ideas including (1) check with the teacher every day about assignments and (2) do his assignments in study hall or as soon as possible.
  - *How does his solution help to solve his problem?* He turns in his homework every day by tracking and prioritizing his English homework. His grade has gone from an F to C+.

- **Introduce and Define the ABCs of Problem Solving (3 mins)**

  - Pass out and refer to the ABCs of Problem Solving Infographic handout.
  - *Here is an infographic for you to refer to throughout AIMS as we learn about the problem-solving process and how to use these steps when you encounter a problem.*

- Briefly review the ABCs of Problem Solving steps that were discussed in the video by having teens take turns reading the 5 steps.

  - A: Aim – Identify the Problem
  - B: Brainstorm Solutions
  - C: Choose the Best Solution
  - D: Do it! Try Out Solution
  - E: Evaluate How it Worked

- *It is easy to remember the steps for Problem Solving using the acronym ABCDE, which is the first letter of the first word of each of the 5 steps.*

- **A: Aim – Identify the Problem (4 mins)**

  - *Today we will focus on talking about the first step: Aim – Identify the Problem. As you all know, problems may:*

    - *Keep you from meeting your goals – for example, getting a good grade in History.*
    - *Cause arguments with parents/caregivers, teachers, and friends – for example, arguing with your mom about when to get started on homework.*
    - *Take away freedom/choices – for example, your caregiver may have to sit next to you as you complete homework to make sure you do it and stay focused or you may lose screen time until you bring your grades up.*

  - Poll: *How many of you feel like it could be helpful to work on identifying your problems to make your life easier?*

  - *Identifying the specific problem makes it easier to solve. If you can use these problem solving skills to help you stay organized, get good grades, do your homework, and study for tests, you are likely to get more freedom and more privileges like playing video games, going outside, and hanging out with friends!*
  - *To clearly define a problem, it is helpful to break it down by asking the 5 W Questions, or the 5 Ws for short, which are:*

    - *Who?*
    - *What?*
    - *When?*
    - *Where?*
    - *Why?*

  - *Let's go over an example to illustrate the importance of clearly defining a problem using the 5 Ws.*

- **Practice – Identify the Problem (5 mins)**

  - Pass out and refer to the <u>Problem Solving Practice – Messy Room</u> handout.
  - As a large group, go through the following example to illustrate the process of solving a problem. Have teens and their caregivers try to come up with answers to the 5 Ws

to help with breaking down a problem. Support and guidance should be provided as needed.

- *Let's work on helping a teen who has a big problem – his very messy room. He and his parents initially identify his problem as "Aiden's room is a mess." However, that problem is not specific enough, and so Aiden can't figure out exactly what he needs to do to fix it. After discussing the problem in more detail with his parents, they come up with the following*:

  - *He has dirty and clean laundry on the floor and on his bed. Aiden's bed is not made. He has dirty dishes and cups on his desk. Aiden's desk is so cluttered he cannot do his homework there. He also has random books, papers, art supplies, video games, and Legos all over his room. Aiden does not put his belongings where they go in his bedroom every day because he is overwhelmed by his messy, unorganized room.*

- *Using the first step of the ABCs of Problem Solving (AIM – Identify the Problem) and asking the 5 Ws (Who?, What?, When?, Where?, and Why?) will help Aiden and his parents get more specific about his problem and come up with a solution to fix it!*
- *Let's work on identifying the 5 Ws for Aiden as a group.*

  - Leaders should use a whiteboard or large post-it to write down the responses for the 5 Ws and encourage caregivers and teens to write it down on their handout.

- As a group, have the teens take the lead in identifying the 5 Ws and have them complete the Problem Solving Practice – Messy Room handout (see below for answers to the 5 Ws).

  - *Who?* Aiden
  - *What?* puts dirty clothes, clean laundry, books, papers, Legos, dishes and cups, and basically all of his belongings wherever there is space
  - *When?* every day
  - *Where?* his bedroom at home
  - *Why?* is overwhelmed by not having any sort of system to organize his belongings.

- *Thus, the specific problem is that Aiden does not put his belongings where they go in his bedroom every day because he is overwhelmed by his messy, unorganized room.*
- Ask: *Any questions about using the first step of Problem Solving?*

- **B: Brainstorm Solutions (2 mins)**

  - *Once you have identified the problem you want to work on using the 5 Ws, the next step is to Brainstorm Solutions, which means to come up with as many solutions as possible. Here are some things to think about when brainstorming solutions for an identified problem*:

    - *More is better! You want to have a variety of solutions to choose from.*
    - *The process of brainstorming takes time and effort. You will need to think through what is contributing to the problem in order to come up with solutions that will hopefully be effective.*
    - *No idea is a bad idea (yet!). At this point, you want to come up with as many solutions as possible (be creative!). You can eliminate some "bad" or "unrealistic" or "absurd" ideas later.*

- *It is a good rule of thumb to come up with at least 5 solutions for every problem.*

- Ask: *Any questions about brainstorming solutions before we get some practice doing this for Aiden?*

- **Practice – Brainstorm Solutions (7 mins)**

  - *Now, let's think back to Aiden and his problem about his messy room. Let's brainstorm as many solutions as possible to address the very real problem of Aiden's extremely messy room. When brainstorming solutions, it is helpful to come up with a lot of solutions so that you have many, many options before choosing one possible solution to work on.*
  - *As a large group, let's take a few minutes to brainstorm some ideas that can help Aiden with his messy room. You can suggest any solution that comes to mind – even if it's silly or unrealistic, like hiring a maid to clean your room everyday!*

    - As a large group, have the teens and their caregivers provide possible solutions as they continue to complete the Problem Solving Practice – Messy Room handout.
    - Leaders should write all of the ideas on a large post-it or whiteboard so that they can be used when discussing pros and cons of solutions.
    - Teens and caregivers should continue to complete the Problem Solving Practice – Messy Room handout.

  - Possible solutions for the Leader to discuss after teens and caregivers have generated ideas may include the following:

    - If it is not put away, caregivers will put it in the trash
    - Close the door
    - Pay a sibling to clean it
    - Move out
    - Set a consistent day/time to clean room
    - Live in a tent in the backyard
    - Argue about it every day with your family
    - Just throw away everything that is on the floor
    - Switch rooms with another family member
    - Get a daily lecture from your family when your room is not clean
    - Take pictures of a friend's room to prove your room is not the messiest in the world
    - Caregivers can take away the "privilege" of having a room (i.e., you sleep outside or in the hallway)
    - Earn a reward for cleaning your room
    - Sell everything you own
    - Rent a storage unit
    - Clean up room for 5 minutes each night before going to bed.

  - After the solutions have been discussed, ask the teens the following questions:

    - *Are all of the solutions that we came up with good solutions?*

      - Answer – *Probably not. But the process of coming up with a wide range of solutions will help us to figure out how to best tackle the problem.*

- *Are there solutions that may help us with the problem of the messy room?*

  - *Answer – Yes! And that leads us to the next step in the ABCs of Problem Solving.*

- **C: Choose the Best Solution (2 mins)**

  - *The third step in Problem Solving is to Choose the Best Solution. After you have brainstormed several solutions, you can then choose 2–3 possible solutions and determine the pros and cons.*

    - *Pros are good things about the solution.*
    - *Cons are bad things about the solution.*

- **Practice – Choose the Best Solution (5 mins)**

  - *Now let's practice choosing the best solution from the ones that we have identified for Aiden's messy room.*
  - As a large group, the Leader should have teens and caregivers choose 2–3 solutions for the messy room problem from the list that was generated by the large group.

    - It may be helpful to involve caregivers in choosing solutions.
    - It may be necessary to remind teens that we want to choose a few solutions that are the "best" in that they have a high likelihood of being successful.

  - For each of the solutions, teens and caregivers should come up with 2–3 pros and 2–3 cons.

    - Leaders should write the solutions and their pros and cons on a whiteboard or large post-it to demonstrate how to do this step of problem solving.
    - Teens and caregivers should continue to complete the Problem Solving Practice – Messy Room handout.

  - Have the teens and caregivers vote on which solution they would choose based on the pros and cons that they came up with.

    - Leaders can also propose combining solutions or trying out 2 solutions, which is similar to what Michael did in the video.

  - Ask: *Any questions about the ABCs of Problem Solving?*
  - Leaders should have caregivers and teens split into separate groups.

    - Remind teens to file handouts in their AIMS binder and provide assistance as needed.

Teen Group (30 mins)

- **Practice the ABCs of Problem Solving (30 mins)**

  - Leaders can briefly go over the activities that are listed on the Session 2 Schedule handout for the Teen Group. State that teens can cross off activities on the schedule as they are completed.

- Leaders may want to review the AIMS Rules Poster with the teens and remind them that they can earn tickets for following the rules, answering questions, and participating in activities.
- Pass out and refer to the <u>Problem Solving Practice – Math Class</u> handout.
- *We are going to go through another example to illustrate the first 3 steps of the ABCs of Problem Solving. Let's start with the Aim – Identify the Problem by using the 5 Ws.*
- *Natasha and her parents initially identify her problem as "Natasha has bad grades." However, that problem is not specific enough, and so Natasha can't figure out exactly what she needs to do to fix it. After discussing the problem in more detail with her parents, they come up with the following:*

  - *Natasha is doing pretty well in all of her classes, but she has a D in math class. When she asks her math teacher about why her grade is so low, her teacher says that she is missing a lot of homework assignments.*

- *Using the first step of the ABCs of Problem Solving (AIM – Identify the Problem) and asking the 5 Ws (Who?, What?, When?, Where?, and Why?) will help her get more specific about her problem and come up with a solution to fix it!*
- *Let's work on identifying the 5 Ws for Natasha as a group.*

  - Leaders should use a whiteboard or large post-it to write down the responses for the 5 Ws and encourage teens to write it down on their handout.

- As a group, have the teens identify the 5 Ws and complete the <u>Problem Solving Practice – Math Class</u> handout (see below for answers to the 5 Ws).

  - *Who?* Natasha
  - *What?* has a D
  - *When?* teens should **NOT** be able to answer this

    - NOTE: not all of these questions will be applicable to each problem

  - *Where?* in Math class
  - *Why?* due to missing assignments.

- *Thus, saying that "Natasha has a D in math class due to missing assignments" is a more clearly defined problem than "Natasha has bad grades."*

- *Let's move on to the next step of problem solving and take a few minutes to brainstorm some ideas that can help Natasha. Remember to suggest any solution that comes to mind that may help Natasha with her problem!*

  - Leaders should write the teens' ideas on a large post-it or whiteboard so that they can be used when discussing pros and cons of solutions. Teens should continue to use the <u>Problem Solving Practice – Math Class</u> handout.

    - Leaders can also provide suggestions if teens are struggling to identify a range of solutions.

- *Now that we have identified several solutions, let's practice choosing the best solution from the ones that we have identified for Natasha.*

  - As a large group, the Leader should have teens choose 2–3 solutions for the math class problem from the list that was generated by the large group.
  - It may be necessary to remind teens that we want to choose a few solutions that are the "best" in that they have a high likelihood of being successful.

- For each of the solutions, teens should come up with 2–3 pros and 2–3 cons.

  - Leaders should write the solutions and their pros and cons on a whiteboard or large post-it to demonstrate how to do this step of problem solving.
  - Teens should continue to complete the <u>Problem Solving Practice – Math Class</u> handout.

- Have the teens vote on which solution they would choose based on the pros and cons that they came up with.

  - Leaders can also propose combining solutions or trying out 2 solutions, which is similar to what Michael did in the video.

- Ask: *Any questions about the ABCs of Problem Solving?*

- *When we rejoin your caregivers, we will have some of you share the first 3 steps of problem solving that we did for Natasha. Who would like to volunteer to do this?*
- Remind teens to file handouts in their AIMS binder and provide assistance as needed.
- If time allows, Leaders can allow the teens to play a short game that utilizes EF skills. Possible games to play include Stack Attack, Penny Stack, Connect 4, or Uno (see Manual Overview for additional information including instructions and materials needed for games).

  - Leaders may want to set a timer for this activity.

- The teens should rejoin their caregivers for the reunification with the Large Group.

Caregiver Group (30 mins)

- **Applying the ABCs of Problem Solving with Your Teen (10 mins)**

  - Briefly check in with caregivers to see if they have any questions about the content that has been presented thus far.
  - Pass out and refer to <u>Tips for Helping Teens with the ABCs of Problem Solving</u> handout.
  - *While your teens are getting some hands-on practice with using the ABCs of problem solving, we want to talk more about why each step of this process is important. We are walking through the process of problem-solving to provide a clear, detailed set of steps so that with continued use and practice, this process will become more routine and automatic as they apply it to school and homework, but also at home, with friends, with family, and at work. Feel free to take notes or jot down any thoughts on your handouts as we discuss this in more detail.*

- Identifying the Problem

  - *Some of the teen's problems are really big and complex, and caregivers need to be aware that these problems may need to be broken down and worked on gradually.*
  - *Teens may also have more than one problem to solve and may need guidance on how to prioritize problems.*

    - *For example, if a teen is not doing any homework on their own and needs help from you with everything from identifying what needs to be done to how to actually do their homework, a first step might be to just have them prioritize one part of the problem such as correctly writing down their daily assignments in a planner. Once they master this, another problem related to doing homework can be tackled.*

  - Ask: *Any questions about taking a slow and thoughtful approach to big or complex problems?*

  - *You may also need to support your teen in being specific and detailed when identifying the problem they are having because that is what leads to better solutions.*

    - *For example, instead of the teen saying "I'm failing school", a better way to describe the problem is "I'm failing English class." An even better way for the teen to define the problem is, '"I'm failing English because I'm not writing down assignments or turning in a paper". Getting specific and detailed about a problem leads to more and better solutions.*

  - Ask and discuss: *What questions do you have about helping your teens to identify problems related to school and homework?*

- Brainstorming Solutions and Choosing the Best Solution

  - *Let's talk a little about brainstorming solutions to problems and then choosing the best solution.*
  - *You will likely know the solution that will benefit your teen the most and lead to improvement without going through the ABCs of problem solving. However, it is critical for teens to be involved in the process of identifying and choosing solutions, even if this means it will take them longer to actually solve the problem.*
  - *A useful metaphor for giving teens more independence in the area of problem-solving is that we want to teach them to fish, not just give them the fish. In other words, we want to teach them how to solve problems, not just give them the solution.*
  - *It may take time to identify the best solution for the problem, but this will help your teen solve problems more effectively in the future.*
  - Ask: *Any questions about taking an active role in encouraging your teen to identify solutions to their problems?*

  - *Once an effective solution is found, it may be able to be applied to multiple problems. For example, if your teen benefits from using a planner to write down, prioritize, and then check off their homework assignments, they may also benefit from checklists to help with chores or how to do a complex task such as laundry.*

- *In AIMS, we will soon be talking about strategies that we know work for addressing issues such as organization, planning, and prioritizing at school and for homework.*
- Ask and discuss: *What questions do you have about helping your teen to brainstorm solutions and then choose the best solution?*

- **Use of Evidence-Based Strategies to Address EF Challenges (20 mins)**

  - *As we discussed last week, EF challenges are brain-based and your teen is NOT purposely choosing not to plan, prioritize, manage their time, organize their materials, get started and finish tasks.*
  - *As adults, many of us set up systems or use strategies to help us stay organized, manage our time effectively, remember where our belongings are, and keep track of our daily and weekly schedule. This likely took some time and some trial and error to figure out what worked best for us.*
  - Leader should provide an example of a system that they use to address an EF challenge. Examples may include:

    - Using an electronic calendar or paper planner to keep track of work, personal, and family obligations and appointments.
    - Putting the car keys in the same place when entering the house so they never need to look for them.
    - Setting up alarms and reminders to remember things that may be needed for school (e.g., permission slip) or work (e.g., lunch, change of clothes for the gym).

  - Ask and discuss: *What strategies do you use to help yourself plan, prioritize, stay organized, get started on tasks, or remember things?*
  - *When children are younger, caregivers take on the role of managing their child's EF needs – such as reminding them to brush their teeth, reminding them to look both ways before crossing the street, or reminding them about what needs to be packed in their backpack.*
  - *In adolescence, it is expected that teens are becoming more independent at home and school, testing out their judgment, and engaging in more complex problem-solving. However, teens with EF difficulties will need additional guidance. Specifically, they will need to be taught how to use and then practice the tools and strategies to help compensate for EF challenges.*
  - *In upcoming AIMS sessions, we will be discussing strategies that can be implemented to address the EF challenges that affect them at school and when doing homework or studying for tests at home. By practicing using these strategies in middle school, it is more likely that your teen will be able to improve their current outcome – such as building study skills so that they can get good grades now. However, developing an effective system of strategies for EF challenges will also affect long term adult outcomes in areas such as high school and college, and also when they get a part-time or full-time job, as they tackle tasks such as planning for long-term projects, prioritizing assignments and tasks that need to be completed, and getting started on tasks without procrastinating.*
  - Ask: *Any questions?*

- *For the remainder of our time together, let's each discuss your teen's main academic "problems" or challenges at school or home that you would like to possibly address in the coming weeks. This fits with this week's Real World Practice assignment because you and your teen will be working to identify a specific "problem" or challenge that they are having at school or with homework.*

  - The Leader should have each caregiver state 1–2 issues that their teen is having at school or home that may be related to academic EF challenges.
  - It may be helpful for the Leader to write the 5 EFs on a whiteboard or large post-it and then write the academic challenges that caregivers bring up under the relevant EF (e.g., remembering to turn in completed HW may go under Working Memory).

Reunification – Large Group (10 mins)

- **Discussion of Teen Session Material (3 mins)**

  - *In their session, the teens did the first 3 steps of problem solving for a teen who was struggling to get a good grade in her math class.*
  - Have several teens share the first 3 steps of the ABCs of problem solving that they completed in the teen group.

- **Take Home Points (2 mins)**

  - *Let's go over our take home points.*
  - Ask the following questions (if time allows) and discuss as needed:

    - *What are the 5 steps in the ABCs of Problem Solving? Remember the acronym ABCDE.*

      - *Aim – Identify the Problem*
      - *Brainstorm Solutions*
      - *Choose the Best Solution*
      - *Do it!*
      - *Evaluate.*

    - *What are the 5 Ws that the first step (Aim – Identify the Problem) answers?*

      - *Who, What, When, Where, and Why.*

    - *What is the 2nd step of Problem Solving? Remember that this is the step that starts with "B" in the ABCs of Problem Solving.*

      - *Brainstorm all possible solutions to a problem.*

    - *What is the 3rd step of Problem Solving? Remember that this is the step that starts with "C" in the ABCs of Problem Solving.*

      - *Choose the best solution. You want to identify and weigh the pros and cons of at least 2–3 possible solutions before choosing a solution.*

- **Real World Practice Assignment (4 mins)**

  - Pass out and refer to <u>Real World Practice – Session 2</u> handout.

  - *For your Real World Practice Assignment this week, you will work with your caregiver to think about a challenge or problem that you have related to school, which could be things like a messy backpack, missing assignments, or forgetting to do your homework. After identifying a problem, go through the 5 Ws for the first step of Problem Solving – Aim – Identify the Problem. After you have identified a more specific problem, you will brainstorm solutions and then choose the best solution. You will not start trying out the solution just yet. This is a way to get practice with the first 3 steps of the ABCs of problem solving by applying them to yourself.*

  - *It is very important that you take the time to do this in the next week because this will be one of the first solutions that you try out next week when we set up your first Problem Solving Plan.*

  - Ask: *Any questions about your Real World Practice assignment?*

  - *In your AIMS binder, take a moment to file your Real World Practice assignment now in the "To Do" side of the folder. You should also take a moment to file all of your other handouts behind the Session 2 divider.*

  - Ask: *Any final questions before we get ready to trade in your tickets for prizes?*

- **Trade in Tickets (1 min)**

  - The Leader should give all teens who earned a ticket an opportunity to trade them in for prizes using the Prize Menu.

  - Leaders should record the number of remaining tickets on the Ticket Tracker (if used)

Session 2 Schedule

Large Group

❏ Review Group Rules and Prize Menu

❏ Review Real World Practice Assignment

❏ Review of Material from Last Session

❏ Goals for Session 2

❏ How Do You Solve Problems?

❏ A: Aim – Identify the Problem and Practice

❏ B: Brainstorm Solutions and Practice

❏ C: Choose the Best Solution and Practice

Teen Group

❏ Practice the ABCs of Problem Solving

Reunification – Large Group

❏ Discussion of Teen Session Material

❏ Take Home Points

❏ Real World Practice Assignment

❏ Trade in Tickets

The ABCs of Problem Solving

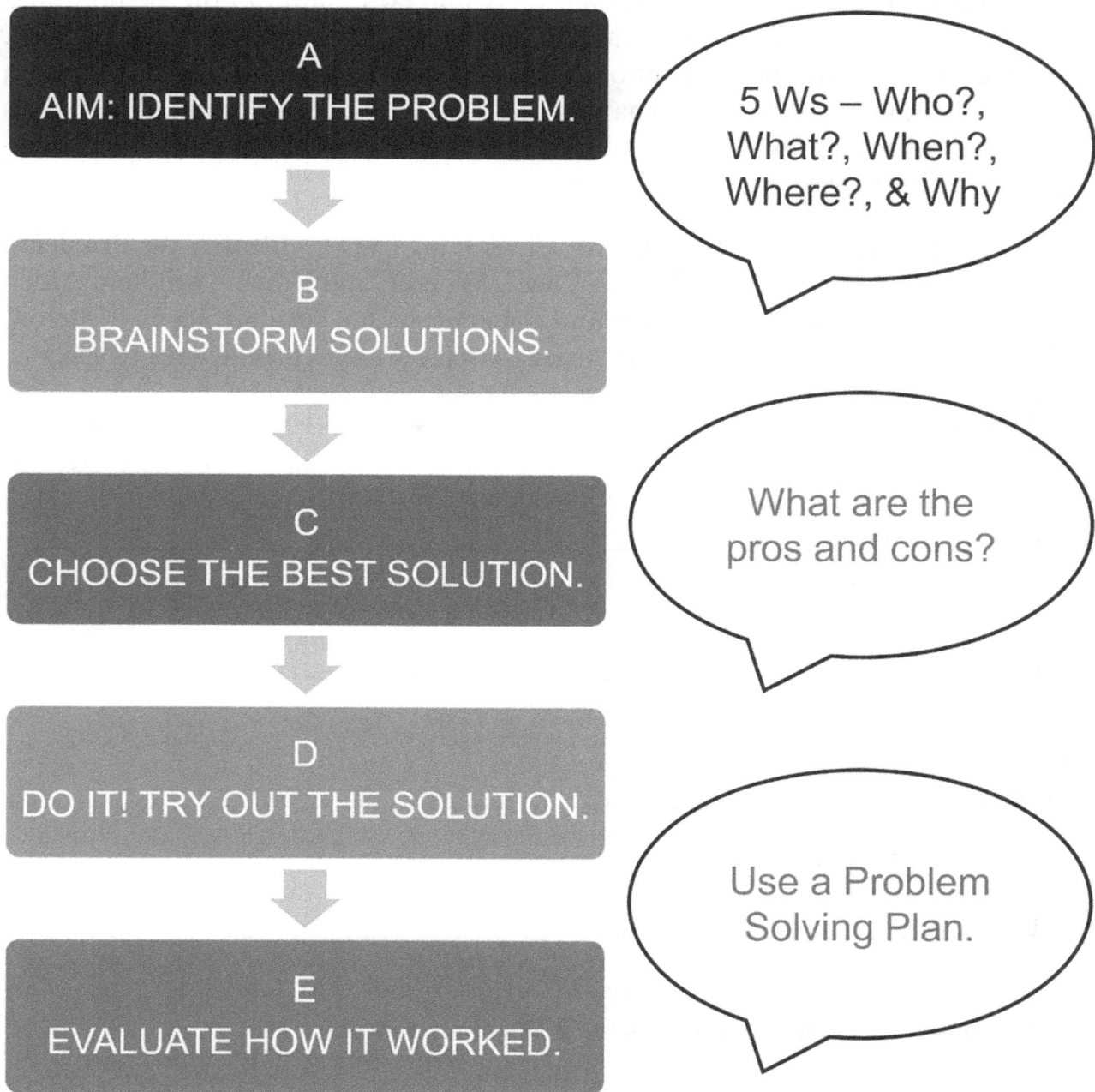

A
AIM: IDENTIFY THE PROBLEM.

5 Ws – Who?, What?, When?, Where?, & Why

B
BRAINSTORM SOLUTIONS.

C
CHOOSE THE BEST SOLUTION.

What are the pros and cons?

D
DO IT! TRY OUT THE SOLUTION.

E
EVALUATE HOW IT WORKED.

Use a Problem Solving Plan.

Problem Solving Practice – Messy Room

Problem: Aiden's room is a mess. He has dirty and clean laundry on the floor and on his bed. Aiden's bed is not made. He has dirty dishes and cups on his desk. Aiden's desk is so cluttered he cannot do his homework there. He also has random books, papers, art supplies, video games, and Legos all over his room. Aiden does not put his belongings where they go in his bedroom every day because he is overwhelmed by his messy, unorganized room.

Using the first step of the ABCs of problem solving (**AIM – Identify the Problem**), and asking the **5 Ws – Who?, What?, When?, Where?, and Why?** – will help Aiden get more specific about the problem and come up with a solution to fix it! Below, write the details you need to know in order to make Aiden's problem more specific:

Who:_____

What:_____

When:_____

Where:_____

Why:_____

More Specific Problem (combines the 5 Ws from above):

_____

_____

_____

_____

Help Aiden <u>BRAINSTORM</u> possible solutions for the problem!

1.
2.
3.
4.
5.
6.
7.
8.

Choose the Best Solution

Solution 1: _____

- Pros –

- Cons –

Solution 2: _____

- Pros –

- Cons –

Solution 3: _____

- Pros –

- Cons –

Choose the Best Solution: _____

_____

Problem Solving Practice – Math Class

Problem: Natasha and her parents initially identify her problem as "Natasha has bad grades." However, that problem is not specific enough, and so Natasha can't figure out exactly what she needs to do to fix it. After discussing the problem in more detail, they come up with following:

Natasha is doing pretty good in all of her other classes, but she has a D in math class. When she asks her math teacher about why her grade is so low, her teacher says that she is missing a lot of homework assignments.

Using the first step of the ABCs of problem solving (**AIM – Identify the Problem**), and asking the **5 Ws – Who?, What?, When?, Where?, and Why?** – will help Natasha get more specific about the problem and come up with a solution to fix it! Below, write the details you need to know in order to make Natasha's problem more specific:

Who:_____

What:_____

When:_____

Where:_____

Why:_____

More Specific Problem (combines the 5 Ws from above):

_____

_____

_____

_____

Help Natasha <u>BRAINSTORM</u> possible solutions for the problem!

1.

2.

3.

4.

5.

6.

7.

8.

Choose the Best Solution

Solution 1: _____

- Pros –

- Cons –

Solution 2: _____

- Pros –

- Cons –

Solution 3: _____

- Pros –

- Cons –

Choose the Best Solution: _____

_____

Tips for Helping Teens with the ABCs of Problem Solving

- **Aim – Identify the Problem**

  - Some of the teen's problems are really big and complex, and may need to be broken down and worked on gradually.

  - Teens may also have more than one problem to solve and may need guidance on how to prioritize problems.

  - Caregivers may need to support their teen in being specific and detailed when identifying the problem because that is what leads to better solutions.

- **Brainstorming Solutions and Choosing the Best Solution**

  - Caregivers will likely know the solution that will benefit their teen the most and lead to improvement without going through the ABCs of problem solving.

    - It is critical for teens to be involved in the process of identifying and choosing solutions, even if this means it will take them longer to actually solve the problem.

    - It may take time to identify the best solution for the problem, but this will help your teen solve problems more effectively in the future.

  - Once an effective solution is found, it may be able to be applied to multiple problems.

  - Teens will need to be taught how to use and then practice the tools and strategies to help compensate for EF challenges.

Real World Practice – Session 2

First, work with your parent/caregiver to think about a challenge or problem that you have related to school – such as messy backpack, missing assignments, forgetting to do your homework. Then, go through the 5 Ws for the first step of Problem Solving – Aim – Identify the Problem. After you have identified a more specific problem, brainstorm solutions and then choose the best solution. *You will not start trying out the solution just yet – we will talk about how to do this next week by setting up a Problem Solving Plan.*

Problem: _____

_____

The 5 Ws:

Who: _____

What: _____

When: _____

Where: _____

Why: _____

More Specific Problem (combines the 5 Ws from above):

_____

_____

_____

_____

_____

<u>BRAINSTORM</u> possible solutions for the problem!

1.

2.

3.

4.

5.

6.

7.

8.

Choose the Best Solution

Solution 1: _____

• Pros –

• Cons –

Solution 2: _____

• Pros –

• Cons –

Solution 3: _____

• Pros –

• Cons –

Choose the Best Solution: _____

_____

Session 3   Using a Problem Solving Plan

Session 3 Preparation

Session Specific Supplies

- None

General AIMS Supplies

- AIMS Rules Poster
- Prize Menu and Prize Box
- Ticket Tracker and tickets
- Real World Practice Tracker
- Whiteboard and dry erase markers OR large Post-It easel pad and markers
- Pens/Pencils
- Game/Activity for Teen Group

Handouts Needed

- Large Group

    - Session 3 Schedule
    - Problem Solving Plan
    - ABCs of Problem Solving for Braden
    - Problem Solving Plan for Braden
    - ABCs of Problem Solving for Natasha
    - Problem Solving Plan for Natasha

- Teen Group

    - Reward Ideas for Teens
    - Problem Solving Plan Examples

- Caregiver Group

    - Tips for a Successful Problem Solving Plan
    - Problem Solving Plan Examples

DOI: 10.4324/9781003500209-4

- Implementing Effective Rewards on the Problem Solving Plan
- Reward Ideas for Teens

- Large Group

  - Real World Practice – Session 3

Important Points for Session 3

- **General Session Notes**

  - This session is highly didactic and the Leader will need to ensure that the teens and caregivers understand the steps of problem solving and how to utilize the Problem Solving Plan.

    - While many of the questions are directed to teens, the Leader can also ask caregivers to provide their thoughts/perspectives – especially if the teens are struggling to come up with responses or give details.
    - Leaders may want to use timers or make a note of when they need to be done with a certain activity to help with managing time during the session.
    - Leaders may want to use the whiteboard or a large post-it to write down teen and caregiver responses during various activities (e.g., Review of Real World Practice Assignment, 5 Ws, etc.). This may increase the attention and focus of teens.

  - Caregivers and teens should be given opportunities to ask questions to ensure that the concepts are understood. However, the Leader should ensure that they are managing time so that they can get through all of the content.
  - Consider rewarding teens who participate by passing out tickets when they:

    - Answer questions during the review
    - Discuss the goals of a Problem Solving Plan
    - Participate in the discussion of the Problem Solving Plan examples
    - Answer the Take Home Points questions
    - File handouts at appropriate times.

  - If needed, the ABCs of Problem Solving video could be shown again to review steps in more detail.

- **Real World Practice**

  - Leaders should allow all caregivers and teens to briefly share the problem that they identified using the 5 Ws, the solutions that they brainstormed, and the solution that they chose after going through the pros and cons. This is important for setting the foundation for discussing how to develop a Problem Solving Plan to target the identified problem.

    - It may be beneficial for Leaders to use a whiteboard or large post-it to write down each teen's identified problem and chosen solution. It is helpful for teens and caregivers to see the different problems and solutions identified prior to utilizing a Problem

Solving Plan. This may also keep other caregivers and teens engaged as each teen discusses their own problem and chosen solution.

- As teens and caregivers share their problem and solution, Leaders should provide some constructive feedback (e.g., making sure the problem is specific and includes all of the information from the 5 Ws, discussing whether the solution is realistic and doable).
- The solution that was identified as part of the Real World Practice assignment may not be the solution that is implemented in the Problem Solving Plan. While the Leader can give some feedback, the current session will be heavily focused on making sure that the caregiver and teen can translate the problem and chosen solution into a Problem Solving Plan.

- **Practice – Problem Solving Plan**

  - Leaders should make sure that teens and caregivers understand how to use the ABCs of problem solving to create a Problem Solving Plan using the examples of Braden and Natasha. These examples can be referred to as the teen and caregiver work together to create their own Problem Solving Plan.

- **Teen Group**

  - It can be helpful to remind teens that the harder that they work and the more focused they are during activities and discussions, the more time they may have to play games or to talk at the end of the teen group.
  - Leaders may want to reward specific behaviors during the teen group by passing out tickets (e.g., teens who raise their hands before speaking, teens who transition quickly and quietly from the large group to the teen group).
  - The Leader should highlight the importance of the teen taking an active role in developing their Problem Solving Plan (e.g., discussing the solution, outlining the plan, identifying motivating rewards).

- **Caregiver Group**

  - The Leader will discuss tips on how to develop and implement an effective Problem Solving Plan to address their teen's academic challenges. It may be beneficial to revisit these tips in future sessions so that caregivers build their confidence in helping their teen to identify specific problems, choose doable and realistic solutions, and identify motivating rewards for the teen as they implement the solution.
  - It can be beneficial for caregivers to talk about strategies and solutions that have worked in the past for their teen because these may be things that could be implemented in their upcoming Problem Solving Plans.
  - Leaders can encourage other caregivers to offer their ideas and experiences when discussing setting up the first Problem Solving Plan (e.g., solutions or strategies that have worked, how to build independence in the teen, reward that may be motivating).
  - Leaders should emphasize the importance of choosing motivating rewards that need to be implemented every time the behavior is demonstrated. This allows teens to make the connection that they receive something positive when they successfully implement a solution or strategy.

- In this or future sessions, it may be helpful to discuss the potential consequences of withholding an unearned reward because some teens may have very negative or strong reactions if they are not able to access a reward that they previously had access to (e.g., now only earn video game time with a Problem Solving Plan when previously they had 1 hour of video game time that did not have to be earned). If caregivers do not feel equipped to do this (e.g., worried about behaviors, worried about ability to be consistent), they should choose a reward that the teen finds motivating and can be earned in addition to other privileges that the teen may already have (e.g., earns an extra 20 minutes of video game time).

Get Ready Checklist for Leaders

❏ Prep the handouts to be passed out
❏ Hang up AIMS Rules Poster
❏ Hang up Prize Menu
❏ Check that Prize Box has range of prizes to be earned
❏ Hang up the Real World Practice Assignment Tracker (if used)
❏ Hang up Ticket Tracker (if used)
❏ Get any supplies for the games to be played in the Teen Group

Session 3 Manual

Large Group – Caregivers and Teens (45 mins)

- **Session Schedule (1 min)**

  - Pass out and refer to <u>Session 3 Schedule</u> handout.
  - *Let's make sure to get started the right way so that we can fully focus on what you will be learning today. Put all materials away except for your AIMS binder and a pen or pencil.*
  - Briefly go over the activities that are listed on the <u>Session 3 Schedule</u> handout. State that teens can cross off activities on the schedule as they are completed.

- **Review Group Rules and Prize Menu (1 min)**

  - Refer to the AIMS Rules Poster and briefly review each of the rules.
  - Remind teens that they will earn tickets that can be traded in for prizes at the end of each session when they:

    - Follow the group rules
    - Participate in the session
    - Complete activities in session
    - Complete Real World Practice Assignments
    - File handouts.

  - Briefly review that the Prize Menu shows how many tickets are needed to earn various prizes.

- **Review Real World Practice Assignment (13 mins)**

  - Instruct teens to get out their Real World Practice Assignment from the Real World Practice folder in their AIMS binder.
  - Ask: *Who completed the Real World Practice Assignment?*

    - If utilizing the Real World Practice Assignment Tracker, Leaders should indicate which teens completed their Real World Practice Assignment.
    - Check that teens filed their Real World Practice Assignment in the "Completed" section of their Real World Practice folder in their AIMS binder.

  - *Your Real World Practice from the last session was to work with your caregiver to think about a challenge or problem that you have related to school – such as a messy backpack, missing assignments, forgetting to do your homework – and then go through the 5 Ws for the first step of Problem Solving – Aim – Identify the Problem. You should have also brainstormed some solutions and then picked the best solution after going through the pros and cons. You can earn a ticket for completing your Real World Practice.*

    - Allow all teens to briefly share the identified problem, the solutions that they brainstormed, and the solution that they picked.

- The Leader should write each teen's problem and chosen solution on a whiteboard or large post-it.
- Leaders can also ask caregivers to provide input as needed.

- The Leader should provide feedback on the identified problem as needed (e.g., Does it answer the 5 Ws?). The Leader can also provide some initial guidance or feedback on the solution (e.g., Is it specific and doable, Is it realistic), but this is something that will also be discussed in more detail throughout the current session.
- Remind teens to file their completed Real World Practice Assignment in their folder.
- If teens completed Real World Practice Assignment, they should be rewarded with 1 ticket.

- **Review of Material from Last Session (2 mins)**

  - Ask the following questions (if time allows) and discuss as needed:

    - *What does EF stand for?*

      - Executive Functioning.

    - *What are the 5 EFs?*

      - Organization – Maintain systems to keep things in order
      - Working Memory – Keep things in mind while you need to use them
      - Planning – Set steps to reach a goal
      - Prioritizing – Organize steps in order of importance
      - Getting Started – Begin tasks without procrastinating.

    - *What are the 5 steps in the ABCs of Problem Solving? Remember the acronym ABCDE.*

      - *Aim – Identify the Problem*
      - *Brainstorm Solutions*
      - *Choose the Best Solution*
      - *Do it!*
      - *Evaluate.*

- **Goals for Session 3 (1 min)**

  - *Our goals for today are the following:*

    - *Learn the D (Do it) and E (Evaluate) steps of the ABCs of Problem Solving.*
    - *Learn why and how to use a Problem Solving Plan.*

- **D: Do It (3 mins)**

  - *We are going to continue talking about the steps of Problem Solving today. The 4th step of the ABCs of Problem Solving is to "Do it." This step involves you doing or trying out the solution to your problem.*
  - *Let's talk about some of the things that may make it difficult for you to solve some of your problems by doing or trying out solutions. For example, what gets in the way of helping you keep your materials at school – such as your binder, locker, or backpack – organized?*

- As a large group, briefly discuss the things that may get in the way of solving problems. Examples can include:

  - Not knowing how to solve a problem
  - Feeling overwhelmed
  - Not knowing what solution might work best
  - Feeling lazy or bored
  - Wanting to do other things
  - Avoiding problems
  - Worrying about consequences.

- Leaders can ask caregivers to give their thoughts about what things may get in the way of their teen being able to effectively solve a problem.
- *We will be using a Problem Solving Plan to make it more likely that you will try out the solution for your problem – which is the "Do it" step of the ABCs of Problem Solving! We will also be talking about how you can earn a reward for trying out a new solution, which also makes it more likely that you will do it!*
- Ask: *Any questions before we talk about the last step of the ABCs of Problem Solving?*

- **E: Evaluate How it Worked (1 min)**

  - *The last step of the ABCs of Problem Solving is "Evaluate How it Worked". We will also be using a Problem Solving Plan as a way to determine if the solution really worked. It is important to take the time to figure out what did work and what did not work when you tried out a solution. For example, you may sit down with your caregiver once a week to talk about whether your solution for turning in missing assignments is working. You will know it is working if you have fewer missing assignments and/or if your grades are going up in specific classes.*
  - Ask: *Any questions about the ABCs of Problem Solving?*

- **Problem Solving Plan (9 mins)**

  - Pass out and refer to the <u>Problem Solving Plan</u> handout.
  - *For your Real World Practice assignment this week, you will set up a Problem Solving Plan to help with a specific problem that you are having related to school. You can use the problem and solution that you identified as part of your Real World Practice assignment from last week.*
  - *Today, we are going to go through several example Problem Solving Plans so that you understand how to use them to try out the solutions to your problems.*
  - *Let's take a few minutes to review why a Problem Solving Plan is effective before we review the parts of a Problem Solving Plan.*

  - Leaders may want to write the reasons a Problem Solving Plan can be effective on a whiteboard or large post-it.
  - *A Problem Solving Plan can be effective because it:*

    - *Defines the problem in a clear and specific way.*
    - *Identifies the solution that you will be trying out to solve your problem, which may be strategies that we teach you in AIMS sessions.*

- *Has a clear plan for monitoring how you are doing. This might include checking in with your caregiver on a daily or weekly basis.*
- *Has a reward that can be earned for using the solution to solve a problem. You will be negotiating this reward with your caregiver.*

- Briefly review the main areas of the Problem Solving Plan. Leaders should use the <u>Problem Solving Plan</u> handout to point out each area as it is discussed.

  - *Problem – It should be specific and answer the 5 Ws: Who, What, When, Where, and Why.*
  - *Solution – It should be chosen after the brainstorming process and after the pros and cons of other solutions have been evaluated. This is the part of the plan in which you will write out what specific strategy you will use when solving your problem. In AIMS, we will be teaching you several strategies, such as using a planner or using a binder to organize your materials for class, that could be the strategies you include under this section of the Problem Solving Plan.*
  - *EFs being targeted – Identifying what EF is being targeted will help you understand what solutions and strategies work for your specific EF challenges.*
  - *Plan and expectations for earning reward – This will include specific details about how the solution you have chosen will address the problem. For example, you may include details about how your caregiver will check in with you to make sure you have worked on the solution. If you follow the plan and meet the expectations, you can earn a reward.*
  - *Reward – You will negotiate a reward with your caregiver that can be earned if you follow the plan and expectations for earning the reward.*
  - *Reward earned – This section allows you to keep track of when you have earned a reward.*
  - *Time frame – This part states when the Problem Solving Plan begins and when you will review it and revise any parts of it.*
  - *Signatures – You and your caregiver will both sign the Problem Solving Plan to hold you both accountable. Specifically, you are agreeing to try out the solution for the problem. Your caregiver is agreeing to provide you with a reward if you do the solution and meet the expectations outlined in the plan.*

- Ask: *Any questions about the parts of a Problem Solving Plan?*

- *Using a Problem Solving Plan may lead to many good things for teens, including:*

  - *Helping you to identify a solution (and strategies) that may solve a problem.*
  - *Giving you more responsibility.*
  - *Giving you more freedom.*
  - *Earning rewards for working to solve a problem.*
  - *Improving performance at school in areas such as organization, completing homework assignments, and studying for tests.*

- Ask: *Any questions before we get some practice with using a Problem Solving Plan?*

- **Practice – Using a Problem Solving Plan (14 mins)**

  - Pass out and refer to the <u>ABCs of Problem Solving for Braden</u> and <u>Problem Solving Plan for Braden</u> handouts.

- First, the Leader should review the identified problem and chosen solution for Braden on the <u>ABCs of Problem Solving for Braden</u> handout. Then, teens should take turns reading each component of the <u>Problem Solving Plan for Braden</u> handout.
- Ask: *Any questions before we go over another example of how to use the ABCs of problem solving to then create a Problem Solving Plan?*
- Pass out and refer to the <u>ABCs of Problem Solving for Natasha</u> and <u>Problem Solving Plan for Natasha</u> handouts.
- First, the Leader should review the identified problem and chosen solution for Natasha on the <u>ABCs of Problem Solving for Natasha</u> handout. Then, teens should take turns reading each component of the <u>Problem Solving Plan for Natasha</u> handout.

- *Over the next several weeks in AIMS, you will be creating Problem Solving Plans as you work to try out strategies that address EF challenges that you have in areas such as organization, keeping track of and prioritizing your homework assignments, and studying for tests.*
- Ask: *Any questions before we break into our separate teen and caregiver groups?*
- Leaders should have caregivers and teens split into separate groups.

  - Remind teens to file handouts in their AIMS binder and provide assistance as needed.

Teen Group (39 mins)

- **Creating a Successful Problem Solving Plan (5 mins)**

  - Leaders can briefly go over the activities that are listed on the <u>Session 3 Schedule</u> handout for the Teen Group. State that teens can cross off activities on the schedule as they are completed.
  - Ask and briefly discuss the following questions:

    - *How are you feeling about using a Problem Solving Plan to tackle a school related problem?*
    - *Have you ever used a contract or agreement like this in the past? For example, some teens may earn money or extra privileges if they do chores around the house.*
    - *The Problem Solving Plan does require you to do the chosen solution, but in return you will earn a reward! It is also likely that as you build EF skills such as organizing and planning and become more independent with managing your schoolwork, your caregiver will bug you less. What are your thoughts on some of these advantages of a Problem Solving Plan?*

  - Refer to the <u>Problem Solving Plan</u> handout.
  - *As you get ready to create your first Problem Solving Plan with your caregiver as part of this week's Real World Practice assignment, let's go over some tips*:

    - *The solution for the problem should be clear and specific.*
    - *The plan and expectations for earning the reward should also be doable and realistic.*
    - *You should choose a reward that is motivating and meaningful to you.*
    - *Your caregiver must give you the reward as soon as you have done the solution and followed the plan and expectations for earning the reward. The reward cannot be taken away if you earned it!*

  - Ask: *Any questions about a Problem Solving Plan?*

- **Possible Rewards (8 mins)**

  - *When you negotiate the Problem Solving Plan with your caregiver this week, you have the power to negotiate what reward you want to earn for completing the solution.*
  - Pass out and refer to <u>Reward Ideas for Teens</u> handout.
  - *Here are several examples of possible rewards that you could earn for doing the solution on your Problem Solving Plan. Take a few minutes to review the rewards listed and circle the ones that you think would be motivating for you.*
  - Ask: *What are some examples of rewards that you would like to earn?*

  - *Rewards can also be earned in different ways, and it can be helpful to think about the following when you are negotiating your reward with your caregiver:*

    - *When can it be earned?*
    - *How early? How late?*
    - *How much can be earned?*
    - *How long can the reward be earned for or how long can it last?*
    - *What days can you earn?*

  - *For example, if your reward is earning video games, you can potentially negotiate (1) when it can be earned – after school, after dinner, after homework; (2) how long you get to play – 1 hour, 20 minutes, 45 minutes; (3) what days/times you get to play; and (4) if you get to play video games earlier or later than usual – before school or after your usual bedtime.*
  - Ask: *Any questions about coming up with rewards for doing the solution on your Problem Solving Plan?*

- **Problem Solving Plan Examples (10 mins)**

  - Pass out and refer to <u>Problem Solving Plan Examples</u> handout.
  - *Here are several examples of simple and doable solutions to common problems that are being worked on using a Problem Solving Plan. Let's review these examples together.*
  - The Leader should go over the problem, solution, plan and expectations for earning the reward, and the identified reward for the first 2 examples on the <u>Problem Solving Plan Examples</u> handout.
  - The Leader should have teens take turns reading the problem, solution, plan and expectations for earning the reward, and the identified reward for the final 2 examples on the <u>Problem Solving Plan Examples</u> handout
  - Ask: *Any questions about using a Problem Solving Plan?*

- **Role Play: Problem Solving Plan (16 mins)**

  - *Now we are going to have one of you role-play how you might create a Problem Solving Plan with your caregiver. This will require you to identify a reward and discuss a plan and expectations for earning a reward.*
  - Have 1 teen volunteer to roleplay negotiating the Problem Solving Plan with the Leader. The goal is to complete an entire Problem Solving Plan during the role play.

    - The volunteer teen should use the target problem and the solution that they identified for last week's Real World Practice assignment. The teen can also use one of the rewards that they identified from the <u>Reward Ideas for Teens</u> handout.

- The Leader should complete each area of a Problem Solving Plan during the role play and write each area on a whiteboard or large post-it.

  - The Leader should provide constructive feedback and tips during and/or after the roleplay.
  - Other teens can be encouraged to provide their thoughts and feedback.

- If needed, the Leader can refer back to the details on the <u>Problem Solving Plan Examples</u> handout to increase teens' understanding.
- Ask: *How are you feeling about creating your first Problem Solving Plan with your caregiver?*
- *When we rejoin your caregivers, we will discuss how you will work together with your caregiver to develop a Problem Solving Plan to target the problem and solution you identified in last week's Real World Practice assignment.*
- Remind teens to file handouts in their AIMS binder and provide assistance as needed.
- If time allows, Leaders can allow the teens to play a short game that utilizes EF skills. Possible games to play include Stack Attack, Penny Stack, Connect 4, or Uno (see Manual Overview for additional information including instructions and materials needed for games).

  - Leaders may want to set a timer for this activity.

- The teens should rejoin their caregivers for the reunification with the Large Group.

Caregiver Group (39 mins)

- **Tips for a Successful Problem Solving Plan (8 mins)**

  - Briefly check in with caregivers to see if they have any questions about the content that has been presented thus far.
  - *You will be creating a Problem Solving Plan with your teen as part of this week's Real World Practice assignment. Let's go over some tips!*
  - Pass out and refer to <u>Tips for a Successful Problem Solving Plan</u> handout.
  - The Leader and caregivers should take turns reading the following tips and helpful hints so that caregivers feel competent and confident in developing and implementing the Problem Solving Plan over the next week:

    - *The solution to tackle the problem should be clear and specific so that the teen knows exactly what they need to do.*
    - *The plan and expectations for earning the reward should be doable and realistic while setting the teen up for success. For example, if a teen has never used their planner to write down and prioritize homework assignments, the solution should include some support and checking in from a caregiver (e.g., reminder to use planner before starting homework, checking accuracy of assignments written in planner, etc.).*
    - *In the plan and expectations for earning the reward section, it can be helpful to add information on (1) how the teen will get started on the solution and (2) how you will check in to make sure that they did the solution correctly. For example, you might specify that the teen should set a reminder on their phone to get started on homework at 4pm.*

You might also specify that they need to show you their completed homework after they are done and have filed it in their homework folder.

- *Do not expect improved behavior to transfer to other settings or skills. For example, if your teen is effectively using a checklist to clean out their backpack each week, this does not mean that they will be able to use a checklist for cleaning their room unless they are taught how to do this.*
- *Set realistic expectations for how long it may take certain behaviors to change or for strategies to be successfully implemented. It can often take several weeks or months for new skills or strategies to become mastered such that they are done automatically and independently.*
- *Targeting 1 solution for a problem can help improve overall performance, but may not solve the entire problem. For example, starting math homework at 4 PM at the kitchen table may not lead to an 'A' in math. However, your teen is making progress in implementing strategies to address their academic EF challenges.*
- *Focus on building independence in your teen – especially if there are behaviors that you have been providing a lot of assistance with. For example, if you are currently helping your teen write down daily assignments in their planner, prioritize what needs to be done, and then checking in on their progress with homework every 15–20 minutes – it would be beneficial to work towards the goal of having the teen independently write down assignments before eventually moving on to the goals of prioritizing assignments and then completing assignments on their own.*
- *Target effort, not just results, as an outcome. For example, if after implementing the solution to a problem, your teen's grade improved by 30% – you would likely be very happy with the effort that they have been demonstrating to bring their grades up. However, if they started at a grade of 35% and improved to 65%, this would still be a failing grade compared to someone starting at 65% and improving to 95%. The same progress may not be actually seen as the same amount of improvement despite the teen putting in significant effort to bring their grade up 30%. Thus, we will focus on effort and use of effective skills rather than grades.*

- Ask: *Any questions about using a Problem Solving Plan?*

- **Identifying Solutions for Teen's Academic Challenges (9 mins)**

  - *Beginning next week, we will talk about several specific strategies that will address the academic EF challenges that many teens face. However, for the Real World Practice assignment this week, you and your teen will begin trying out a solution to address one of their academic challenges by using a Problem Solving Plan. It is often helpful to start with something that is easy – such as writing down homework assignments or getting started on homework – as you get used to using the Problem Solving Plan. Let's go through some examples together.*
  - Pass out and refer to <u>Problem Solving Plan Examples</u> handout.
  - *Here are several examples of doable solutions to common problems that are being worked on using a Problem Solving Plan. Let's review these examples together.*

- The Leader should go over the problem, solution, plan and expectations for earning the reward, and the identified reward for the first 2 examples on the <u>Problem Solving Plan Examples</u> handout.
- The Leader should have several caregivers read the problem, solution, plan and expectations for earning the reward, and the identified reward for the final 2 examples on the <u>Problem Solving Plan Examples</u> handout.
- Ask: *Any questions before we move on to discussing rewards?*

- **Effective Rewards (12 mins)**

  - Pass out and refer to the <u>Implementing Effective Rewards on the Problem Solving Plan</u> handout.
  - *We are going to talk about the importance of using rewards when building new skills. It may be helpful to take some notes during this discussion.*
  - *Caregivers should use rewards rather than punishment because rewards motivate teens and strengthen the likelihood that teens will continue to do a behavior. As an example, many of us go to work each day in order to be rewarded with a paycheck. Our reward for going to work when we are supposed to and completing the required tasks is that we consistently receive a paycheck.*

  - *Rewards are also worded in a more positive way than punishment, which may also increase buy-in and motivation from your teen.*

    - *Punishment – If you don't do your homework, you cannot watch TV.*
    - *Reward – If you do your homework, then you can watch TV.*

  - *As you can probably tell, the way that the reward is worded is likely more motivating to most people.*

  - *We are using rewards to provide external motivation in order to build the necessary strategies that lead to an increase in EF skills and academic functioning. The target outcome is not completing homework, writing daily assignments in a planner, or putting completed assignments in the homework folder – but this is the solution that is rewarded. However, these solutions to problems will lead to the teen mastering effective strategies that compensate for EF challenges such as organization and planning.*
  - Ask: *Any questions about the use of reward to increase your teen's likelihood to do the solution on their Problem Solving Plan?*

  - *Let's review a few more points regarding rewards:*

    - *Rewards should be motivating and meaningful so that they are strong enough to change behavior. For example, 5 minutes of screen time may not motivate a teen to complete their math homework, but 20 minutes of screen may serve as a strong motivator.*

      - *If teens do not care about earning a reward or do not seem upset when they do not earn it, the reward is likely not meaningful or motivating to them.*
      - *Rewards may also need to be changed on a regular basis because a reward may be motivating one week, but not as motivating the following week.*

- *Rewards must be implemented every time the target solution on the Problem Solving Plan is completed.*

  - *This will build buy-in from the teen.*
  - *It is very important that you provide this reward if it is earned and it CANNOT be taken away. For example, if the teen does the solution by starting their homework at 4 PM at the kitchen, they earn their reward even if they then get in trouble for fighting with their sibling or not doing their chores.*

- *You must be willing to withhold the reward if the teen does not demonstrate the solution.*
- *You need to balance the strength of the reward and the feasibility of implementing the reward. For example, it is likely easier to implement the reward of playing a video game for 15 minutes each day as opposed to buying a new video game each week.*
- *Rewards should not be easily replaceable. For example, screen time may not be a motivating reward if the teen is able to access it regardless of whether they do the solution on their Problem Solving Plan.*

- *Rewards can also be earned in different ways, and it can be helpful to think about the following when negotiating your reward with your teen:*

  - *When can it be earned?*
  - *How early? How late?*
  - *How much? How long?*
  - *What days?*

- *For example, if a teen's reward is earning video games, you can potentially negotiate (1) when it can be earned – after school, after dinner, after homework; (2) how long they get to play – 1 hour, 20 minutes, 45 minutes; (3) what days/times they get to play; and (4) if they get to play video games earlier or later than usual – before school or after their usual bedtime.*

- Pass out and refer to <u>Reward Ideas for Teens</u> handout.
- *Here are several examples of possible rewards that your teen could earn for doing the solution on their Problem Solving Plan. Take a minute to review the rewards listed and circle the ones that you think would be motivating for your teen.*
- As a group, briefly discuss the rewards that 2–3 caregivers think their teen would be interested in earning.
- *The teens are also discussing this in their session, which will be helpful as you work together to choose a reward to use on the Problem Solving Plan.*

- **Collaborating with Teens to Create a Problem Solving Plan (10 mins)**

  - *For this week's Real World Practice assignment, you will work with your teen to develop the first Problem Solving Plan. It can often be difficult to communicate and negotiate with your teen as you work on developing and changing the Problem Solving Plan over the next several sessions. It will be important to keep communication barriers in mind while working with teens.*

- *Some common communication barriers that caregivers express concern about include*:

  - *Decision making abilities*
  - *Easily overwhelmed*
  - *Managing and coping with emotions*
  - *Problem solving skills*
  - *Flexibility*
  - *Impulsivity*
  - *Cooperation and collaboration.*

- Ask and discuss: *Are there things that you are concerned about as you get ready to start working on your teen's first Problem Solving Plan?*
- *Some effective communication strategies that may help to address some of the above challenges include:*

  - *Active ignoring – you can choose to ignore mild behaviors such as eye rolling and complaining as you are working on developing the Problem Solving Plan.*
  - *Engaging the teen – you can choose to emphasize how the Problem Solving Plan actually benefits the teen. Specifically, you could highlight that teens are involved in choosing the problem and the solution, and also get to choose the reward that they are working towards. It can be helpful to point out how the teen is in control of earning the reward by doing the solution on the Problem Solving Plan.*
  - *Negotiating with patience – you can keep in mind that teens can often be impulsive, single solution-focused, uncooperative, and inflexible. It may be helpful to identify a time when teens are most likely to participate in developing the Problem Solving Plan. If the teen gets upset or frustrated, it may be helpful to take a break and come back to the Problem Solving Plan later.*

- *For the remainder of our time together, let's each briefly discuss what you think your teen's Problem, Solution, Plan and Expectations for Earning the Reward, and Reward will be on the Problem Solving Plan. Keep in mind that you also want to make sure that your teen feels heard and involved in this process – so it is likely that what you are planning may change slightly.*
- Allow each caregiver to briefly discuss their thoughts for what solutions that they would like to implement on their teen's Problem Solving Plan.
- Leaders may want to write each caregiver's Problem, Solution, Plan and Expectations for Earning the Reward, and Reward on the whiteboard or a large post-it.

Reunification – Large Group (6 mins)

- **Discussion of Teen Session Material (1 min)**

  - *In their session, the teens discussed some tips for setting up the first Problem Solving Plan. We role played how to set up a Problem Solving Plan, including how to negotiate for rewards.*
  - The Teen Leaders can share any additional details about how the role play and discussion went in the Teen Group.

- **Take Home Points (2 mins)**

  - *Let's go over our take home points.*
  - Ask the following questions (if time allows) and discuss as needed:

    - *What are the benefits of using a Problem Solving Plan?*

      - *Helps you identify solutions to help target a problem*
      - *Allows you to earn a reward*
      - *May increase independence*
      - *May lead to better grades.*

    - *What are the parts of the Problem Solving Plan?*

      - *Problem*
      - *EFs being targeted*
      - *Solution*
      - *Plan and expectations for earning reward*
      - *Reward*
      - *Checklist for whether reward was earned throughout the week*
      - *When it begins and when it will be reviewed*
      - *Signatures.*

- **Real World Practice Assignment (2 mins)**

  - Pass out and refer to <u>Real World Practice – Session 3</u> handout.
  - *For your Real World Practice Assignment this week, you will work with your caregiver to complete your first Problem Solving Plan and start working on the solution that you identify for the problem. You should use the problem and solution you identified for your Real World Practice assignment last week. After our discussion today, it is possible that you may want to make your solution more specific, clear, and doable, and you can also outline this in the "plan and expectations for earning the reward" section of the Problem Solving Plan.*
  - Ask: *Any questions about your Real World Practice assignment?*
  - *You and your caregiver should set aside time either tonight or tomorrow to create the Problem Solving Plan so that you have some time to work on it over the next week and get a chance to earn a reward. Take a moment to discuss when you can complete your Problem Solving Plan with your caregiver.*
  - *In your AIMS binder, take a moment to file your Real World Practice assignment now in the "To Do" side of the folder. You should also take a moment to file all of your other handouts behind the Session 3 divider.*
  - Ask: *Any final questions before we get ready to trade in your tickets for prizes?*

- **Trade in Tickets (1 min)**

  - The Leader should give all teens who earned a ticket an opportunity to trade them in for prizes using the Prize Menu.
  - Leaders should record the number of remaining tickets on the Ticket Tracker (if used).

Session 3 Schedule

Large Group

❏ Review Group Rules and Prize Menu

❏ Review Real World Practice Assignment

❏ Review of Material from Last Session

❏ Goals for Session 3

❏ D: Do It

❏ E: Evaluate How it Worked

❏ Problem Solving Plan and Practice

Teen Group

❏ Creating a Successful Problem Solving Plan

❏ Possible Rewards

❏ Problem Solving Plan Examples

❏ Role Play: Problem Solving Plan

Reunification – Large Group

❏ Discussion of Teen Session Material

❏ Take Home Points

❏ Real World Practice Assignment

❏ Trade in Tickets

Problem Solving Plan

Date: _____

Problem Who, What, Where, When, & Why	Solution	EF(s) Being Targeted	Plan and Expectations for Earning Reward	Reward	Reward Earned?
		Getting Started Planning Prioritizing Organizing Working Memory			☐ Monday ☐ Tuesday ☐ Wednesday ☐ Thursday ☐ Friday ☐ Saturday ☐ Sunday
		Getting Started Planning Prioritizing Organizing Working Memory			☐ Monday ☐ Tuesday ☐ Wednesday ☐ Thursday ☐ Friday ☐ Saturday ☐ Sunday

This agreement begins on _____ and we will review the agreement again on _____.

_____
Teen

_____
Parent/Caregiver

© 2026 Amie Duncan and Leanne Tamm, *Improving Academic Executive Functioning for Autistic Middle Schoolers*

ABCs of Problem Solving for Braden

What is happening?
Braden goes to his locker before catching the bus to go home, but he realizes that he did not write any of his homework assignments in his planner. He is not sure what he should bring home, so he just decides to bring all of his books, notebooks, and folders home so he can figure it out later.

Aim – Identify the Problem:
I don't know the materials I need for homework and bring all of my books, notebooks, and other school materials home each day.

Brainstorm Solutions:

1. Always bring home all books, notebooks, and folders.

   - Pros – I will always have the materials I need, it is easy to figure out what I need to pack at the end of the day.
   - Cons – My backpack will be really heavy, I will not actually use most of the materials I bring home.

2. Don't bring any materials home to study or do homework.

   - Pros – Easy to do.
   - Cons – I will not be able to study for tests and do homework assignments, will affect my grades.

3. Write down the materials I need for homework and studying in my planner.

   - Pros – I will only bring home what I need, my planner can be a checklist for what I need to bring home.
   - Cons – I have to make sure I fill this out after every class, somewhat time-consuming.

4. Ask my classmate next to my locker what books he is taking home and just do the same thing.

   - Pros – Easy.
   - Cons – My classmate may not always have the same homework as I do.

Choose a Solution: Write down the specific school materials I need for homework and studying in my planner.

Problem Solving Plan for Braden

Date: Oct 8-12

Problem Who, What, Where, When, & Why	Solution	EF(s) Being Targeted	Plan and Expectations for Earning Reward	Reward	Reward Earned?
I don't know the materials I need for homework and bring all of my books, notebooks, and other school materials home each day.	Write down the specific materials I need for homework and studying in my planner.	Getting Started <u>Planning</u> Prioritizing <u>Organizing</u> Working Memory	After each class, I will write down the school materials I need to bring home in my planner. I will ask for help from my teacher if I am not sure. I will use the list in my planner at the end of the day to pack my backpack.	My mom will check my list and make sure I brought home all of the materials. I can earn 15 minutes of screen time after dinner.	☐ Monday ☐ Tuesday ☐ Wednesday ☐ Thursday ☐ Friday ☐ Saturday ☐ Sunday
		Getting Started Planning Prioritizing Organizing Working Memory			☐ Monday ☐ Tuesday ☐ Wednesday ☐ Thursday ☐ Friday ☐ Saturday ☐ Sunday

This agreement begins on __10/8__ and we will review the agreement again on __10/12__.

_____
Teen

_____
Parent/Caregiver

Natasha Example

What is happening?

Natasha is doing pretty well in all of her classes, except for math class where she has a D. When she asks her math teacher about why her grade is so low, her teacher says that she is missing a lot of homework assignments.

Aim – Identify the Problem:

Natasha has a "D" in math class due to missing assignments.

Brainstorm Solutions:

1. Drop out of math class.

- Pros – I will not be getting a "D" in math anymore, will not have to do any math homework or take math test.
- Cons – Math is a required class that I have to take.

2. Check online portal everyday after school.

- Pros – I will know what math assignments I need to do, it is pretty quick to look up my assignments.
- Cons – I will have to remember to do this everyday.

3. Use a homework folder to keep track of math assignments.

- Pros – I will always have the assignments I need to complete for math, can also put my completed math assignments back in the folder.
- Cons – I need to remember to bring my homework folder to each class and to bring it home each day.

4. Ask my sister to do my math homework for me.

- Pros – I will not have to do any math homework.
- Cons – I will have to pay my sister, I will still have to take math tests.

Choose a Solution: Use a homework folder to keep track of math assignments and check online portal every day after school to make sure there are no missing assignments.

© 2026 Amie Duncan and Leanne Tamm, *Improving Academic Executive Functioning for Autistic Middle Schoolers*

Problem Solving Plan for Natasha

Date: <u>Oct 8-12</u>

Problem Who, What, Where, When, & Why	Solution	EF(s) Being Targeted	Plan and Expectations for Earning Reward	Reward	Reward Earned?
I have a D in math class due to missing assignments.	Use a homework folder to keep track of math assignments and check online portal every day after school to make sure there are no missing assignments.	Getting Started Planning Prioritizing Organizing Working Memory	After math class, I will put worksheets in the "To Do" pocket of my HW folder. I will check the online portal every day after school to make sure I am not missing any HW. I will put completed math worksheets in the "To Turn In" pocket of my HW folder.	After my mom checks that I have used my homework folder and that all math assignments are completed in the online portal, I can earn an extra snack of my choice.	☐ Monday ☐ Tuesday ☐ Wednesday ☐ Thursday ☐ Friday ☐ Saturday ☐ Sunday
		Getting Started Planning Prioritizing Organizing Working Memory			☐ Monday ☐ Tuesday ☐ Wednesday ☐ Thursday ☐ Friday ☐ Saturday ☐ Sunday

This agreement begins on <u>10/8</u> and we will review the agreement again on <u>10/12</u>.

_____   Parent/Caregiver

_____
Teen

Session 3 – Handout 6 – p. 1 of 1

AIMS

Reward Ideas for Teens

Video and computer games	Watching YouTube videos
Dessert or favorite snacks	Watching/renting/streaming a movie
Money	Extra screen time
Time or an activity with a family member or sibling	Sleeping in on the weekends
Going out to eat at a restaurant	Having a family member cook your favorite meal
Buying a new book	Going to a favorite store
Choosing dinner or take-out	Buying a clothing item of choice
Music	Buying something for hobby (e.g., Legos)
Spending time with a friend	Going to a special event
Outdoor activities (e.g., basketball)	Going to the library
Taking time off from chores	Staying up late
Helping to plan an activity/outing	Taking lessons

Problem Solving Plan Examples

Date: 9/1 – 9/5

Problem Who, What, Where, When, & Why	Solution	EF(s) Being Targeted	Plan and Expectations for Earning Reward	Reward	Reward Earned?
I do not know what assignments I need to complete when I begin my homework each day.	Write down and prioritize all homework assignments in my planner each day.	<u>Getting Started</u> <u>Planning</u> <u>Prioritizing</u> Organizing Working Memory	By 3:30pm on Monday-Friday, I will look up all of my assignments in my online portal and write them in my planner. My dad will help me prioritize the order I need to complete my assignments.	Stay up 20 minutes past my bedtime.	☐ Monday ☐ Tuesday ☐ Wednesday ☐ Thursday ☐ Friday ☐ Saturday ☐ Sunday
I often forget to bring my materials (e.g., folders, binder, lunch, water bottle) to school each day.	Create a checklist of all of the things that I need to pack in my backpack every morning.	Getting Started <u>Planning</u> Prioritizing <u>Organizing</u> <u>Working Memory</u>	I will use a checklist by 7:55am on Monday-Friday to check that I have packed all of my materials in my backpack. My mom will check that I have used the checklist at 8am on Monday-Friday.	15 minutes of screen time from 8-8:15am until we need to leave for school	☐ Monday ☐ Tuesday ☐ Wednesday ☐ Thursday ☐ Friday ☐ Saturday ☐ Sunday

This agreement begins on <u>9/1</u> _____ and we will review the agreement again on <u>9/7</u> _____ .

_____
Teen

_____
Parent/Caregiver

Problem Solving Plan Examples

Date: 9/1 – 9/5

Problem Who, What, Where, When, & Why	Solution	EF(s) Being Targeted	Plan and Expectations for Earning Reward	Reward	Reward Earned?
I forget to turn in my homework assignments in several classes.	Put all completed homework assignments in my Homework Folder in my binder.	Getting Started _Planning_ Prioritizing _Organizing_ _Working Memory_	By 8pm on Sunday – Thursday, I will make sure that all of my homework worksheets are in my homework folder. My grandma will check my folder at 8pm on Sunday – Thursday before I put it in my backpack.	Choice of dessert	☐ Monday ☐ Tuesday ☐ Wednesday ☐ Thursday ☐ Friday ☐ Saturday ☐ Sunday
My backpack is very messy and I cannot find the materials I need.	On Friday night, I will clean out my backpack using a checklist of what I need to keep, file, or throw away.	Getting Started Planning Prioritizing _Organizing_ Working Memory	I will set an alarm on Friday at 7pm to clean out my backpack using the checklist. I will show my backpack and the completed checklist to a parent.	Choice of movie for family movie night	☐ Monday ☐ Tuesday ☐ Wednesday ☐ Thursday ☐ Friday ☐ Saturday ☐ Sunday

This agreement begins on 9/1 _____ and we will review the agreement again on 9/7 _____.

Teen _____

Parent/Caregiver _____

AIMS

Tips for a Successful Problem Solving Plan

- The <u>solution</u> to tackle the problem should be clear and specific so that the teen knows exactly what they need to do.
- The <u>plan and expectations for earning the reward</u> should be doable and realistic while setting the teen up for success.

  - Caregivers may need to provide some support and fade back this support as their teen becomes more independent.

- In the <u>plan and expectations for earning the reward</u> section, it can be helpful to add information on (1) how the teen will get started on the solution and (2) how you will check in to make sure that they did the solution correctly.
- Do not expect improved behavior to transfer to other settings or skills.
- Set realistic expectations for how long it may take certain behaviors to change or for strategies to be successfully implemented.

  - It can often take several weeks or months for new skills or strategies to become mastered such that they are done automatically and independently.

- Targeting 1 solution for a problem can help improve overall performance, but may not solve the entire problem.
- Focus on building independence in your teen – especially if there are behaviors that you have been providing a lot of assistance with.
- Target effort, not just results, as an outcome.

AIMS

Implementing Effective Rewards on the Problem Solving Plan

- Rewards are worded in a more positive way than punishment, which may increase buy-in and motivation from your teen.

  - Punishment – If you don't do your homework, you cannot watch TV.
  - Reward – If you do your homework, then you can watch TV.

- Rewards provide the external motivation to build the necessary strategies that lead to an increase in EF skills and academic functioning.

  - The target outcome is not completing homework, writing daily assignments in a planner, or putting completed assignments in the homework folder – but this is the solution that is rewarded on the Problem Solving Plan.

- Rewards should be motivating and meaningful so that they are strong enough to change behavior.

  - If teens do not care about earning a reward or do not seem upset when they do not earn it, the reward is likely not meaningful or motivating to them.
  - Rewards may need to be changed on a regular basis.

- Rewards must be implemented every time the target solution on the Problem Solving Plan is completed.

  - This will build buy-in from the teen.
  - It is very important that caregivers provide this reward if it is earned and it CANNOT be taken away.

- Caregivers must be willing to withhold the reward if the teen does not demonstrate the solution.
- Caregivers need to balance the strength of the reward and the feasibility of implementing the reward.
- Rewards should not be easily replaceable.

  - Rewards can also be earned in different ways:

    - When can it be earned?
    - How early? How late?
    - How much? How long? What days?

© 2026 Amie Duncan and Leanne Tamm, *Improving Academic Executive Functioning for Autistic Middle Schoolers*

Real World Practice - Session 3

Work with your caregiver to complete your first Problem Solving Plan and start working on the solution that you identify for the problem. You should use the problem and solution you identified for your Real World Practice assignment last week.

After our discussion today, it is possible that you may want to make your solution more specific, clear, and doable, and you can also outline this in the Plan and Expectations for Earning Reward section of the Problem Solving Plan.

Problem Solving Plan

Date: _____

Problem Who, What, Where, When, & Why	Solution	EF(s) Being Targeted	Plan and Expectations for Earning Reward	Reward	Reward Earned?
		Getting Started Planning Prioritizing Organizing Working Memory			☐ Monday ☐ Tuesday ☐ Wednesday ☐ Thursday ☐ Friday ☐ Saturday ☐ Sunday
		Getting Started Planning Prioritizing Organizing Working Memory			☐ Monday ☐ Tuesday ☐ Wednesday ☐ Thursday ☐ Friday ☐ Saturday ☐ Sunday

This agreement begins on _____ and we will review the agreement again on _____.

_____
Teen

_____
Parent/Caregiver

© 2026 Amie Duncan and Leanne Tamm, *Improving Academic Executive Functioning for Autistic Middle Schoolers*

Session 4   Developing a Homework System

Session 4 Preparation

Session Specific Supplies

- None

General AIMS Supplies

- AIMS Rules Poster
- Prize Menu and Prize Box
- Ticket Tracker and tickets
- Real World Practice Tracker
- Whiteboard and dry erase markers OR large Post-It easel pad and markers
- Pens/Pencils
- Game/Activity for Teen Group

Handouts Needed

- Large Group

  - Session 4 Schedule
  - Homework System

- Teen Group

  - Problem Solving Plan Examples for Homework System

- Caregiver Group

  - Problem Solving Plan
  - Problem Solving Plan Examples for Homework System

- Large Group

  - Real World Practice – Session 4

DOI: 10.4324/9781003500209-5

Important Points for Session 4

- **General Session Notes**

  - Leaders should ensure that they are addressing any questions that caregivers and teens have about using the Problem Solving Plan over the last week. There is time in the large group, the teen group, and the caregiver group to address any issues, questions, or concerns.

  - As the Leader discusses each teen's Problem Solving Plan, they should provide feedback on each component (e.g., solution, plan/expectations, reward) and also provide suggestions to increase the likelihood of success (e.g., specific, doable, realistic, appropriate amount of detail, motivating reward).

  - Leaders should encourage teens and caregivers to add or modify a solution on the Problem Solving Plan for this sessions' Real World Practice assignment. Specifically, teens and caregivers should add in a goal for their Homework System if feasible so that they get some practice incorporating one of the solutions discussed in the current session.

    - If the teen incorporated a solution related to their homework system on the Problem Solving Plan last week, they may need to modify it based on what is discussed in the current session.

  - Consider rewarding teens who participate by passing out tickets when they:

    - Answer questions during the review
    - Discuss how their Problem Solving Plan went from the Real World Practice assignment
    - Answer the Take Home Points questions.

- **Real World Practice**

  - During the large group, caregivers and teens will all have the opportunity to discuss the Real World Practice task of completing the Problem Solving Plan in great detail including discussion of any challenges, successes, or questions. It is likely that most teens' Problem Solving Plan will need to be modified, and time should be devoted to refining the solution, plan/expectations, and reward.

    - Leaders are encouraged to use a whiteboard or large post-it to write down each teen's identified problem, chosen solution, EFs being targeted, plan and expectations for earning the reward, and the reward. It is helpful for teens and caregivers to see the different problems, solutions, plans/expectations, and rewards on the Problem Solving Plans of other teens. This may also keep other caregivers and teens engaged as each teen discusses their Problem Solving Plan.

    - It may be helpful to have the Caregiver Leader facilitate the discussion with the teens and for another Leader to write down the details of the Problem Solving Plan on the whiteboard or a large post-it.

- Common challenges for the first Problem Solving Plan include:

  - Being too vague or too ambitious when identifying the solution
  - Not specifying a clear and doable plan and expectations for earning the reward
  - Not identifying a reward that motivates the teen
  - The caregiver withholding the reward or not delivering it immediately or consistently.

- Caregivers will also have the opportunity to discuss the Problem Solving Plan away from the teens, and it can be helpful to remind caregivers about this if they start to express frustration or negativity towards or about their teen.

- **Teen Group**

  - Leaders may want to facilitate a smooth transition from the large group to the teen group by having teens get in the habit of writing down on a whiteboard or large post-it what went well over the last week as they implemented their Problem Solving Plan.
  - It can be helpful to remind teens that the harder that they work and the more focused they are during activities and discussions, the more time they may have to play games or to talk at the end of the teen group.
  - The Leader should highlight the importance of teens taking an active role in developing their Problem Solving Plan (e.g., discussing the solution, outlining the plan, identifying motivating rewards).

- **Caregiver Group**

  - The Leader will revisit any questions or challenges that the caregivers had as they worked with their teen to implement the Problem Solving Plan at home.

    - It can be helpful for Leaders to refer to the whiteboard or large post-it notes that document each teen's Problem Solving Plan.
    - Leaders can encourage caregivers to jot down notes of things that they may want to modify or discuss on a blank Problem Solving Plan.

  - The Leader will also discuss if each caregiver wants to modify their current Problem Solving Plan by modifying the solution from last week and also adding a solution that is focused on the components of a homework system.
  - Teens will have different goals depending on their challenges and also how quickly they are able to implement new solutions.
  - Leaders should encourage caregivers and teens to try out 2 solutions on the Problem Solving Plan and emphasize that even small changes (e.g., targeting starting homework everyday at 4pm) can lead to big improvements (e.g., homework getting done earlier in the day, less arguing between caregiver and teen about starting homework).

    - While it may feel like a lot for caregivers and teens to add another solution to their Problem Solving Plan, it can be something feasible or doable that allows them to build good habits and increase independence around their homework.

Get Ready Checklist for Leaders

❏ Prep the handouts to be passed out

❏ Hang up AIMS Rules Poster

❏ Hang up Prize Menu

❏ Check that Prize Box has range of prizes to be earned

❏ Hang up the Real World Practice Assignment Tracker (if used)

❏ Hang up Ticket Tracker (if used)

❏ Get any supplies for the games to be played in the Teen Group

Session 4 Manual

Large Group – Caregivers and Teens (50 mins)

- **Session Schedule (1 min)**

  - Pass out and refer to <u>Session 4 Schedule</u> handout.
  - *Let's make sure to get started the right way so that we can fully focus on what you will be learning today. Put all materials away except for your AIMS binder and a pen or pencil.*
  - Briefly go over the activities that are listed on the <u>Session 4 Schedule</u> handout. State that teens can cross off activities on the schedule as they are completed.

- **Review Group Rules and Prize Menu (1 min)**

  - Refer to the AIMS Rules Poster and briefly review each of the rules.
  - Remind teens that they will earn tickets that can be traded in for prizes at the end of each session when they:

    - Follow the group rules
    - Participate in the session
    - Complete activities in session
    - Complete Real World Practice Assignments.

  - Briefly review that the Prize Menu shows how many tickets are needed to earn various prizes.

- **Review Real World Practice Assignment (22 mins)**

  - Instruct teens to get out their Real World Practice Assignment from their AIMS binder.
  - Ask: *Who completed the Real World Practice Assignment?*

    - If utilizing the Real World Practice Assignment Tracker, Leaders should indicate which teens completed their Real World Practice Assignment. This can be done by asking teens to raise their hands if they completed the assignment and/or walking around the room to check on whether the teens completed it.
    - Check that teens filed their Real World Practice Assignment in the "Completed" section of their Real World Practice folder in their AIMS binder.

  - *Your Real World Practice from the last session was to work with your caregiver to complete your first Problem Solving Plan and start working on the solution that you identified for the problem. You can earn a ticket for completing your Real World Practice.*
  - To assess what caregivers and teens thought about using the Problem Solving Plan, poll the large group by asking the following questions:

    - *Was it easy to set up the Problem Solving Plan?*
    - *Was it doable to work on the solution you chose on your Problem Solving Plan?*
    - *Teens – were you able to negotiate the reward that you wanted?"*
    - *Teens – did you earn a reward?"*

- *Teens – did your caregiver give you the reward if you earned it?*
- *Teens – did you make progress towards becoming independent with your schoolwork?*
- *Teens – did you have more free time to do the things you wanted to do?*

- Ask each caregiver/teen dyad to share their Problem Solving Plan. Specifically, first have each teen share the details of their Problem Solving Plan (i.e., problem, solution, EFs being targeted, plan and expectations for earning reward, and reward).
- Leaders should write each teen's Problem Solving Plan components (i.e., problem, solution, EFs being targeted plan and expectations for earning reward, and reward) on the whiteboard or a large post-it.
- The following questions can be asked of each teen when reviewing their Problem Solving Plan and writing it on the whiteboard or large post-it:

  - *What was the target problem?*
  - *What was the solution?*
  - *What was the plan and expectations for earning the reward?*
  - *What was the reward?*
  - *How did it go trying out the solution?*

    - *Did it address your problem?*
    - *Was it worth it?*

  - *Did you earn a reward?*
  - *Did you feel you had more independence?*
  - *What worked well or what was successful about your Problem Solving Plan?*
  - *What did not work or what was challenging about your Problem Solving Plan?*

- While the caregiver can weigh in, they will have time to discuss their thoughts and experiences in the caregiver group session. Ask the caregiver the following questions (if time allows):

  - *How did it go trying out the solution?*

    - *Did they make progress towards addressing the problem?*

  - *Did you feel that your teen showed more independence?*

- Leaders should allow each teen to share the progress on their Problem Solving Plan. If a teen did not complete the Problem Solving Plan, the Leader should briefly brainstorm ideas for how to complete this for the following week (e.g., choose a doable goal, set a reminder to complete the Problem Solving Plan, set a reminder to work on solution of Problem Solving Plan).
- *Each week, we will spend some time discussing the Problem Solving Plan as a group in order to address any difficulties with identifying the problem, defining and then implementing the solution and plan and expectations for earning a reward, and choosing a reward. This will help you with making any changes to the Problem Solving Plan for the following week. It does take time to figure out how to make the Problem Solving Plan work, and we can also learn a lot from hearing the experiences of other teens.*

- Remind teens to file their completed Real World Practice Assignment in their folder.
- If teens completed the Real World Practice Assignment, they should be rewarded with 1 ticket.

- **Review of Material from Last Session (2 mins)**

  - Ask the following questions (if time allows) and discuss as needed:

    - *What does AIMS stand for?*

      - Achieving Independence and Mastery in School.

    - *What are the 5 EFs?*

      - Organization – Maintain systems to keep things in order
      - Working Memory – Keep things in mind while you need to use them
      - Planning – Set steps to reach a goal
      - Prioritizing – Organize steps in order of importance
      - Getting Started – Begin tasks without procrastinating.

    - *What are the benefits of using a Problem Solving Plan?*

      - *Helps you identify solutions to help target a problem*
      - *Allows you to earn a reward*
      - *May increase independence*
      - *May lead to better grades.*

- **Goals for Session 4 (1 min)**

  - *Our goals for today are the following*:

    - *Discuss the rationale for creating an effective homework system.*
    - *Discuss the essential components of a homework system.*

- **Why Set Up a Homework System? (8 mins)**

  - Ask and discuss the following question with teens and caregivers: *What challenges do you have with getting started and then completing homework assignments?*

    - Some example responses from teens and caregivers might include the following:

      - Caregivers argue with and complain about their teen getting homework started/finished
      - Homework assignments are too difficult
      - Teens do not understand the homework assignment
      - Homework takes too long
      - Teens have little motivation to do homework
      - Teens are not organized with homework assignments and materials
      - Teens forget materials in their locker
      - Teens struggle to use a planner or to check their assignments online

- Teens get easily distracted (e.g., music, television, siblings, etc.)
- Teens do not use an efficient organization system (e.g., using binders for different classes, using a homework folder)
- Caregivers try to or feel that they have to provide significant support for homework and studying.

- *Most middle schoolers and their caregivers struggle with homework in one way or another. EF skills such as organization, planning, prioritizing, and time management do not come naturally to most teens, but instead these skills need to be learned and practiced until they are mastered.*
- *One way to tackle the challenges that often come up with homework is to use a homework system, which is a set of consistent and individualized strategies and supports that can make the process of getting homework started and completed much easier and more efficient for teens.*
- *It is important to individualize the homework system for each teen based on what works and does not work for them. It will also be critical to use the homework system consistently once it is established so that it is more likely to become a routine.*
- *As your caregivers know, staying organized and efficient is a lifelong pursuit and takes some practice. Throughout this session, we will be discussing components of a homework system that could be implemented at home.*
- *There are many benefits to setting up a homework system that is individualized to the teen, consistently implemented, and also designed to build independence. Let's discuss some of the benefits.*
- Pass out and refer to <u>Homework System</u> handout.
- Have caregivers and teens take turns reading the following benefits of a homework system from the <u>Homework System</u> handout (see below) and discuss as needed:

  - Helps develop organization skills
  - Helps develop time management skills
  - Increases ability to focus and stay on task by minimizing distractions
  - Helps get homework and studying done faster
  - Increases likelihood of turning in homework that is completed
  - Increases teens' independence by completing homework assignments on their own
  - Decreases arguing between caregivers and teens
  - Increases the amount of time to do fun things.

- **Essential Components of an Effective Homework System (15 mins)**

  - Refer to <u>Homework System</u> handout.

    - Leaders may also want to write the components of an effective homework system on the whiteboard or a large post-it to increase engagement of caregivers and teens. Teens can also take turns writing the components on the whiteboard or large post-it.

    - *Let's review the essential components for developing an effective homework system. These are strategies that are meant to increase organization, time management, and focus and concentration while also building your independence. This will help you get your homework done quicker and more efficiently so you have more time to do the things you want to do in your free time!*

- *Most teens have some problems when it comes to homework, so as we discuss these essential components of a homework system, think about whether there are solutions that may be particularly helpful to add to your Problem Solving Plan.*

- Set Up a Dedicated Homework Space

  - *The first "must have" of an effective homework system is to have a dedicated homework space. It is important to have a consistent location to do your homework, which can be at a desk, at the kitchen counter, in your bedroom, or at the dining room table. Ideally the homework space is in an area where you can work on assignments or study while having all of your supplies out and available to use. It should also be a calm and quiet place so that the teen can focus and maintain attention.*

  - *Before you start doing your homework each day, set up all of your supplies so that they are available, and you do not have to get up to use them. While some of these supplies may be in your backpack, such as books, notebooks, and folders, other supplies can be kept at your dedicated homework space such as pens, pencils, and paper.*

  - Ask: *How many of you have a dedicated homework space now?*

    - The Leader can briefly discuss teens' homework spaces. Leaders can also note that this may be a solution to incorporate on this week's Problem Solving Plan if teens do not have a dedicated homework space.

- Minimize Distractions at your Homework Space

  - *The second "must have" of creating an effective homework system is to minimize any distractions so that you can stay focused – which will help you get your homework done faster.*

  - *While the homework space should be in a calm and quiet area, it is essential to turn off any unnecessary electronic devices such as phones, tablets, and televisions that may be distracting. If a computer needs to be used for homework, it will be important to only use it for the assignment and to not do any other activities while on the computer.*

  - *While some teens like to listen to music while studying or doing homework, this can actually be a distraction and decrease concentration when working. One possible solution is to listen to instrumental or classical music because this has been shown to actually help with maintaining attention during studying or homework.*

  - *Other distractions that may impact the ability to do homework effectively include older or younger siblings or even other family members who may be doing other activities such as getting dinner started or playing a game.*

  - *It may take some time to figure out the best environment for the homework space and what distractions may need to be removed or turned off when working on assignments.*

  - Ask: *How many of you get distracted when doing your homework or studying?*

    - The Leader can briefly discuss teens' responses. Leaders can also note that this may be a solution to incorporate on this week's Problem Solving Plan if teens are frequently distracted.

- Choose a Consistent Time to Start Homework

  - *It can be beneficial to get into a consistent routine by starting homework at a specific time each day.*
  - *Many teens need a 30–60 minute break after being at school all day, so it may be best to start homework after a short break. For example, the teen could come home from school and get started on doing their homework everyday at 4pm after a snack.*
  - *Ask: How many of you get started on your homework at the same time each day?*

    - The Leader can briefly discuss teens' responses. Leaders can also note that this may be a solution to incorporate on this week's Problem Solving Plan if teens do not start their homework at a specific time.

- Designate a Block of Time to Do Homework

  - *It can also be helpful to designate a consistent block of time to do homework each day, which can be changed based on other activities or commitments. For example, a teen may do their homework from 4–5:30 on Monday–Wednesday and then 7–8:30 on Thursday because of karate practice.*
  - *Ask: How many of you do your homework within a specific block of time each day?*

    - The Leader can briefly discuss teens' responses. Leaders can also note that this may be a solution to incorporate on this week's Problem Solving Plan if teens do not have a designated block of time to do their homework.

- Decide When to Take Breaks

  - *It is a good idea to identify when breaks can be taken, how long a break will last, and what can be done during breaks from homework.*
  - *Most teens should be able to maintain focus and concentration to do homework in 30–45 minute increments.*
  - *Many teens also benefit from using a timer or alarm to indicate when to begin a break and when a break is over. For example, a teen may take a 10 minute break after working for 40 minutes. They can get a drink and watch a video on their phone during the break and must return to the homework space when the timer goes off.*
  - *Ask: How many of you take breaks when doing your homework or studying?*

    - The Leader can briefly discuss teens' responses. Leaders can also note that this may be a solution to incorporate on this week's Problem Solving Plan if teens do not consistently take breaks when doing their homework or studying.

- Use a Homework Folder

  - *In the same way that we are using a folder to file Real World Practice assignments, it can be helpful to have a specific folder to file all homework assignments.*
  - *For example, teens can place all of their assignments in the "To Do" pocket of their homework folder after it is assigned in class. Then, after they complete the homework assignment at home, they can file the assignment in the "To Turn In" pocket. Thus, all*

homework assignments are kept in the homework folder, and teens are more likely to remember to bring them home and then turn them in after they complete the assignments.
- Ask: *How many of you have a homework folder?*

  - The Leader can briefly discuss teens' responses. Leaders can also note that this may be a solution to incorporate on this week's Problem Solving Plan if teens do not have a homework folder for their assigned and completed homework.

- Discuss How to Ask for Help

  - *It is important to encourage teens to be as independent as possible when completing homework. However, if they are struggling or need help, caregivers can help them identify how to ask for help. For example, caregivers could help teens problem solve how to look up something that they are confused about in a textbook or in their notebook.*
  - *Caregivers can also provide some assistance to teens if needed, but should be mindful of how much help they are providing so that the teen continues to become independent. For example, caregivers can specify that they will check the teen's math homework after they complete 5 problems independently.*
  - Ask: *How many of you feel like it could be helpful to discuss how to ask for help when doing homework?*

    - The Leader can briefly discuss teens' responses. Leaders can also note that this may be a solution to incorporate on this week's Problem Solving Plan if teens need some guidelines about when and how to ask for help.

- *For your Real World Practice assignment this week, you will be adding in a solution that relates to a problem you may be having with getting started, doing, or turning in homework. For example, if you are struggling to stay focused when doing homework, if you procrastinate doing homework assignments, or if you forget to turn completed assignments in, several of the essential components of a homework system may be a solution to address these problems.*
- *In upcoming AIMS sessions, we will also add on strategies that may be helpful when completing homework assignments including organizing your backpack, using a binder organization system, and using a planner to write down homework assignments and break down long-term assignments and studying for tests.*
- Ask: *Any questions before we break into our separate teen and caregiver groups?*
- Leaders should have caregivers and teens split into separate groups.

  - Remind teens to file handouts in their AIMS binder and provide assistance as needed.

Teen Group (30 mins)

- **Modifying Your Problem Solving Plan (20 mins)**

  - In order to facilitate a smooth and quick transition from the large group to the teen group, Leaders can ask teens to write down one thing that worked or was successful about using the Problem Solving Plan over the last week. Leaders can have the teens read their responses and briefly discuss.

- Leaders can briefly go over the activities that are listed on the <u>Session 4 Schedule</u> handout for the Teen Group. State that teens can cross off activities on the schedule as they are completed.

- *We discussed the Problem Solving Plan that you worked on with your caregiver over the last week at the beginning of today's session in great detail.*
- Ask: *Are there any additional questions or comments that you have about continuing to try out solutions to your problems by using a Problem Solving Plan?*

- Pass out and refer to <u>Problem Solving Plan Examples for Homework System</u> handout.
- *On this handout, there are additional examples of how set up a homework system using a Problem Solving Plan.*
- The Leader should have teens read the problem, solution, EFs being targeted, plan and expectations for earning the reward, and identified reward for the first 2 examples on the <u>Problem Solving Plan Examples</u> handout.
- Ask: *Any questions about using a Problem Solving Plan to set up a homework system?*

- *You may be changing or adding to your current Problem Solving Plan by working on a solution that is related to setting up a homework system.*

  - *For example, if you struggle with turning your homework assignments in, you may try out the solution of using a single homework folder to store all your assigned and completed homework assignments in.*
  - *As another example, if you tend to procrastinate with getting started on your homework each day, you may try out the solution of starting your homework at 4pm.*

- Ask the following questions and write teens' responses on the whiteboard or a large post-it:

  - *What solution that we talked about today might be helpful for you for setting up an effective homework system?*
  - *What EF challenge would this solution address?*
  - *What reward could you earn for working on the solution?*

- *When we rejoin your caregivers, we will discuss your Real World Practice assignment. You will work together with your caregiver to continue using a Problem Solving Plan to continue targeting the solution from last week, but also add in a solution related to your homework system.*
- Remind teens to file handouts in their AIMS binder and provide assistance as needed.

- **EF Game (10 mins)**

  - If time allows, the Leader can allow the teens to play a short game that utilizes EF skills. Possible games to play include Stack Attack, Penny Stack, Connect 4, or Uno (see Manual Overview for additional information including instructions and materials needed for games).
  - The Leader should pass out tickets for teens who participate in the EF game to encourage participation.
  - The teens should rejoin their caregivers for the reunification with the Large Group.

Caregiver Group (30 mins)

- **Discussion of Problem Solving Plan (15 mins)**

  - *We discussed the Problem Solving Plan that you worked on with your teen over the last week at the beginning of today's session in great detail. I am going to pass out a blank Problem Solving Plan so that you can jot down any notes about things you may want to add or edit for the upcoming week. Also, it can be helpful to review the <u>Tips for a Successful Problem Solving Plan</u> handout that we discussed last week.*
  - Pass out <u>Problem Solving Plan</u> handout.

  - Ask: *Are there any questions or comments that you have about continuing to try out solutions to your teen's problems by using a Problem Solving Plan?*
  - *You and your teen may be changing or adding to the current Problem Solving Plan by working on a solution that is related to setting up a successful homework system.*

    - *For example, if your teen struggles with turning their homework assignments in, it may be helpful to try out the solution of using a single homework folder to store all of their assigned and completed homework assignments in.*
    - *As another example, if your teen tends to procrastinate with getting started on their homework each day, it may be helpful for them to try out the solution of starting their homework at 4pm.*

  - Pass out and refer to <u>Problem Solving Plan Examples for Homework System</u> handout.
  - *On this handout, there are additional examples of how to target setting up an effective homework system using a Problem Solving Plan.*
  - Ask: *What solution that we talked about today might be helpful for setting up a successful homework system for your teen?*

    - Leaders should write caregivers' responses on the whiteboard or large post-it.

- **Collaborating with Teens to Create a Problem Solving Plan (15 mins)**

  - *When the teens rejoin, we will discuss this week's Real World Practice assignment. You will work together with your teen to continue using a Problem Solving Plan to target the solution from last week, but also add in a solution related to a problem your teen is having with their current homework system. If your solution from last week targeted your teen's homework system, you can edit the solution to be more specific or to implement one of the strategies we discussed today.*
  - *For the remainder of our time together, let's each briefly discuss what you think your teen's Problem, Solution, EFs being Targeted, Plan and Expectations for Earning the Reward, and Reward will be on the Problem Solving Plan. Keep in mind that you also want to make sure that your teen feels heard and involved in this process – so it is likely that what you are planning may change slightly.*

    - *We also want to make sure that the teen's solution and plan for earning the reward is specific and doable so that they are set up for success as they build effective strategies for addressing their EF challenges.*
    - *We also want to make sure that it is feasible for you to implement the solution this week.*

- As each caregiver discusses their teen's Problem Solving Plan, the Leader should write the Problem Solving Plan components (i.e., problem, solution, EFs being targeted plan and expectations for earning reward, and reward) on the whiteboard or a large post-it.

- Leaders should allow each caregiver to briefly discuss their thoughts for what solutions they would like to implement on their teen's Problem Solving Plan. They may keep the solution the same, modify a solution, and/or add a solution to a target problem.

Reunification – Large Group (10 mins)

- **Discussion of Teen Session Material (1 min)**

  - *In their session, the teens discussed their thoughts on the first week of using a Problem Solving Plan and also discussed what solution they may want to use for tackling any challenges with their homework routine and space.*
  - The Teen Leaders can share any additional details about the discussion and activities in the Teen Group.

- **Take Home Points (2 mins)**

  - *Let's go over our take home points.*
  - Ask the following questions (if time allows) and discuss as needed:

    - *What are some essential components of a homework system?*

      - *Set up a dedicated homework space that includes a consistent location that is calm, quiet, and has all of your needed school supplies and materials.*
      - *Minimize distractions at your homework space.*
      - *Choose a consistent time to start homework.*
      - *Designate a consistent block of time to do homework.*
      - *Decide when to take breaks, how long breaks will last, and what can be done during breaks from homework.*
      - *Use a homework folder with a "To Do" pocket and a "To Turn In" pocket.*

    - *What are the parts of a Problem Solving Plan?*

      - *Problem*
      - *EFs being targeted*
      - *Solution*
      - *Plan and expectations for earning reward*
      - *Reward*
      - *Checklist for whether reward was earned throughout the week*
      - *When it begins and when it will be reviewed*
      - *Signatures.*

- **Real World Practice Assignment (6 mins)**

  - Pass out and refer to <u>Real World Practice – Session 4</u> handout.

- *For your Real World Practice Assignment this week, you will work with your caregiver on creating your Problem Solving Plan and start working on the solutions that you identify for your problems. Many of you will be working on two solutions – the one from last week and a new solution addressing your homework system.*

  - *After our discussion today, it is possible that you may want to make your solution more specific, clear, and doable and you can also outline this in the "plan and expectations for earning the reward" section of the Problem Solving Plan.*

- Ask: *Any questions about your Real World Practice assignment?*
- *You and your caregiver should set aside time either tonight or tomorrow to create the new Problem Solving Plan so that you have some time to work on it over the next week and get a chance to earn a reward. Take a minute to discuss when you can complete your Problem Solving Plan with your caregiver.*

- *Also, we would like you to bring in your backpacks next week with any supplies that you use for homework or classes including notebooks, folders, a planner, binder, and pens and pencils. You should also bring in a copy of your class schedule. We will be discussing how to organize your backpack and binder and will do some organizing during our session!*
- *In your AIMS binder, take a moment to file your Real World Practice assignment now in the "To Do" side of the folder. You should also take a moment to file all of your other handouts behind the Session 4 divider.*
- Ask: *Any final questions before we get ready to trade in your tickets for prizes?*

- **Trade in Tickets (1 min)**

  - The Leader should give all teens who earned a ticket an opportunity to trade them in for prizes using the Prize Menu.
  - Leaders should record the number of remaining tickets on the Ticket Tracker (if used).

Session 4 Schedule

Large Group

❏ Review Group Rules and Prize Menu

❏ Review Real World Practice Assignment

❏ Review of Material from Last Session

❏ Goals for Session 4

❏ Why Set Up a Homework System?

❏ Essential Components of an Effective Homework System

Teen Group

❏ Modifying Your Problem Solving Plan

❏ EF Game

Reunification – Large Group

❏ Discussion of Teen Session Material

❏ Take Home Points

❏ Real World Practice Assignment

❏ Trade in Tickets

Benefits of a Homework System

- Helps develop organization skills
- Helps develop time management skills
- Increases ability to focus and stay on task by minimizing distractions
- Helps get homework and studying done faster
- Increases likelihood of turning in homework that is completed
- Increases teens' independence by completing homework assignments on their own
- Decreases arguing between caregivers and teens
- Increases the amount of time to do fun things.

Essential Components of a Homework System

- Set up a dedicated homework space that includes a consistent location that is calm, quiet, and has all of your needed school supplies and materials.
- Minimize distractions at your homework space by:

  - Turning off any electronic devices such as phones, tablets, and television
  - Only using a computer or tablet when needed for homework
  - Turning off any music
  - It may be necessary to move locations if there are household distractions (e.g., sibling watching TV, parent cooking dinner).

- Choose a consistent time to start homework.
- Designate a consistent block of time to do homework.
- Decide when to take breaks, how long breaks will last, and what can be done during breaks from homework.
- Use a homework folder with a "To Do" pocket and a "To Turn In" pocket.
- Discuss how to ask for help from others.

Problem Solving Plan

Date: _____

Problem Who, What, Where, When, & Why	Solution	EF(s) Being Targeted	Plan and Expectations for Earning Reward	Reward	Reward Earned?
		Getting Started Planning Prioritizing Organizing Working Memory			☐ Monday ☐ Tuesday ☐ Wednesday ☐ Thursday ☐ Friday ☐ Saturday ☐ Sunday
		Getting Started Planning Prioritizing Organizing Working Memory			☐ Monday ☐ Tuesday ☐ Wednesday ☐ Thursday ☐ Friday ☐ Saturday ☐ Sunday

This agreement begins on _____ and we will review the agreement again on _____.

Teen _____

Parent/Caregiver _____

Session 4 – Handout 3 – p. 1 of 1

Problem Solving Plan Examples for Homework System

Date: 9/1 – 9/5

Problem Who, What, Where, When, & Why	Solution	EF(s) Being Targeted	Plan and Expectations for Earning Reward	Reward	Reward Earned?
I am easily distracted by my phone and other electronic devices when I start working on my homework.	Work at the dining room table with only the supplies and materials I need to do my homework.	Getting Started Planning Prioritizing Organizing Working Memory	I will start doing homework at 4pm at the dining room table. I will set an alarm to remind me. I can take a 10-min break every 45 minutes. I will set an alarm to remind me when to take a break and when my break is finished.	I can look at my phone during each homework break. I can have 15 minutes of extra screen time when my homework is completed.	☐ Monday ☐ Tuesday ☐ Wednesday ☐ Thursday ☐ Friday ☐ Saturday ☐ Sunday
I argue with my mom about when to start homework and often wait until after 8pm to start my assignments.	Start my homework at 4:30pm each day.	Getting Started Planning Prioritizing Organizing Working Memory	I will set an alarm to go off at 4:30pm each day. I will start my homework at my desk and will work until it is completed.	I can choose a television show to watch after dinner if my homework is done.	☐ Monday ☐ Tuesday ☐ Wednesday ☐ Thursday ☐ Friday ☐ Saturday ☐ Sunday

This agreement begins on 9/1 _____ and we will review the agreement again on 9/7 _____ .

_____ _____
Teen   Parent/Caregiver

Session 4 – Handout 4 – p. 1 of 1

Real World Practice – Session 4

- Work with your caregiver to modify your Problem Solving Plan and start working on the solutions that you identify for any problems. After our discussion today, it is possible that you may want to make your solution more specific, clear, and doable, and you can also outline this in the Plan and Expectations for Earning the Reward section of the Problem Solving Plan. Over the next week, you should do the following:

  - Add on a solution to target building an effective homework system.

  - Continue working on any solutions from your previous Problem Solving Plan.

- Bring in your backpack next week with any supplies that you use for homework or for your classes including notebooks, folders, a planner, binder, and pens and pencils. You should also bring a copy of your class schedule. We will be discussing how to organize your backpack and binder and will do some organizing during our session!

Problem Solving Plan

Date: _____

Problem Who, What, Where, When, & Why	Solution	EF(s) Being Targeted	Plan and Expectations for Earning Reward	Reward	Reward Earned?
		Getting Started Planning Prioritizing Organizing Working Memory			☐ Monday ☐ Tuesday ☐ Wednesday ☐ Thursday ☐ Friday ☐ Saturday ☐ Sunday
		Getting Started Planning Prioritizing Organizing Working Memory			☐ Monday ☐ Tuesday ☐ Wednesday ☐ Thursday ☐ Friday ☐ Saturday ☐ Sunday

This agreement begins on _____ and we will review the agreement again on _____.

Teen _____

Parent/Caregiver _____

Session 5   Backpack and Binder Organization Systems

Session 5 Preparation

Session Specific Supplies

- Projector/computer for video
- Backpack Organization Video
- Binder Organization System Video
- Example Binder Organization System
- Supplies for teens to create and organize school binders (see <u>Binder Organization System</u> handout)

  - 2" or 3" binder
  - 7 subject class planner
  - HW folder (2 pockets)
  - Folders for each class
  - Notebooks for each class
  - Dividers with pockets (one color for each class)
  - Pencil case
  - Looseleaf paper

General AIMS Supplies

- AIMS Rules Poster
- Prize Menu and Prize Box
- Ticket Tracker and tickets
- Real World Practice Tracker
- Whiteboard and dry erase markers OR large Post-It easel pad and markers
- Pens/Pencils
- Game/Activity for Teen Group

DOI: 10.4324/9781003500209-6

Handouts Needed

- Large Group

  - Session 5 Schedule
  - The Big Dump – Backpack
  - Binder Organization System

- Teen Group

  - Problem Solving Plan Examples for School Organization Systems

- Caregiver Group

  - Problem Solving Plan
  - Problem Solving Plan Examples for School Organization Systems

- Large Group

  - Real World Practice – Session 5

Important Points for Session 5

- **General Session Notes**

  - Backpack Organization

    - Leaders should consider teens' existing systems within their school and classrooms when highlighting the importance of keeping their backpack organized. For example, having an organized backpack might help teens to remember what needs to be taken home (e.g., permission slips for caregivers to sign).

  - Binder Organization System

    - It will be important to be mindful of any current binder organization systems that are being utilized by the teen at school or in specific classes (e.g., a specific binder is required for Math class) because this may impact how they create and then use a larger binder organization system.
    - All materials necessary to create a binder organization system should be provided to teens in the current session (see Session Specific Supplies). However, teens should be encouraged to utilize any materials that they currently have or that their teachers are requiring them to utilize.
    - If teens already have a binder organization system that they are using, they can choose to reorganize their current binder using the steps in the <u>Binder Organization System</u> handout.
    - It will be important to use the planner/assignment notebook system that is supported by the teen's classroom teachers. If the teen's school has a specific planner that they use, this should be utilized. Teens will learn strategies for utilizing a planner in Session 6.

- Leaders should directly address teen and caregiver buy-in to the Binder Organization System and emphasize that this is a system that can help them now (e.g., have all folders and notebooks in one place, use of a homework folder) and in the future (e.g., once they get to high school). However, this system often requires consistent and daily check-ins to ensure that things are being filed and stored appropriately.

- Leaders should ensure that they are addressing any questions that caregivers and teens have about using the Problem Solving Plan over the last week. There is time in the large group, the teen group, and the caregiver group to address any issues, questions, or concerns.

- As the Leader discusses each teen's Problem Solving Plan, they should provide feedback on each component (e.g., solution, plan/expectations, reward) and also provide suggestions to increase the likelihood of success (e.g., specific, doable, realistic, appropriate amount of detail, motivating reward).

- Consider rewarding teens who participate by passing out tickets when they:

  - Answer questions during the review
  - Discuss how their Problem Solving Plan went from the Real World Practice assignment
  - Demonstrate insight into their current organization strategies and what organization areas they may need to improve
  - Use the <u>Binder Organization System</u> handout to put together their binder
  - Answer the Take Home Points questions.

- **Real World Practice**

  - During the large group, caregivers and teens will all have the opportunity to discuss the Real World Practice task of completing the Problem Solving Plan in detail including discussion of any challenges, successes, or questions. It is likely that most teens' Problem Solving Plan will need to be modified, and time should be devoted to refining the solution, plan/expectations, and reward.

    - Leaders are encouraged to use a whiteboard or large post-it to write down each teen's identified problem, chosen solution, EFs being targeted, plan and expectations for earning the reward, and the reward. It is helpful for teens and caregivers to see the different problems, solutions, plans/expectations, and rewards on the Problem Solving Plans of other teens. This may also keep other caregivers and teens engaged as each teen discusses their Problem Solving Plan.

    - It may be helpful to have the Caregiver Leader facilitate the discussion with the teens and for another Leader to write down the details of the Problem Solving Plan on the whiteboard or a large post-it.

  - Caregivers will also have the opportunity to discuss the Problem Solving Plan away from the teens, and it can be helpful to remind caregivers about this if they start to express frustration or negativity towards or about their teen.

- **Teen Group**

    - Leaders may want to facilitate a smooth transition from the large group to the teen group by having teens get in the habit of writing down on a whiteboard or large post-it what went well over the last week as they implemented their Problem Solving Plan.

    - The Leader should highlight the importance of the teens taking an active role in developing their Problem Solving Plan (e.g., discussing the solution, outlining the plan, identifying motivating rewards).

    - The Leader should provide direct support and feedback as the teens work to organize their binders using the <u>Binder Organization System</u> handout.

    - Leaders will need to individualize the binder organization system for some teens depending on what they are currently doing at school and home. It will be important for teens to incorporate strategies/systems that are required by their school (e.g., planner) or teacher (e.g., specific math folder). However, teens should still be encouraged to develop a binder organization system so that all of their materials for each class are organized and easy to locate.

        - Leaders should encourage the teens to check-in with their caregivers about how the binder was organized, and that modifications may need to be made after the session.

- **Caregiver Group**

    - The Leader will revisit any questions or challenges that the caregivers had as they worked with their teen to implement the Problem Solving Plan at home.

        - It can be helpful for Leaders to refer to the whiteboard or large post-it notes that document each teen's Problem Solving Plan.

        - Leaders can encourage caregivers to jot down notes of things that they may want to modify or discuss on a blank Problem Solving Plan.

    - The Leader will also discuss if each caregiver wants to modify their current Problem Solving Plan by modifying the solution from last week and also adding a solution that is focused on organizing the backpack or binder.

    - Teens will have different goals depending on their challenges and also how quickly they are able to implement new solutions.

    - Leaders should encourage caregivers and teens to try out 2–3 solutions on the Problem Solving Plan and emphasize that even small changes (e.g., targeting starting homework everyday at 4pm, organizing the teen's backpack weekly) can lead to big improvements (e.g., homework getting done earlier in the day, not losing assignments or materials).

        - While it may feel like a lot for caregivers and teens to add another solution to their Problem Solving Plan, it can be something feasible or doable that allows them to build good habits and increase independence around organizing their materials (e.g., checking that they have their planner in their backpack each morning).

Get Ready Checklist for Leaders

❏ Prep the handouts to be passed out
❏ Hang up AIMS Rules Poster
❏ Hang up Prize Menu
❏ Check that Prize Box has range of prizes to be earned
❏ Hang up the Real World Practice Assignment Tracker (if used)
❏ Hang up Ticket Tracker (if used)
❏ Set up projector and/or computer
❏ Open the Backpack Organization video
❏ Open the Binder Organization video
❏ Prep Example Binder Organization system with planner, binder, class schedule, HW folder, folders, dividers, pencil case, paper, and notebooks
❏ Gather supplies needed for each teen to create their binder system (i.e., 2" or 3" binder, planner, HW folder, folders, notebooks, dividers, pencil case, and paper)
❏ Get any supplies for the games to be played in the Teen Group

Session 5 Manual

Large Group – Caregivers and Teens (50 mins)

- **Session Schedule (1 min)**

  - Pass out and refer to <u>Session 5 Schedule</u> handout.
  - *Let's make sure to get started the right way so that we can fully focus on what you will be learning today. Put all materials away except for your AIMS binder and a pen or pencil.*
  - Briefly go over the activities that are listed on the <u>Session 5 Schedule</u> handout. State that teens can cross off activities on the schedule as they are completed.

- **Review Group Rules and Prize Menu (1 min)**

  - Refer to the AIMS Rules Poster and briefly review each of the rules.
  - Remind teens that they will earn tickets that can be traded in for prizes at the end of each session when they:

    - Follow the group rules
    - Participate in the session
    - Complete activities in session
    - Complete Real World Practice Assignments.

  - Briefly review that the Prize Menu shows how many tickets are needed to earn various prizes.

- **Review Real World Practice Assignment (22 mins)**

  - Instruct teens to get out their Real World Practice Assignment from their AIMS binder.
  - Ask: *Who completed the Real World Practice Assignment?*

    - If utilizing the Real World Practice Assignment Tracker, Leaders should indicate which teens completed their Real World Practice Assignment. This can be done by asking teens to raise their hands if they completed the assignment and/or walking around the room to check on whether the teens completed it.
    - Check that teens filed their Real World Practice Assignment in the "Completed" section of their Real World Practice folder in their AIMS binder.

  - *Your Real World Practice from the last session was to work with your caregiver to modify your Problem Solving Plan and start working on the solution that you identified for the problem. Last week, we talked about the essential components of a homework system, so we encouraged you to choose a solution to address any problems you were having with doing homework. You can earn a ticket for completing your Real World Practice.*
  - To assess what caregivers and teens thought about using the Problem Solving Plan, poll the large group by asking the following questions:

    - *Was it easy to set up the Problem Solving Plan?*
    - *Was it doable to work on the solution you chose on your Problem Solving Plan?*

- *Teens – were you able to negotiate the reward that you wanted?*
- *Teens – did you earn a reward?*
- *Teens – did your caregiver give you the reward if you earned it?*
- *Teens – did you make progress towards becoming independent with your schoolwork?*
- *Teens – did you have more free time to do the things you wanted to do?*

- Ask each caregiver/teen dyad to share their Problem Solving Plan. Specifically, first have each teen share the details of their Problem Solving Plan (i.e., problem, solution, EFs being targeted, plan and expectations for earning reward, and reward).

  - Due to time constraints, teens should share 1–2 of the solutions that they are targeting. If applicable, Leaders should encourage teens to discuss the use of a solution for their homework space.

- Leaders should write each teen's Problem Solving Plan components (i.e., problem, solution, EFs being targeted plan and expectations for earning reward, and reward) on the whiteboard or a large post-it.
- The following questions can be asked of each teen when reviewing their Problem Solving Plan and writing it on the whiteboard or large post-it:

  - *What was the target problem?*
  - *What was the solution?*
  - *What was the plan and expectations for earning the reward?*
  - *What was the reward?*
  - *How did it go trying out the solution?*

    - *Did it address your problem?*
    - *Was it worth it?*

  - *Did you earn a reward?*
  - *Did you feel you had more independence?*
  - *What worked well or what was successful about your Problem Solving Plan?*
  - *What did not work or what was challenging about your Problem Solving Plan?*

- While the caregiver can weigh in, they will have time to discuss their thoughts and experiences in the caregiver group session. Ask the caregiver the following questions (if time allows):

  - *How did it go trying out the solution?*

    - *Did they make progress towards addressing the problem?*

  - *Did you feel that your teen showed more independence?*

- Leaders should allow each teen to share the progress on their Problem Solving Plan. If a teen did not complete the Problem Solving Plan, the Leader should briefly brainstorm ideas for how to complete this for the following week (e.g., choose a doable goal, set a reminder to complete the Problem Solving Plan, set a reminder to work on solution of Problem Solving Plan).

- *As a reminder, each week we will spend some time discussing the Problem Solving Plan as a group in order to address any difficulties with identifying the problem, defining and then implementing the solution and plan and expectations for earning a reward, and choosing a reward.*

  - Remind teens to file their completed Real World Practice Assignment in their folder.
  - If teens completed the Real World Practice Assignment, they should be rewarded with 1 ticket.

- **Review of Material from Last Session (2 mins)**

  - Ask the following questions (if time allows) and discuss as needed:

    - *What are the benefits of using a Problem Solving Plan?*

      - *Helps you identify solutions to help target a problem*
      - *Allows you to earn a reward*
      - *May increase independence*
      - *May lead to better grades.*

    - *What are some essential components of a homework system?*

      - *Set up a dedicated homework space that includes a consistent location that is calm, quiet, and has all of your needed school supplies and materials.*
      - *Minimize distractions at your homework space.*
      - *Choose a consistent time to start homework.*
      - *Designate a consistent block of time to do homework.*
      - *Decide when to take breaks, how long breaks will last, and what can be done during breaks from homework.*
      - *Use a homework folder with a "To Do" pocket and a "To Turn In" pocket.*

- **Goals for Session 5 (1 min)**

  - *Our goals for today are the following*:

    - *Learn how to organize your backpack using the Big Dump strategy.*
    - *Learn how to organize the materials and supplies from your classes using a Binder Organization System.*

- **Organizing Your Backpack (7 mins)**

  - Ask the teens the following questions about their backpack and briefly discuss their responses:

    - *What do you carry in your backpack each day?*
    - *Is your backpack messy?*
    - *How often do you clean out your backpack?*
    - *Do you have an organization system that you use for your backpack?*

- *Do you use any accessories (e.g., keychain, pencil case, backpack pockets) to help with organizing your backpack?*

- *We are going to use the Big Dump strategy to organize the things in your backpack and then keep it organized.*
- Show Backpack Organization video (2m 53s).

  - NOTE: If the teens are having difficulty paying attention or staying engaged, the video can be paused and the Leader can ask questions (e.g., What are the main steps of The Big Dump? What items would you trash? What items would you file?) to increase the likelihood that they will understand the concepts.

- **The Big Dump – Backpack (3 mins)**

  - Pass out and refer to <u>The Big Dump – Backpack</u> handout.
  - Have 2–3 teens read through the main steps for The Big Dump – Backpack that were also covered in the video (see below) and discuss as needed:

    - Gather your backpack and all materials that you carry in your backpack (e.g., binder, planner, textbooks, notebooks, folders, etc.).
    - Remove all items from your backpack so that it is completely empty.
    - Examine each item and determine which of the 3 Main Steps to do:

      - Act on it – Make a plan for any papers that need to be completed (e.g., math worksheet, permission slip, etc.).
      - File it – Organize and file any papers or materials that you may need for classes (e.g., study guide for an upcoming test, worksheets, homework to be turned in, etc.).
      - You could also use accessories to help with keeping things organized. For example, a pencil case could be used to hold all of your pens and pencils. A keychain could be used to hold your keys or your water bottle.
      - Trash it – Throw away or recycle items that you no longer need in the trash (e.g., old papers no longer needed for class, wrappers, food or drinks, etc.).

    - Choose a time each week to do the 3 main steps of The Big Dump – Backpack. It can be helpful to set up a reminder to do this (e.g., Sunday night after dinner).
    - If you keep your backpack organized, you will have to do The Big Dump – Backpack less often (e.g., once per month).

  - *While we do not have time today to practice the Big Dump, this is something that you could potentially add to your Problem Solving Plan this week to work on. For example, if one of your problems is keeping your backpack organized, you could add the solution of the Big Dump and commit to doing it one time per week on your Problem Solving Plan.*

- **Binder Organization System (13 mins)**

  - Pass out and refer to the <u>Binder Organization System</u> handout.
  - The Leader should refer to the Example Binder Organization System when pointing out the various features described below.

- *The next organization strategy we are going to learn about is how to develop a Binder Organization System, which will keep all of the materials for your classes organized in a very simple way.*
- *We are going to encourage you to use a single binder to store all folders, notebooks, papers, assignments, notes, study guides, and other materials from your classes.*
- *We are going to work together to figure out how to make and then use a Binder Organization System that works for you based on your classes. It will take some time to get used to a new organization system, but it will help you keep things organized, save you time looking for materials, and keep track of your assignments and quizzes/tests.*

- *Let's watch a video together on how to create a Binder Organization System.*
- Show the Binder Organization video (2m 17s).

  - NOTE: If the teens are having difficulty paying attention or staying motivated, the video can be paused and the Leader can ask questions (e.g., What materials do you need to organize a binder? What materials should go at the front of the binder?) to increase the likelihood that they will understand the concepts.

- *Let's go over some of the features of a binder organization system that we saw in the video.*

  - *Individual subjects will have their own colored divider with pockets that will be stored in the binder. For example, you may use a red folder for Language Arts and a green folder for Science. The front subject divider pocket can be used to store class handouts while the back pocket can be used for graded papers and tests. If you have notebooks or folders for these classes, you should also put these in your binder.*
  - *There will be a homework folder that is brought home daily and includes all of the papers and assignments that need to be brought home.*

- Ask: *Any questions about how you will be creating a binder organization to use at school?*

  - Leaders may need to answer questions about how to individualize the binder for teens based on their individual school or teacher preferences.
  - The overall goal is to use to a binder to organize the teen's current class materials.

- *We will work on creating a Binder Organization System in the teen group and this is also something that you could add to your Problem Solving Plan this week.*
- Ask: *Any questions before we break into our separate teen and caregiver groups?*
- Leaders should have caregivers and teens split into separate groups.

  - Remind teens to file handouts in their AIMS binder and provide assistance as needed.

Teen Group (30 mins)

- **Modifying Your Problem Solving Plan (10 mins)**

  - In order to facilitate a smooth and quick transition from the large group to the teen group, Leaders can ask teens to write down one thing that worked or was successful about using the Problem Solving Plan over the last week. Leaders can have the teens read their responses and briefly discuss.

- Leaders can briefly go over the activities that are listed on the <u>Session 5 Schedule</u> handout for the Teen Group. State that teens can cross off activities on the schedule as they are completed.

- *We discussed the Problem Solving Plan that you worked on with your caregiver over the last week at the beginning of today's session in great detail.*
- Ask: *Are there any questions or comments that you have about continuing to try out solutions to your problems by using a Problem Solving Plan?*
- Pass out and refer to <u>Problem Solving Plan Examples for School Organization Systems</u> handout.
- *On this handout, there are additional examples of how to set up a binder or backpack organization system using a Problem Solving Plan.*
- The Leader should have teens read the problem, solution, EFs being targeted, plan and expectations for earning the reward, and identified reward for the first 2 examples on the <u>Problem Solving Plan Examples for School Organization Systems</u> handout.
- Ask: *Any questions about using a Problem Solving Plan to set up an organization system for your backpack or binder?*

- *For your Real World Practice assignment this week, You may be changing or adding to your current Problem Solving Plan by working on a solution that is related to using an organization system for your backpack or binder.*

  - *For example, if you struggle with keeping all of the materials for your classes organized and often lose papers, you may try out the solution of using a binder organization system.*

- Ask the following questions and write teens' responses on the whiteboard or a large post-it:

  - *What solution that we talked about today might be helpful for you for setting up an effective organization system for your backpack, binder, or class materials?*
  - *What EF challenge would this solution address?*
  - *What reward could you earn for working on the solution?*

- *When we rejoin your caregivers, we will discuss your Real World Practice assignment. You will work together with your caregiver to continue using a Problem Solving Plan to continue targeting the solution from last week, but will also add in a solution related to using an organization system.*

- **Creating a Binder Organization System (20 mins)**

  - *Let's start working on creating your own binder organization system. We will use the steps on the Binder Organization System handout, and if we do not finish in session, this is something that you can also do with your caregiver at home.*
  - Refer to the <u>Binder Organization System</u> handout.
  - Pass out materials for teens to create a binder organization system based on what they need.
  - *You should have all of the materials necessary to create your own Binder Organization System including a binder, dividers, folders, planner, notebooks, loose leaf paper, and pencil case. You will also need to incorporate any materials that you have in your backpack.*

- Leaders may need to work with individual students to determine what materials they need (e.g., they are using their school's planner but they need a HW folder).

- The Leader should read each step on the <u>Binder Organization System</u> handout to assist teens with understanding and applying each step. The Leader should also demonstrate each step using the Example Binder Organization System and answer questions as needed.

  - Leaders should provide guidance as needed. It may be beneficial to split teens up into smaller groups so that Leaders can help with putting together the binder organization systems.
  - Teens can use the handout as a checklist to indicate that each step has been completed.
  - Encourage teens to help one another or refer to how other teens are putting their binders together.

- *You have all shown good organizational skills by putting together a binder that you can use every day to keep track of all of your class materials! When we rejoin your caregivers, we will show them the progress you made by creating your binder.*
- Remind teens to file handouts in their AIMS binder and provide assistance as needed.
- The Leader should pass out tickets for teens who actively worked on organizing their binder.
- The teens should rejoin their caregivers for the reunification with the Large Group.

Caregiver Group (30 mins)

- **Discussion of Problem Solving Plan (10 mins)**

  - *We discussed the Problem Solving Plan that you worked on with your teen over the last week at the beginning of today's session in great detail. I am going to pass out a blank Problem Solving Plan so that you can jot down any notes about things you may want to add or edit for the upcoming week. Also, it can be helpful to review the <u>Tips for a Successful Problem Solving Plan</u> handout that we discussed a few weeks ago.*
  - Pass out <u>Problem Solving Plan</u> handout.

  - Ask: *Are there any questions or comments that you have about continuing to try out solutions to your teen's problems by using a Problem Solving Plan?*
  - *You and your teen may be changing or adding to the current Problem Solving Plan by working on a solution that is related to using a system to organize their backpack or binder.*

    - *For example, if your teen struggles with organizing the various folders, notebooks and papers for their classes, it may be helpful to try out the solution of using a binder organization system.*

  - Pass out and refer to <u>Problem Solving Plan Examples for School Organization System</u> handout.
  - *On this handout, there are additional examples of how to target setting up an effective organization system using a Problem Solving Plan.*

- Ask: *What solution that we talked about today might be helpful for setting up a successful organization system for your teen?*

- Leaders should write caregivers' responses on the whiteboard or large post-it.

- **Collaborating with Teens to Create a Problem Solving Plan (20 mins)**

  - *Your teen is working on creating a binder organization system in the teen group session. They may not complete all of the steps, but will likely have a lot of the components completed. This is something that you can help them finish setting up at home – especially if this is a solution you would like for them to implement as a solution on their Problem Solving Plan.*

    - *You may also need to individualize the binder organization system based on any requirements of your child's school or classroom teachers.*
    - *The important thing is that your teen has a binder that they can use to organize and then easily locate all class materials.*

  - *When the teens rejoin us, we will discuss this week's Real World Practice assignment. You will work together with your teen to continue using a Problem Solving Plan to target the solution or solutions from last week, but also add in a solution related to a problem your teen is having with their current school organization system.*
  - *For the remainder of our time together, let's each briefly discuss what you think your teen's Problem, Solution, EFs being Targeted, Plan and Expectations for Earning the Reward, and Reward will be on the Problem Solving Plan. Keep in mind that you also want to make sure that your teen feels heard and involved in this process – so it is likely that what you are planning may change slightly.*

    - *We also want to make sure that the teen's solution and plan for earning the reward is specific and doable so that they are set up for success as they build effective strategies for addressing their EF challenges.*
    - *We also want to make sure that it is feasible for you to implement the solution this week.*

  - *We understand that it can feel like a lot to be working on 2–3 solutions on the Problem Solving Plan, but even adding in a solution that is easy and quick can have a big impact and may help build up to larger solutions down the road.*

    - *For example, it may only be doable to add in using a binder that has the teen's planner and homework folder in it. However, after the teen is using the binder consistently, you could add in that the teen also keeps their notebooks and folders for each class in the binder.*

  - As each caregiver discusses their teen's Problem Solving Plan, the Leader should write the Problem Solving Plan components (i.e., problem, solution, EFs being targeted plan and expectations for earning reward, and reward) on the whiteboard or a large post-it.

    - Leaders should allow each caregiver to briefly discuss their thoughts for what solutions they would like to implement on their teen's Problem Solving Plan. They may keep the solution the same, modify a solution, and/or add a solution to target a problem.

Reunification – Large Group (10 mins)

- **Discussion of Teen Session Material (4 mins)**

  - *In their session, the teens discussed their thoughts on using a Problem Solving Plan and also discussed what solution they may want to address for any challenges they have with organizing their binder or backpack. The teens also worked on creating a binder organization system that they could use at school. Let's take a minute to allow the teens to share their binder organization system with their caregiver.*
  - The Leader should have teens share the parts of their binder organization system with the caregiver and briefly address any questions or comments that caregivers may have. It is likely that several of the teens may need to finish their binder organization system at home – especially if they did not bring all of the necessary materials to the session.
  - The Teen Leaders can share any additional details about the discussion and activities in the Teen Group.

- **Take Home Points (1 min)**

  - *Let's go over our take home points.*
  - Ask the following questions (if time allows) and discuss as needed:

    - *What are the steps of The Big Dump – Backpack?*

      - *Empty backpack*
      - *Act on it*
      - *File it*
      - *Trash it*
      - *Pick a time each week to do the 3 main steps (Act on it, File it, Trash it).*

    - *Why would you use a Binder Organization System?*

      - *To keep all of your classroom materials (e.g., notebooks, folders, planner) organized*
      - *To more easily locate worksheets, study guides, graded tests/quizzes, etc. for each class*
      - *To have access to your planner/assignment notebook in each class so that assignments and upcoming tests/quizzes can be written down*
      - *To have a consistent place to put homework that needs to be completed and homework that has been completed.*

- **Real World Practice Assignment (4 mins)**

  - Pass out and refer to <u>Real World Practice – Session 5</u> handout.
  - *For your Real World Practice Assignment this week, you will work with your caregiver on creating your Problem Solving Plan and start working on the solutions that you identify for your problems. Many of you will be working on three solutions – the two solutions from last week and a new solution addressing your organization system for your backpack and binder.*

- *After our discussion today, it is possible that you may want to make your solution more specific, clear, and doable and you can also outline this in the plan and expectations for earning the reward section of the Problem Solving Plan.*

- Ask: *Any questions about your Real World Practice assignment?*
- *You and your caregiver should set aside time either tonight or tomorrow to create the new Problem Solving Plan so that you have some time to work on it over the next week and get a chance to earn a reward. Take a minute to discuss when you can complete your Problem Solving Plan with your caregiver.*

- *Also, we would like you to bring in your planner or assignment notebook next week because we will be discussing how to write down and prioritize daily assignments, including studying for tests and working on long-term assignments.*
- *In your AIMS binder, take a moment to file your Real World Practice assignment now in the "To Do" side of the folder. You should also take a moment to file all of your other handouts behind the Session 5 divider.*
- Ask: *Any final questions before we get ready to trade in your tickets for prizes?*

- **Trade in Tickets (1 min)**

  - The Leader should give all teens who earned a ticket an opportunity to trade them in for prizes using the Prize Menu.
  - Leaders should record the number of remaining tickets on the Ticket Tracker (if used).

Session 5 Schedule

Large Group

❏ Review Group Rules and Prize Menu

❏ Review Real World Practice Assignment

❏ Review of Material from Last Session

❏ Goals for Session 5

❏ Organizing Your Backpack

❏ The Big Dump – Backpack

❏ Binder Organization System

Teen Group

❏ Modifying Your Problem Solving Plan

❏ Creating a Binder Organization System

Reunification – Large Group

❏ Discussion of Teen Session Material

❏ Take Home Points

❏ Real World Practice Assignment

❏ Trade in Tickets

The Big Dump – Backpack

Steps	Complete?
Gather your backpack and all materials that you carry in your backpack (e.g., binder, planner, textbooks, notebooks, folders, etc.).	
Remove all items from your backpack so that it is completely empty.	
Examine each item and determine which of the 3 Main Steps to do: 1. **ACT ON IT** – Make a plan for any papers or materials that need to be completed (e.g., math worksheet, permission slip, etc.). 2. **FILE IT** – Organize and file any papers or materials that you may need for class (e.g., study guide for upcoming class, worksheets, homework to be turned in, etc.). 3. **TRASH IT** – Throw away any items that you no longer need in the trash (e.g., papers no longer needed for class, wrappers, food or drinks, etc.).	
Choose a time each week to do the 3 Main Steps. It can be helpful to set a reminder to do this at the same day and time each week.	

Binder Organization System

Materials Needed

- One large binder (2" or 3") for all classes
- Copy of class schedule
- Pencil case
- Planner or Assignment Notebook
- One folder with 2 pockets for homework
- Notebooks and/or folders (one color for each class)
- Subject dividers with pockets (one color for each class)
- Loose leaf paper

How to Make Binder:

1. Insert class schedule in the front of the binder.

2. Insert pencil case.

3. Insert planner or assignment notebook.

4. Insert homework folder:

   - Label left side "Homework to do"
   - Label right side "Homework to turn in".

5. Insert subject divider with notebooks and/or folders for each class in the order that your classes are on your schedule.

   - Choose a different color for each subject (e.g., green for Science, red for Math).

6. Label the subject divider pockets.

   - Front: Class Handouts.
   - Back: Graded Papers and Tests.

7. Insert loose leaf paper at the back of your binder to be used as needed.

Problem Solving Plan

Date: _____

Problem Who, What, Where, When, & Why	Solution	EF(s) Being Targeted	Plan and Expectations for Earning Reward	Reward	Reward Earned?
		Getting Started Planning Prioritizing Organizing Working Memory			☐ Monday ☐ Tuesday ☐ Wednesday ☐ Thursday ☐ Friday ☐ Saturday ☐ Sunday
		Getting Started Planning Prioritizing Organizing Working Memory			☐ Monday ☐ Tuesday ☐ Wednesday ☐ Thursday ☐ Friday ☐ Saturday ☐ Sunday

This agreement begins on _____ and we will review the agreement again on _____ .

_____
Parent/Caregiver

_____
Teen

Session 5 – Handout 4 – p. 1 of 1

AIMS

Problem Solving Plan Examples for School Organization System

Date: 9/1 – 9/5

Problem Who, What, Where, When, & Why	Solution	EF(s) Being Targeted	Plan and Expectations for Earning Reward	Reward	Reward Earned?
I often lose things or cannot find things in my backpack.	Do the steps of the Big Dump – Backpack every Sunday night at 7:30pm as a way to get ready for the week.	Getting Started Planning Prioritizing <u>Organizing</u> Working Memory	I will set an alarm to remind me to do the Big Dump – Backpack every Sunday at 7:30pm. I will use the Big Dump – Backpack checklist to make sure I do all of the steps. My dad will check my backpack to make sure I did all of the steps.	I can earn $3.	☐ Monday ☐ Tuesday ☐ Wednesday ☐ Thursday ☐ Friday ☐ Saturday ☐ Sunday
I do not have any way to organize my notes, worksheets, and study guides, and I often lose things because I misplace them or put them in the incorrect place.	Use a binder organization system to organize my notebooks, folders, and homework folder for all of my classes.	<u>Getting Started</u> <u>Planning</u> Prioritizing Organizing Working Memory	I will file any papers in the correct subject folder after class. I will use the correct notebook for each class that is in my binder. My mom and I will check how I am doing using the binder after school each day.	I can choose an extra after school snack of my choice if I correctly used the binder organization system during the school day.	☐ Monday ☐ Tuesday ☐ Wednesday ☐ Thursday ☐ Friday ☐ Saturday ☐ Sunday

This agreement begins on 9/1 _____ and we will review the agreement again on 9/7 _____ .

_____   _____
Teen   Parent/Caregiver

Session 5 – Handout 5 – p. 1 of 1

Real World Practice – Session 5

1. Work with your caregiver to modify your Problem Solving Plan and start working on the solutions that you identify for the problems. After our discussion today, it is possible that you may want to make your solution more specific, clear, and doable, and you can also outline this in the Plan and Expectations for Earning Reward section of the Problem Solving Plan. Over the next week, you should do the following:

   a. Add on a solution to target building an effective school organization system for your backpack or binder.

   b. Continue working on any solutions from your previous Problem Solving Plan.

2. Bring in your planner or assignment notebook next week. We will be discussing how to plan and prioritize your homework assignments, including studying for tests and working on long-term assignments or projects.

   a. If your school uses an online portal for managing assignments or grades, make sure that you are able to log in before next week's session!

Problem Solving Plan

Date: _____

Problem Who, What, Where, When, & Why	Solution	EF(s) Being Targeted	Plan and Expectations for Earning Reward	Reward	Reward Earned?
		Getting Started Planning Prioritizing Organizing Working Memory			❑ Monday ❑ Tuesday ❑ Wednesday ❑ Thursday ❑ Friday ❑ Saturday ❑ Sunday
		Getting Started Planning Prioritizing Organizing Working Memory			❑ Monday ❑ Tuesday ❑ Wednesday ❑ Thursday ❑ Friday ❑ Saturday ❑ Sunday

This agreement begins on _____ and we will review the agreement again on _____.

_____
Teen

_____
Parent/Caregiver

AIMS

Problem Solving Plan

Date: _____

Problem Who, What, Where, When, & Why	Solution	EF(s) Being Targeted	Plan and Expectations for Earning Reward	Reward	Reward Earned?
		Getting Started Planning Prioritizing Organizing Working Memory			☐ Monday ☐ Tuesday ☐ Wednesday ☐ Thursday ☐ Friday ☐ Saturday ☐ Sunday
		Getting Started Planning Prioritizing Organizing Working Memory			☐ Monday ☐ Tuesday ☐ Wednesday ☐ Thursday ☐ Friday ☐ Saturday ☐ Sunday

This agreement begins on _____ and we will review the agreement again on _____.

_____
Teen

_____
Parent/Caregiver

Session 6   Using a Planner for Homework Assignments

Session 6 Preparation

Session Specific Supplies

- Example planner
- Computer to look up homework assignments in the teen's online portal

General AIMS Supplies

- AIMS Rules Poster
- Prize Menu and Prize Box
- Ticket Tracker and tickets
- Real World Practice Tracker
- Whiteboard and dry erase markers OR large Post-It easel pad and markers
- Pens/Pencils
- Game/Activity for Teen Group

Handouts Needed

- Large Group

  - Session 6 Schedule
  - Weekly Planner
  - Weekly Planner Example
  - Keeping Track of Homework Assignments Using a Planner
  - Prioritizing Planner Tasks

- Teen Group

  - Problem Solving Plan Examples for Using a Planner
  - Have to Do vs. Want to Do Tasks

- Caregiver Group

  - Problem Solving Plan
  - Problem Solving Plan Examples for Using a Planner

DOI: 10.4324/9781003500209-7

- Large Group
  - Real World Practice – Session 6

Important Points for Session 6

- **General Session Notes**

  - This session is highly didactic and teens are more likely to understand how to use a planner and prioritize assignments the more they actively participate. Leaders are encouraged to reward teens with tickets when they participate throughout.
  - Keeping Track of Assignments with a Planner

    - It will also be important to use the planner/assignment notebook system that is supported by the teen's classroom teachers. If the teen's school has a specific planner that they use, this should be utilized. If not, it may be helpful to utilize a student planner that has room to write and prioritize assignments for at least 7 subjects (similar to what was used in Session 5). Further, if teens are using an online portal, planner, or calendar to manage their assignments, the concepts in this session can still be applied.
    - We highly encourage teens to use a paper planner (even if the school uses an online portal) because writing down and prioritizing assignments in a planner makes these tasks more concrete and visual.

      - Teens are only encouraged to transition to an electronic planner if they demonstrate consistent success using a paper planner.

    - If any teens forgot their planner, the Leader can provide them with the <u>Weekly Planner</u> handout so that they can get some practice writing down and prioritizing their assignments.
    - If the teen is already using a planner, the Leader can discuss how to use it even more efficiently and/or have the teen demonstrate how they are using their planner.
    - Teens who do not have homework, projects, or tests/quizzes to write in their planners should be encouraged to write down AIMS Real World Practice assignments, extra-curricular activities, and school/family events in their planner. This will ensure that they still get practice using a planner to keep track of and prioritize tasks.
    - Leaders should directly address teen and caregiver buy-in to using a planner and emphasize that this is a system that can help them now (e.g., keep track of daily assignments, learn how to prioritize tasks) and can also be used in the future (e.g., high school, college, etc.). However, this system often requires consistent and daily check-ins to ensure that teens are correctly writing down all assignments and tests/quizzes and prioritizing them appropriately.

- **Prioritizing Tasks**

  - Leaders may need to provide some assistance in helping teens with prioritizing assignments and talking through how/why assignments are prioritized in a specific way.
  - Leaders should encourage teens to first prioritize assignments that are due the next day, and then determine which assignments to do based on preference and/or how long it will take.

- Teens who do not have assignments or tests/quizzes should still practice prioritizing tasks such as chores, extracurricular activities, and free time activities. Teens should consider the differences between "Have to Do" vs. "Want to Do" tasks and put tasks in order of importance in their planners.

- Leaders should ensure that they are addressing any questions that caregivers and teens have about using the Problem Solving Plan over the last week. There is time in the large group, the teen group, and the caregiver group to address any issues, questions, or concerns.
- As the Leader discusses each teen's Problem Solving Plan, they should provide feedback on each component (e.g., solution, plan/expectations, reward) and also provide suggestions to increase the likelihood of success (e.g., specific, doable, realistic, appropriate amount of detail, motivating reward).
- Consider rewarding teens who participate by passing out tickets when they:

  - Answer questions during the review
  - Discuss how their Problem Solving Plan went from the Real World Practice assignment
  - Participate in identifying Have to Do vs. Want to Do tasks
  - Answer the Take Home Points questions.

- **Real World Practice**

  - During the large group, caregivers and teens will all have the opportunity to discuss the Real World Practice task of completing the Problem Solving Plan in detail including discussion of any challenges, successes, or questions. It is likely that most teens' Problem Solving Plan will need to be modified, and time should be devoted to refining the solution, plan/expectations, and reward.

    - Leaders are encouraged to use a whiteboard or large post-it to write down each teen's identified problem, chosen solution, EFs being targeted, plan and expectations for earning the reward, and the reward. It is helpful for teens and caregivers to see the different problems, solutions, plans/expectations, and rewards on the Problem Solving Plans of other teens. This may also keep other caregivers and teens engaged as each teen discusses their Problem Solving Plan.
    - It may be helpful to have the Caregiver Leader facilitate the discussion with the teens and for another Leader to write down the details of the Problem Solving Plan on the whiteboard or a large post-it.

  - Caregivers will also have the opportunity to discuss the Problem Solving Plan away from the teens, and it can be helpful to remind caregivers about this if they start to express frustration or negativity towards or about their teen.

- **Teen Group**

  - Leaders may want to facilitate a smooth transition from the large group to the teen group by having teens get in the habit of writing down on a whiteboard or large post-it what went well over the last week as they implemented their Problem Solving Plan.
  - The Leader should highlight the importance of the teens taking an active role in developing their Problem Solving Plan (e.g., discussing the solution, outlining the plan, identifying motivating rewards).

- The goal of the "Have to Do" and "Want to Do" activity is to build teen's understanding of the tasks that need to be completed each day (e.g., homework, study for quizzes, work on a project) and the tasks that are more related to their hobbies or interests. Leaders may have to provide guidance and support to help teens understand the distinction.
- Leaders should encourage the teens to check-in with their caregivers about how they can utilize their planner for writing down and prioritizing homework assignments, tests, and quizzes.

- **Caregiver Group**

  - The Leader will revisit any questions or challenges that the caregivers had as they worked with their teen to implement the Problem Solving Plan at home.

    - It can be helpful for Leaders to refer to the whiteboard or large post-it notes that document each teen's Problem Solving Plan.
    - Leaders can encourage caregivers to jot down notes of things that they may want to modify or discuss on a blank Problem Solving Plan.

  - The Leader will also discuss if each caregiver wants to modify their current Problem Solving Plan by modifying the solution from last week and also adding a solution that is focused on organizing the backpack or binder.
  - Teens will have different goals depending on their challenges and also how quickly they are able to implement new solutions.
  - Leaders should encourage caregivers and teens to continue to try out 3–4 solutions on the Problem Solving Plan and emphasize that even small changes (e.g., writing down daily assignments in a planner, putting completed assignments in a homework folder) can lead to big improvements (e.g., independently writing assignments and upcoming tests in planner, having fewer missing assignments).

    - While it may feel like a lot for caregivers and teens to add another solution to their Problem Solving Plan, it can be something feasible or doable that allows them to build good habits and increase independence around organizing their materials (e.g., making a list of their daily homework assignments in their planner when they get home from school).

Get Ready Checklist for Leaders

❏ Prep the handouts to be passed out

❏ Hang up AIMS Rules Poster

❏ Hang up Prize Menu

❏ Check that Prize Box has range of prizes to be earned

❏ Hang up the Real World Practice Assignment Tracker (if used)

❏ Hang up Ticket Tracker (if used)

❏ Prep Example Planner

❏ Get any supplies for the games to be played in the Teen Group

Session 6 Manual

Large Group – Caregivers and Teens (55 mins)

- **Session Schedule (1 min)**

  - Pass out and refer to <u>Session 6 Schedule</u> handout.
  - *Let's make sure to get started the right way so that we can fully focus on what you will be learning today. Put all materials away except for your AIMS binder and a pen or pencil.*
  - Briefly go over the activities that are listed on the <u>Session 6 Schedule</u> handout. State that teens can cross off activities on the schedule as they are completed.

- **Review Group Rules and Prize Menu (1 min)**

  - Refer to the AIMS Rules Poster and briefly review each of the rules.
  - Remind teens that they will earn tickets that can be traded in for prizes at the end of each session when they:

    - Follow the group rules
    - Participate in the session
    - Complete activities in session
    - Complete Real World Practice Assignments.

  - Briefly review that the Prize Menu shows how many tickets are needed to earn various prizes.

- **Review Real World Practice Assignment (15 mins)**

  - Instruct teens to get out their Real World Practice Assignment from their AIMS binder.
  - Ask: *Who completed the Real World Practice Assignment?*

    - If utilizing the Real World Practice Assignment Tracker, Leaders should indicate which teens completed their Real World Practice Assignment. This can be done by asking teens to raise their hands if they completed the assignment and/or walking around the room to check on whether the teens completed it.
    - Check that teens filed their Real World Practice Assignment in the "Completed" section of their Real World Practice folder in their AIMS binder.

  - *Your Real World Practice from the last session was to work with your caregiver to modify your Problem Solving Plan and start working on the solution that you identified for the problem. Last week, we talked about the Big Dump – Backpack strategy and a binder organization system, so we encouraged you to choose a solution to address any problems you were having with organizing your school materials. You can earn a ticket for completing your Real World Practice.*
  - To assess what caregivers and teens thought about using the Problem Solving Plan, poll the large group by asking the following questions:

    - *Was it easy to set up the Problem Solving Plan?*
    - *Was it doable to work on the solution you chose on your Problem Solving Plan?*

- *Teens – were you able to negotiate the reward that you wanted?*
- *Teens – did you earn a reward?*
- *Teens – did your caregiver give you the reward if you earned it?*
- *Teens – did you make progress towards becoming independent with your schoolwork?*
- *Teens – did you have more free time to do the things you wanted to do?*

- Ask each caregiver/teen dyad to share their Problem Solving Plan. Specifically, first have each teen share the details of their Problem Solving Plan (i.e., problem, solution, EFs being targeted, plan and expectations for earning reward, and reward).

  - Due to time constraints, teens should share 1–2 of the solutions that they are targeting. If applicable, Leaders should encourage teens to discuss the use of a solution for backpack or binder organization systems.

- Leaders should write each teen's Problem Solving Plan components (i.e., problem, solution, EFs being targeted, plan and expectations for earning reward, and reward) on the whiteboard or a large post-it.
- The following questions can be asked of each teen when reviewing their Problem Solving Plan and writing it on the whiteboard or large post-it:

  - *What was the target problem?*
  - *What was the solution?*
  - *What was the plan and expectations for earning the reward?*
  - *What was the reward?*
  - *How did it go trying out the solution?*

    - *Did it address your problem?*
    - *Was it worth it?*

  - *Did you earn a reward?*
  - *Did you feel you had more independence?*
  - *What worked well or what was successful about your Problem Solving Plan?*
  - *What did not work or what was challenging about your Problem Solving Plan?*

- While the caregiver can weigh in, they will have time to discuss their thoughts and experiences in the caregiver group session. Ask the caregiver the following questions (if time allows):

  - *How did it go trying out the solution?*

    - *Did they make progress towards addressing the problem?*

  - *Did you feel that your teen showed more independence?*

- Leaders should allow each teen to share the progress on their Problem Solving Plan. If a teen did not complete the Problem Solving Plan, the Leader should briefly brainstorm ideas for how to complete this for the following week (e.g., choose a doable goal, set a reminder to complete the Problem Solving Plan, set a reminder to work on solution of Problem Solving Plan).

- *As a reminder, each week we will spend some time discussing the Problem Solving Plan as a group in order to address any difficulties with identifying the problem, defining and then implementing the solution and plan and expectations for earning a reward, and choosing a reward. You may eventually have 3–5 solutions that you are implementing on your Problem Solving Plan to address problems you may be having with organizing, planning, and doing homework and studying for tests.*

  - Remind teens to file their completed Real World Practice Assignment in their folder.
  - If teens completed the Real World Practice Assignment, they should be rewarded with 1 ticket.

- **Review of Material from Last Session (2 mins)**

  - Ask the following questions (if time allows) and discuss as needed:

    - *What are the steps of The Big Dump – Backpack?*

      - *Empty backpack*
      - *Act on it*
      - *File it*
      - *Trash it*
      - *Pick a time each week to do the 3 main steps (Act on it, File it, Trash it).*

    - *Why would you use a Binder Organization System?*

      - *To keep all of your classroom materials (e.g., notebooks, folders, planner) organized*
      - *To more easily locate worksheets, study guides, graded tests/quizzes, etc. for each class*
      - *To have access to your planner/assignment notebook in each class so that assignments and upcoming tests/quizzes can be written down*
      - *To have a consistent place to put homework that needs to be completed and homework that has been completed.*

- **Goals for Session 6 (1 min)**

  - *Our goals for today are the following:*

    - *Learn how to keep track of homework assignments by using a planner.*
    - *Learn how to prioritize assignments using a planner.*
    - *Learn the difference between a "Have to Do" Task and a "Want to Do" Task.*

- **Keeping Track of Homework Assignments (7 mins)**

  - *We are going to discuss how to use a paper planner or assignment notebook not only to keep track of homework assignments but also to prioritize assignments.*
  - *The benefits of using a planner are that you will create a daily to-do list of what needs to be completed in each of your classes that will then help you stay on top of studying for tests/quizzes and completing long-term projects.*
  - Ask and briefly discuss the following questions with several teens:

- *Do you use a planner or assignment notebook?*
- *Do you use an online portal to look up homework assignments?*
- *What do you use your planner for?*
- *How often do you use your planner?*

- *We asked you to bring your planner to the session today so that we could talk about some helpful strategies for planning and prioritizing homework assignments and get some hands-on practice using your planner.*
- Ask teens to get out their planner.
- Pass out and refer to <u>Weekly Planner</u> handout.
- *We are also passing out a handout that likely looks very similar to your own planner. You can use this if you forgot your planner at home.*

- The Leader should use the example planner to show teens each part of the planner as it is discussed.

  - It may be helpful for other Leaders to walk around the room and assist teens as needed (e.g., help them locate the monthly calendar) as the parts of the planner are reviewed.

- Pass out and refer to <u>Weekly Planner Example</u> handout.
- *The main goal of using a planner is to write down what you need to do for each of your classes. I will walk you through how I would do this in my planner, and you can also look at this handout as an example of how you could fill out your planner each week.*

  - *Open up the planner and find today's date in your planner.*
  - *Write down each of your classes at the beginning of each row. This will allow you to keep track of everything you need to do in all of your classes.*

    - *In this example planner, your classes are already filled in. If one of the classes is not one that you take, you could cross it out and write in the class you are taking. For example, if you are not taking a world language, you could cross it out and write a class that you are taking.*

  - *You should write down daily assignments, upcoming quizzes and tests, and upcoming assignments and projects in the Monday–Friday columns.*

    - *If you do NOT have anything to do for a class, you can leave it blank or mark an "X" for that day.*

  - *It is helpful to write down assignments after each class so that you remember them.*

- *There is also a monthly calendar in most planners that you could use to write down any tests, quizzes, and long-term project due dates. This will then help you figure out which specific days you need to study or work on the project.*
- *You can also write down any events or activities such as piano lessons, soccer practice, band concert, and dentist appointments on your monthly or weekly calendar. This can help you figure out what days you will be able to work on long-term assignments or study for tests/quizzes.*

  - *In this example planner, you could write any events or activities in the Notes section.*

- *It can be helpful to store your planner in the front of your binder organization system and to make sure that you bring it to school and then back home each day.*
- Ask and discuss: *Any questions before we discuss more about using a planner?*

- **Steps to Keeping Track of Homework Assignments (5 mins)**

  - Pass out and refer to the <u>Keeping Track of Homework Assignments Using a Planner</u> handout.
  - *Now let's discuss how to use your planner in more detail. This is a strategy that can really help if you have difficulties with the EFs of planning or prioritizing!*
  - Have teens take turns reading aloud the key points (see below) from the <u>Keeping Track of Homework Assignments Using a Planner</u> handout and discuss as needed:

    - Write down each daily homework assignment immediately after it is given. The assignment should be recorded in the column of the correct day and the row of the specific class subject.
    - If you have an online portal, your daily assignments can be double-checked in a study hall, resource or skills class, or at home.
    - When you write down homework assignments, make sure to be as detailed and specific as possible!

      - For example, writing down "Do Math Problems" is not as specific or detailed as "Math book pg 21, problems 5–20."

    - Any tests, quizzes, or long-term project due dates should be written down as soon as they are assigned. These should be written down on BOTH the monthly calendar and also on the weekly calendar.

      - Clearly mark tests, quizzes, and other due dates by using a different color pen, highlighting it, drawing a circle or box around the due date, using a due date sticker, and/or writing it larger so that it stands out.

    - Write down any school or after-school obligations or activities that you have on the monthly calendar. These might include school clubs, practices or games for sports, music lessons, or orthodontist appointments. This will help you determine when you may be able to study for tests/quizzes and work on long-term projects.

  - If you use your planner correctly, you will have a to-do list for what assignments need to be completed and what tests/quizzes need to be studied for at the end of each day.
  - Ask and discuss: *Any questions about using a planner to keep track of homework assignments?*

- **Practice Using a Planner (7 mins)**

  - *With your caregiver, you should practice writing down homework assignments, projects, and upcoming tests and quizzes in your planner.*

    - *This is a skill that can take some time to learn and your caregiver can help by demonstrating, instructing, and giving feedback on how to write down your assignments.*

- *You may need to get out your classroom materials or check your online portal in order to write down homework assignments and upcoming tests/quizzes in your planner.*

- *You can also write down any after school activities or events in your planner for the rest of the week.*
- *You can also write down the Real World Practice assignments you are going to complete on the days that you have AIMS sessions.*
- It may be helpful for Leaders to set a timer for this activity.
- The Leader should walk around and assist caregiver and teen dyads as they practice writing down the teen's homework assignments, upcoming tests/quizzes, and extracurricular activities and appointments in their planner. It will be important to:

  - Double-check that teens are correctly writing down assignments on the correct day and in the correct column for each of their class subjects.
  - Confirm that teens know how to utilize an online portal (if applicable) to double-check upcoming assignments and quizzes/tests.
  - Support teens by determining how many days they need to study for an upcoming test/quiz or work on a long-term project. This task could then be written down in the planner (e.g., "Study for Biology" for 3 days prior to the actual test).
  - If time allows, have caregivers demonstrate how to look up whether teens have any missing assignments in the online portal. Teens could then add these missing assignments to their daily or weekly to-do list.

- Have 2–3 teens share some of the upcoming assignments, tests/quizzes, or activities/events that they wrote in the planners.

- **Prioritizing Homework Assignments (6 mins)**

  - *Now that you have some practice writing down your daily homework assignments, we are going to talk about how you prioritize your assignments.*
  - Ask and briefly discuss the following with the teens:

    - *How do you know which homework assignment to work on first?*
    - *Are there certain subjects that you prefer to work on first?*
    - *Are there certain subjects that you prefer to work on last?*
    - *Do you like to do short assignments first or last?*
    - *Do you like to do long assignments first or last?*

  - Leaders should make a "Have To Do" column and a "Want To Do" column on a whiteboard or large post-it and then write the definitions and examples as they are discussed with the teens.
  - *Most assignments, tests/quizzes, and projects can be broken down into "Have to Do" and "Want to Do" tasks. Knowing whether something is a "Have to Do" vs. a "Want to Do" task will help you figure out when you need to complete the task.*
  - *"Have to Do Tasks" are assignments that need to be completed and are typically due the next day. For example, completing the math problems that are due tomorrow and reading Chapter 2 in your History textbook for tomorrow's class discussion are both "Have to Do" tasks.*

- *These also include studying for upcoming tests and quizzes and working on long-term projects. For example, studying 5 vocabulary words for English and writing the Introduction paragraph for a Biology report are both "Have to Do" tasks. While your teacher may not always check that you have done these tasks, they will make it easier for you to break up studying for tests, writing papers, or finishing big projects.*

- Ask: *What assignments have you written down in your planner today or over the last few weeks that are "Have to Do" tasks?*

- *"Want to Do Tasks" are assignments that you may want to do or could do, but are not typically due the following day. For example, you may want to read more chapters in the book you are reading in Language Arts even if it has not been assigned by the teacher.*

  - *When doing your homework at home, other "Want To Do" tasks might be things like watching television, playing video games, hanging out with friends, etc.*
  - *It can be helpful to have a "Want To Do" space in your planner where you can write down the "Want To Do" tasks that can be done after you complete the "Have To Do" tasks.*
  - *It can also be motivating to think about the "Want To Do" tasks that you will get to do once you finish your "Have To Do" tasks!*

- Ask: *What are some examples of "Want to Do" tasks that you have done in the last few weeks?*

- **Have to Do vs. Want To Do Tasks (5 mins)**

  - *An easy way to indicate "Have To Do" vs. "Want To Do" tasks in your planner is to number your "Have To Do" daily assignments in the order of importance.*
  - *For example, if you had 3 homework assignments that were due the next day, you would write #1, #2, and #3 next to the assignments that need to be completed so that you know which order to do them in.*
  - *You get to decide which one you want to do first or last – and this might be based on which one you will complete the fastest, which one you like the most, etc. After you have prioritized your "Have to Do" assignments, you could then add in your "Want to Do" Tasks in order of importance.*

  - Pass out and refer to the <u>Prioritizing Planner Tasks</u> handout.
  - *In this planner, you can see that the "Have to Do" homework assignments are numbered in order of importance. The "Want to Do" tasks are listed after and can be completed if there is enough time.*
  - *Any assignments that were given on Friday can either be done on Friday or can be done on Saturday and/or Sunday.*
  - Using the <u>Prioritizing Planner Tasks</u> handout, have a teen read the "Have to Do" assignments for Thursday in the order that they were prioritized.

    - Have another teen read the "Want to Do" task in the Notes section for Wednesday.

  - *If there are several assignments that need to be completed because they are due the next day, you have the flexibility to choose which one you want to do first. Some things to consider might include:*

- *When do you want to do your favorite or preferred subjects?*
- *When do you want to do your least favorite or non-preferred subjects?*
- *When do you want to do the assignment that will take you the longest?*
- *When do you want to do the assignment that will take you the shortest?*

- **Practice Prioritizing Tasks (5 mins)**

  - *With your caregiver, prioritize the assignments that you wrote down in your planner. Think about whether tasks are "Have to Do" vs. "Want to Do." You also need to consider the order you want to do tasks in and then number your tasks based on the order you would like to do them in. Let me know if you need help or have any questions!*
  - It may be helpful for Leaders to set a timer for this activity.
  - Leaders should provide feedback and support as needed to the caregiver/teen dyads.
  - Have 2–3 teens share how they prioritized the upcoming assignments, tests/quizzes, or activities/events that they wrote in the planners.
  - *The teens will continue to work on identifying "Have to Do" vs. "Want to Do" tasks in the teen group.*
  - Ask: *Any questions before we break into our separate teen and caregiver groups?*
  - Leaders should have caregivers and teens split into separate groups.

    - Remind teens to file handouts in their AIMS binder and provide assistance as needed.

Teen Group (28 mins)

- **Modifying Your Problem Solving Plan (10 mins)**

  - In order to facilitate a smooth and quick transition from the large group to the teen group, Leaders can ask teens to write down one thing that worked or was successful about using the Problem Solving Plan over the last week. Leaders can have the teens read their responses and briefly discuss.
  - Leaders can briefly go over the activities that are listed on the <u>Session 6 Schedule</u> handout for the Teen Group. State that teens can cross off activities on the schedule as they are completed.

  - *We discussed the Problem Solving Plan that you worked on with your caregiver over the last week at the beginning of today's session in detail.*
  - Ask: *Are there any questions or comments that you have about continuing to try out solutions to your problems by using a Problem Solving Plan?*
  - Pass out and refer to <u>Problem Solving Plan Examples for Using a Planner</u> handout.
  - *On this handout, there are additional examples of how to build the skill of writing down and prioritizing assignments with a planner using a Problem Solving Plan.*
  - The Leader should have teens read the problem, solution, EFs being targeted, plan and expectations for earning the reward, and identified reward for the first 2 examples on the <u>Problem Solving Plan Examples for Using a Planner</u> handout.
  - Ask: *Any questions about using a Problem Solving Plan to use a planner to write down and prioritize assignments?*

- *For your Real World Practice assignment this week, You may be changing or adding to your current Problem Solving Plan by working on a solution that is related to using your planner.*

  - *For example, if you struggle with knowing what assignments you need to do each day, you could use your planner to keep a list of homework assignments.*

- Ask the following questions and write teens' responses on the whiteboard or a large post-it:

  - *Would it be helpful to use a planner to write down and/or prioritize your assignments?*
  - *What EF challenge would this solution address?*
  - *What reward could you earn for working on the solution?*

- *When we rejoin your caregivers, we will discuss your Real World Practice assignment. You will work together with your caregiver to keep using a Problem Solving Plan to continue targeting the solution from last week, but will also add in a solution related to using your planner.*

- **Practice – Have to Do vs. Want to Do Tasks (12 mins)**

  - Pass out and refer to <u>Have to Do vs. Want to Do Tasks</u> handout.
  - *Now we are going to get some more practice with figuring out whether activities are "Have to Do" or "Want to Do." You will need a pencil for this activity. We will complete this together as a large group and then discuss the correct answers. It is possible that we may have very different ideas about which activities are "Have to Do" or "Want to Do."*
  - The Leader should read each question on the <u>Have to Do vs. Want to Do Tasks</u> handout and encourage teens to quickly respond. Teens should be encouraged to take their best guess if they are not sure.
  - After all of the teens have completed the handout, the Leader should go through each activity and take a poll of whether the teens identified it as a "Have to Do" or "Want to Do" activity. The Leader should discuss the rationale for the correct answer (see below) and answer any questions that the teens have about the distinction between "Have to Do" and "Want to Do."

    - The "Have to Do" activities include all school assignments and school-related activities (e.g., basketball practice, practice instrument, read for 30 minutes).
    - The "Want to Do" activities include hobbies or interests (e.g., video games, social media).
    - As a group, discuss any disputed items so that teens clearly understand the difference between which tasks are "Have to Do" or "Want to Do."

  - *You have all done a great job building your understanding of "Have to Do" and "Want to Do" tasks. When we rejoin your caregivers, we will briefly discuss what we worked on and that this is a skill that you can start using as you write down and prioritize assignments, tests, and activities in your planner.*
  - Remind teens to file handouts in their AIMS binder and provide assistance as needed.

- **EF Game (6 mins)**

  - If time allows, the Leader can allow the teens to play a short game that utilizes EF skills. Possible games to play include Stack Attack, Penny Stack, Connect 4, or Uno (see Manual Overview for additional information including instructions and materials needed for games).
  - The Leader should pass out tickets for teens who participate in the EF game to encourage participation.
  - The teens should rejoin their caregivers for the reunification with the Large Group.

Caregiver Group (28 mins)

- **Discussion of Problem Solving Plan (12 mins)**

  - *We discussed the Problem Solving Plan that you worked on with your teen over the last week at the beginning of today's session in great detail. I am going to pass out a blank Problem Solving Plan so that you can jot down any notes about things you may want to add or edit for the upcoming week. Also, it can be helpful to review the <u>Tips for a Successful Problem Solving Plan</u> handout that we discussed a few weeks ago.*
  - Pass out <u>Problem Solving Plan</u> handout.
  - Ask: *Are there any questions or comments that you have about continuing to try out solutions to your teen's problems by using a Problem Solving Plan?*
  - *You and your teen may be changing or adding to the current Problem Solving Plan by working on a solution that is related to using a planner to write down and prioritize assignments.*

    - *For example, if your teen struggles with knowing what their assignments are and what tests they need to study for, it may be helpful to try out the solution of using a planner. Using a planner to write down and prioritize tasks in order of importance is also a very valuable skill that they will use in high school, and also in college and in the workplace.*

  - Pass out and refer to <u>Problem Solving Plan Examples for Using a Planner</u>.
  - *On this handout, there are additional examples of how to target the use of a planner to write down and prioritize assignments using a Problem Solving Plan.*
  - Ask: *What solution related to using a planner to write down and/or prioritize assignments might be helpful for your teen?*

    - Leaders should write caregivers' responses on the whiteboard or large post-it.

- **Collaborating with Teens to Create a Problem Solving Plan (16 mins)**

  - *Your teen is working on building their understanding of what a "Have to Do" and a "Want to Do" task is so that they can become better at prioritizing what they need to do each day.*

  - *When the teens rejoin us, we will discuss this week's Real World Practice assignment. You will work together with your teen to continue using a Problem Solving Plan to target the solution or solutions from last week, but also add in a solution related to a problem your teen is having with writing down and prioritizing their homework assignments.*

- *For the remainder of our time together, let's each briefly discuss what you think your teen's Problem, Solution, EFs being Targeted, Plan and Expectations for Earning the Reward, and Reward will be on the Problem Solving Plan. Keep in mind that you also want to make sure that your teen feels heard and involved in this process – so it is likely that what you are planning may change slightly.*

  - *We also want to make sure that the teen's solution and plan for earning the reward is specific and doable so that they are set up for success as they build effective strategies for addressing their EF challenges.*
  - *We also want to make sure that it is feasible for you to implement the solution this week.*

- *We would really like to add in a goal related to using a planner because this ensures that your teen is able to practice the skill that they were taught. We understand that it can feel like a lot to be working on 3–4 solutions on the Problem Solving Plan, but we are here to provide support and figure out how to make this work for you and your teen.*

  - *For example, it may only be doable to add in writing down 1 subject's homework assignment in the planner each day. However, after the teen is consistently writing down homework for 1 subject, they can increase it slowly so that they are eventually keeping track of all homework assignments.*

- As each caregiver discusses their teen's Problem Solving Plan, the Leader should write the Problem Solving Plan components (i.e., problem, solution, EFs being targeted plan and expectations for earning reward, and reward) on the whiteboard or a large post-it.

  - Leaders should allow each caregiver to briefly discuss their thoughts for what solutions they would like to implement on their teen's Problem Solving Plan. They may keep the solution the same, modify a solution, and/or add a solution to a target problem.

Reunification – Large Group (7 mins)

- **Discussion of Teen Session Material (1 min)**

  - *In their session, the teens discussed their thoughts on using a Problem Solving Plan and also discussed what solution they may want to address for any challenges they have with writing down and prioritizing homework assignments. The teens also worked on building their understanding of the difference between a "Have to Do" Task and a "Want to Do" Task.*
  - The Teen Leaders can share any additional details about the discussion and activities in the Teen Group.

- **Take Home Points (2 mins)**

  - *Let's go over our take home points.*
  - Ask the following questions (if time allows) and discuss as needed:

    - *What are the benefits of using a planner?*

      - *Quickly and easily create a daily to-do list of what needs to be completed in each of your classes*

- *Stay on top of studying for tests/quizzes and completing long-term projects*
- *May lead to better grades – getting all assignments completed, studying for upcoming tests, and completing long-term projects*
- *May lead to more free time – getting things done more quickly and efficiently.*

- *What is a "Have to Do" Task?*

  - *These are assignments that need to be completed and are typically due the next day.*

- *What is a "Want to Do" Task?*

  - *These are assignments that you may want to do but are not due the following day. When doing your homework at home, other "Want To Do" tasks might be things like watching television, playing video games, hanging out with friends, etc.*

- **Real World Practice Assignment (3 mins)**

  - Pass out and refer to <u>Real World Practice – Session 6</u> handout.
  - *For your Real World Practice Assignment this week, you will work with your caregiver on creating your Problem Solving Plan and start working on the solutions that you identify for your problems. Many of you will be working on 3–4 solutions – the 2–3 solutions from last week and a new solution addressing planning and prioritizing your homework assignments.*

    - *After our discussion today, it is possible that you may want to make your solution more specific, clear, and doable, and you can also outline this in the Plan and Expectations for Earning the Reward section of the Problem Solving Plan.*

  - Ask: *Any questions about your Real World Practice assignment?*
  - *You and your caregiver should set aside time either tonight or tomorrow to create the new Problem Solving Plan so that you have some time to work on it over the next week and get a chance to earn a reward. Take a minute to discuss when you can complete your Problem Solving Plan with your caregiver.*

  - *In your AIMS binder, take a moment to file your Real World Practice assignment now in the "To Do" side of the folder. You should also take a moment to file all of your other handouts behind the Session 6 divider.*
  - Ask: *Any final questions before we get ready to trade in your tickets for prizes?*

- **Trade in Tickets (1 min)**

  - The Leader should give all teens who earned a ticket an opportunity to trade them in for prizes using the Prize Menu.
  - Leaders should record the number of remaining tickets on the Ticket Tracker (if used).

Session 6 Schedule

Large Group

❑ Review Group Rules and Prize Menu

❑ Review Real World Practice Assignment

❑ Review of Material from Last Session

❑ Goals for Session 6

❑ Keeping Track of Homework Assignments

❑ Practice Using a Planner

❑ Prioritizing Homework Assignments

❑ Have To Do vs. Want To Do Tasks

❑ Practice Prioritizing Tasks

Teen Group

❑ Modifying Your Problem Solving Plan

❑ Practice – Have To Do vs. Want to Do Tasks

❑ EF Game

Reunification – Large Group

❑ Discussion of Teen Session Material

❑ Take Home Points

❑ Real World Practice Assignment

❑ Trade in Tickets

Weekly Planner

WEEKLY ASSIGNMENTS	MONDAY	TUESDAY	WEDNESDAY	THURSDAY	FRIDAY
MATH					
SCIENCE					
LANGUAGE ARTS					
HISTORY/SS					
WORLD LANG					
ART/MUSIC					
OTHER:					
NOTES					

WEEK OF: _____

Weekly Planner Example

WEEKLY ASSIGNMENTS	MONDAY	TUESDAY	WEDNESDAY	THURSDAY	FRIDAY
				WEEK OF: 9/24 – 9/28	
MATH			Pg 51 #s 1–14		
SCIENCE		Complete worksheet			
LANGUAGE ARTS				Study spelling words	SPELLING TEST
HISTORY/SS	Read Chap 2 Pgs 30–42		Pg 48, Answer #s 4–12		
WORLD LANG		Make 5 Study Cards	Make 5 Study Cards	Make 5 Study Cards	VOCAB TEST
ART/MUSIC		Practice cello – 15 mins		Practice cello – 15 mins	
OTHER:		Karate at 4:30pm	Spanish Club at 3:15pm		
NOTES					Hang out with Sam

Tips for Keeping Track of Homework Assignments Using a Planner

- Write down each daily homework assignment immediately after it is given. The assignment should be recorded in the column of the correct day and the row of the specific class subject.

- If you have an online portal, your daily assignments can be double checked in a study hall, resource or skills class, or at home.

- When you write down homework assignments, make sure to be as detailed and specific as possible!

  - For example, writing down "Do Math Problems" is not as specific or detailed as "Math pg 21, problems 5–20."

- Any tests, quizzes, or long-term project due dates (e.g., essays) should be written down as soon as they are assigned. These should be written down on BOTH the monthly calendar and also on the weekly calendar.

  - Clearly mark tests, quizzes, and other due dates by using a different color pen, highlighting it, drawing a circle or box around the due date, using a due date sticker, and/or writing it larger so that it stands out.

- Write down any school or after-school obligations or activities that you have on the monthly calendar. This will help you determine when you may be able to study for tests/quizzes and work on long term projects.

Have to Do vs. Want to Do

Here is a big list of tasks for a middle schooler. Determine whether each activity is a "Have to Do Task" or a "Want to Do Task."

Steps	Have to Do?	Want to Do?
Write a book report on *The Giver* for English.	❑	❑
Take a nap.	❑	❑
Math worksheets.	❑	❑
Play video games with Samir.	❑	❑
Band practice after school on Tuesday and Thursday.	❑	❑
Science fair submission.	❑	❑
Watch YouTube videos.	❑	❑
Read for 30 minutes a day.	❑	❑
Algebra study review problems from chapter 3.	❑	❑
Do a social media dance challenge.	❑	❑
Read chapter 4 in my textbook for social studies.	❑	❑
Basketball practice Monday and Wednesday at 4:30.	❑	❑
Practice baritone for 30 minutes a day for the band.	❑	❑
Bake cookies at Maria's house.	❑	❑
Draw in my sketchbook.	❑	❑
Use the computer to research my History essay.	❑	❑
Check the online portal for missing math assignments.	❑	❑

Prioritizing Planner Tasks

WEEKLY ASSIGNMENTS	MONDAY	TUESDAY	WEDNESDAY	THURSDAY	FRIDAY
				WEEK OF: 9/24 – 9/28	
MATH			**2** Pg 51 #s 1–14		
SCIENCE		**1** Complete worksheet			
LANGUAGE ARTS				**1** Study spelling words	SPELLING TEST
HISTORY/SS	**1** Read Chap 2 Pgs. 30–42		**1** Pg 48 #s 4–12		
WORLD LANG		**2** Make 5 Study Cards	**3** Make 5 Study Cards	**2** Make 5 Study Cards	VOCAB TEST
ART/MUSIC		**3** Practice cello – 15 mins		**3** Practice cello – 15 mins	
OTHER:		Karate at 4:30pm	Spanish Club at 3:15pm		
NOTES					Hang out with Sam

Session 6 – Handout 6 – p. 1 of 1

AIMS

Problem Solving Plan

Date: _____

Problem Who, What, Where, When, & Why	Solution	EF(s) Being Targeted	Plan and Expectations for Earning Reward	Reward	Reward Earned?
		Getting Started Planning Prioritizing Organizing Working Memory			☐ Monday ☐ Tuesday ☐ Wednesday ☐ Thursday ☐ Friday ☐ Saturday ☐ Sunday
		Getting Started Planning Prioritizing Organizing Working Memory			☐ Monday ☐ Tuesday ☐ Wednesday ☐ Thursday ☐ Friday ☐ Saturday ☐ Sunday

This agreement begins on _____ and we will review the agreement again on _____ .

_____
Teen

_____
Parent/Caregiver

Problem Solving Plan Examples for Using a Planner

Date: 9/1 – 9/5

Problem Who, What, Where, When, & Why	Solution	EF(s) Being Targeted	Plan and Expectations for Earning Reward	Reward	Reward Earned?
I don't know what my homework assignments are when I get home from school.	Use a planner to write down my homework after every class.	Getting Started Planning Prioritizing Organizing Working Memory	Bring my planner home. Use my planner as a checklist as I work on each assignment.	30 minutes of extra screen time.	☐ Monday ☐ Tuesday ☐ Wednesday ☐ Thursday ☐ Friday ☐ Saturday ☐ Sunday
I am not able to figure out which assignments I need to do and which assignments I can wait to do.	After writing down my assignments in my planner, I will prioritize the ones that are due tomorrow.	Getting Started Planning Prioritizing Organizing Working Memory	I will do the assignments that are due tomorrow and number them in the order I want to do them. I will write down and prioritize the other "have to do" assignments and "want to do" activities in my planner. My mom will check my planner after school.	$1 towards an amusement park pass.	☐ Monday ☐ Tuesday ☐ Wednesday ☐ Thursday ☐ Friday ☐ Saturday ☐ Sunday

This agreement begins on 9/1 _____ and we will review the agreement again on 9/7 _____ .

_____
Teen

_____
Parent/Caregiver

© 2026 Amie Duncan and Leanne Tamm, *Improving Academic Executive Functioning for Autistic Middle Schoolers*

Real World Practice – Session 6

- Work with your caregiver to modify your Problem Solving Plan and start working on the solutions that you identify for the problems. After our discussion today, it is possible that you may want to make your solution more specific, clear, and doable and you can also outline this in the Plan and Expectations for Earning the Reward section of the Problem Solving Plan. Over the next week, you should do the following:

  - Add on a solution to target writing down and prioritizing homework assignments in your planner.

  - Continue working on any solutions from your previous Problem Solving Plan.

Problem Solving Plan

Date: _____

Problem Who, What, Where, When, & Why	Solution	EF(s) Being Targeted	Plan and Expectations for Earning Reward	Reward	Reward Earned?
		Getting Started Planning Prioritizing Organizing Working Memory			☐ Monday ☐ Tuesday ☐ Wednesday ☐ Thursday ☐ Friday ☐ Saturday ☐ Sunday
		Getting Started Planning Prioritizing Organizing Working Memory			☐ Monday ☐ Tuesday ☐ Wednesday ☐ Thursday ☐ Friday ☐ Saturday ☐ Sunday

This agreement begins on _____ and we will review the agreement again on _____ .

_____
Teen

_____
Parent/Caregiver

Problem Solving Plan

Date: _____

Problem Who, What, Where, When, & Why	Solution	EF(s) Being Targeted	Plan and Expectations for Earning Reward	Reward	Reward Earned?
		Getting Started Planning Prioritizing Organizing Working Memory			☐ Monday ☐ Tuesday ☐ Wednesday ☐ Thursday ☐ Friday ☐ Saturday ☐ Sunday
		Getting Started Planning Prioritizing Organizing Working Memory			☐ Monday ☐ Tuesday ☐ Wednesday ☐ Thursday ☐ Friday ☐ Saturday ☐ Sunday

This agreement begins on _____ and we will review the agreement again on _____.

_____
Parent/Caregiver

_____
Teen

Session 7   Building Effective Study Strategies

Session 7 Preparation

Session Specific Supplies

- Projector/computer for video
- AIMS Study Cards video
- Index cards

General AIMS Supplies

- AIMS Rules Poster
- Prize Menu and Prize Box
- Ticket Tracker and tickets
- Real World Practice Tracker
- Whiteboard and dry erase markers OR large Post-It easel pad and markers
- Pens/Pencils
- Game/Activity for Teen Group

Handouts Needed

- Large Group

    - Session 7 Schedule
    - Effective Study Strategies and the Importance of Defining Studying
    - My Study Strategies
    - Study Card vs. Flash Card
    - Steps for Creating a Study Card
    - Teleport Study Card

- Teen Group

    - Problem Solving Plan Examples for Building Study Strategies
    - Study Cards Practice

DOI: 10.4324/9781003500209-8

- Caregiver Group
  - Problem Solving Plan
  - Problem Solving Plan Examples for Building Study Strategies
- Large Group
  - Real World Practice – Session 7

Important Points for Session 7

- **General Session Notes**

  - This session is highly didactic, and teens are more likely to understand how to utilize effective study strategies the more they actively participate. Leaders are encouraged to reward teens with tickets when they participate throughout.
  - Leaders should present material on the 4–7 rule, Stickiness Factor, and creating a study card at a dynamic pace to keep the teens engaged while also demonstrating the key concepts.

    - It will be extremely beneficial for the Leaders to be very familiar with the content of the activities so that they can execute it smoothly.

  - Activity – Stickiness Factor

    - The goal of this activity is to allow teens to practice using the 4–7 rule to define the word "bicycle". Leaders should encourage teens to identify only the most relevant keywords to the definition of "bicycle", using the fewest words possible. Leaders should then demonstrate that putting the 4–7 keywords together creates a definition that will "stick" in their brain because it follows the 4–7 rule and contains only the most critical information.
    - This activity should be done as a large group on a whiteboard or large post-it, and Leaders should provide feedback to ensure keywords are concise and critical to the definition.

      - Leaders can test and demonstrate the power of the stickiness factor throughout Session 7 and in Session 8 by periodically asking teens to give the definition of "bicycle."

  - Activity – Making a Study Card

    - This activity allows teens to practice the process of identifying 4–7 keywords, which is a key part of making a study card. Leaders should read the definition aloud and provide feedback to teens about the most important 4–7 keywords for the definition, referring back to the "bicycle" example when emphasizing the important features of a keyword.
    - Leaders should then emphasize that the process of identifying keywords itself is studying, and results in a short, concise definition to use on their study card that will also stick in their brain.

- Leaders should directly address teen and caregiver buy-in to using study cards by emphasizing that by taking the time to study when making the study cards, teens will spend less time actively studying (i.e., reviewing the study cards).
- Teens should be encouraged to only make 4–7 study cards per night because this makes it more likely that these will stick in their brain. This may mean that teens need to break up studying across several days.

- Leaders should ensure that they are addressing any questions that caregivers and teens have about using the Problem Solving Plan over the last week. There is time in the large group, the teen group, and the caregiver group to address any issues, questions, or concerns.
- As the Leader discusses each teen's Problem Solving Plan, they should provide feedback on each component (e.g., solution, plan/expectations, reward) and also provide suggestions to increase the likelihood of success (e.g., specific, doable, realistic, appropriate amount of detail, motivating reward).
- Consider rewarding teens who participate by passing out tickets when they:

  - Answer questions during the review
  - Discuss how their Problem Solving Plan went from the Real World Practice assignment
  - Participate in the 4–7 rule activity
  - Participate in making study cards
  - Answer the Take Home Points questions.

- **Real World Practice**

  - During the large group, caregivers and teens will all have the opportunity to discuss the Real World Practice task of completing the Problem Solving Plan in detail including discussion of any challenges, successes, or questions. It is likely that most teens' Problem Solving Plan will need to be modified, and time should be devoted to refining the solution, plan/expectations, and reward.

    - Leaders are encouraged to use a whiteboard or large post-it to write down each teen's identified problem, chosen solution, EFs being targeted, plan and expectations for earning the reward, and the reward. It is helpful for teens and caregivers to see the different problems, solutions, plans/expectations, and rewards on the Problem Solving Plans of other teens. This may also keep other caregivers and teens engaged as each teen discusses their Problem Solving Plan.
    - It may be helpful to have the Caregiver Leader facilitate the discussion with the teens and for another Leader to write down the details of the Problem Solving Plan on the whiteboard or a large post-it.

  - Caregivers will also have the opportunity to discuss the Problem Solving Plan away from the teens, and it can be helpful to remind caregivers about this if they start to express frustration or negativity towards or about their teen.

- **Teen Group**

  - Leaders may want to facilitate a smooth transition from the large group to the teen group by having teens get in the habit of writing down on a whiteboard or large post-it what went well over the last week as they implemented their Problem Solving Plan.
  - The Leader should highlight the importance of the teens taking an active role in developing their Problem Solving Plan (e.g., discussing the solution, outlining the plan, identifying motivating rewards).
  - Leaders should ensure that teens follow the 5 steps for making a study card (e.g., underline all keywords, choose 4–7 keywords, etc.) and transfer the term and 4–7 keywords onto an index card.
  - Leaders should provide feedback about the keywords that teens identify (e.g., making sure that they are critical to the term, are not repetitive, etc.) and ensure that teens are only adding 4–7 keywords onto the index card.
  - Leaders should encourage the teens to check-in with their caregivers about how they can utilize study cards to study for specific tests or quizzes in their classes.

- **Caregiver Group**

  - The Supplemental Materials contains additional terms that can be used to practice making study cards at home. This may be helpful for caregivers who want to increase their understanding to help their teen identify the 4–7 keywords from terms.
  - The Leader will revisit any questions or challenges that the caregivers had as they worked with their teen to implement the Problem Solving Plan at home.

    - It can be helpful for Leaders to refer to the whiteboard or large post-it notes that document each teen's Problem Solving Plan.
    - Leaders can encourage caregivers to jot down notes of things that they may want to modify or discuss on a blank Problem Solving Plan.

  - The Leader will also discuss if each caregiver wants to modify their current Problem Solving Plan by modifying the solution from last week and also adding a solution that is focused on organizing the backpack or binder.
  - Teens will have different goals depending on their challenges and also how quickly they are able to implement new solutions.
  - Leaders should encourage caregivers and teens to continue to try out 4–5 solutions on the Problem Solving Plan and emphasize that even small changes (e.g., making 3 study cards to study for the Spanish test) can lead to big improvements (e.g., learning Spanish vocabulary, performing better on upcoming quizzes and tests).

    - While it may feel like a lot for caregivers and teens to add another solution to their Problem Solving Plan, it can be something feasible or doable that allows them to build good habits and increase independence around organizing their materials (e.g., making 3 study cards each night for their vocabulary test).

Get Ready Checklist for Leaders

❑ Prep the handouts to be passed out

❑ Hang up AIMS Rules Poster

❑ Hang up Prize Menu

❑ Check that Prize Box has range of prizes to be earned

❑ Hang up the Real World Practice Assignment Tracker (if used)

❑ Hang up Ticket Tracker (if used)

❑ Set up projector and/or computer

❑ Open the AIMS Study Cards video

❑ Write the word "bicycle" on a large post-it or whiteboard in preparation for the Stickiness Factor Activity

❑ Get any supplies for the games to be played in the Teen Group

Session 7 Manual

Large Group – Caregivers and Teens (68 mins)

- **Session Schedule (1 min)**

  - Pass out and refer to <u>Session 7 Schedule</u> handout.
  - *Let's make sure to get started the right way so that we can fully focus on what you will be learning today. Put all materials away except for your AIMS binder and a pen or pencil.*
  - Briefly go over the activities that are listed on the <u>Session 7 Schedule</u> handout. State that teens can cross off activities on the schedule as they are completed.

- **Review Group Rules and Prize Menu (1 min)**

  - Refer to the AIMS Rules Poster and briefly review each of the rules.
  - Remind teens that they will earn tickets that can be traded in for prizes at the end of each session when they:

    - Follow the group rules
    - Participate in the session
    - Complete activities in session
    - Complete Real World Practice Assignments.

  - Briefly review that the Prize Menu shows how many tickets are needed to earn various prizes.

- **Review Real World Practice Assignment (15 mins)**

  - Instruct teens to get out their Real World Practice Assignment from their AIMS binder.
  - Ask: *Who completed the Real World Practice Assignment?*

    - If utilizing the Real World Practice Assignment Tracker, Leaders should indicate which teens completed their Real World Practice Assignment. This can be done by asking teens to raise their hands if they completed the assignment and/or walking around the room to check on whether the teens completed it.
    - Check that teens filed their Real World Practice Assignment in the "Completed" section of their Real World Practice folder in their AIMS binder.

  - *Your Real World Practice from the last session was to work with your caregiver to modify your Problem Solving Plan and start working on the solution that you identified for the problem. Last week, we talked about using a planner to write down and prioritize your homework assignments, so we encouraged you to choose a solution to address any problems you were having with using your planner. You can earn a ticket for completing your Real World Practice.*
  - To assess what caregivers and teens thought about using the Problem Solving Plan, poll the large group by asking the following questions:

    - *Was it easy to set up the Problem Solving Plan?*
    - *Was it doable to work on the solution you chose on your Problem Solving Plan?*

- *Teens – were you able to negotiate the reward that you wanted?*
- *Teens – did you earn a reward?*
- *Teens – did your caregiver give you the reward if you earned it?*
- *Teens – did you make progress towards becoming independent with your schoolwork?*
- *Teens – did you have more free time to do the things you wanted to do?*

- Ask each caregiver/teen dyad to share their Problem Solving Plan. Specifically, first have each teen share the details of their Problem Solving Plan (i.e., problem, solution, EFs being targeted, plan and expectations for earning reward, and reward).

  - Due to time constraints, teens should share 1–2 of the solutions that they are targeting. If applicable, Leaders should encourage teens to discuss the use of a solution for backpack or binder organization systems.

- Leaders should write each teen's Problem Solving Plan components (i.e., problem, solution, EFs being targeted plan and expectations for earning reward, and reward) on the whiteboard or a large post-it.
- The following questions can be asked of each teen when reviewing their Problem Solving Plan and writing it on the whiteboard or large post-it:

  - *What was the target problem?*
  - *What was the solution?*
  - *What was the plan and expectations for earning the reward?*
  - *What was the reward?*
  - *How did it go trying out the solution?*

    - *Did it address your problem?*
    - *Was it worth it?*

  - *Did you earn a reward?*
  - *Did you feel you had more independence?*
  - *What worked well or what was successful about your Problem Solving Plan?*
  - *What did not work or what was challenging about your Problem Solving Plan?*

- While the caregiver can weigh in, they will have time to discuss their thoughts and experiences in the caregiver group session. Ask the caregiver the following questions (if time allows):

  - *How did it go trying out the solution?*

    - *Did they make progress towards addressing the problem?*

  - *Did you feel that your teen showed more independence?*

- Leaders should allow each teen to share the progress on their Problem Solving Plan. If a teen did not complete the Problem Solving Plan, the Leader should briefly brainstorm ideas for how to complete this for the following week (e.g., choose a doable goal, set a reminder to complete the Problem Solving Plan, set a reminder to work on solution of Problem Solving Plan).

- *As a reminder, each week we will spend some time discussing the Problem Solving Plan as a group in order to address any difficulties with identifying the problem, defining and then implementing the solution and plan and expectations for earning a reward, and choosing a reward. You may eventually have 3–5 solutions that you are implementing on your Problem Solving Plan to address problems you may be having with organizing, planning, and doing homework and studying for tests.*

  - Remind teens to file their completed Real World Practice Assignment in their folder.
  - If teens completed the Real World Practice Assignment, they should be rewarded with 1 ticket.

- **Review of Material from Last Session (2 mins)**

  - Ask the following questions (if time allows) and discuss as needed:

    - *What are the benefits of using a planner?*

      - *Quickly and easily create a daily to-do list of what needs to be completed in each of your classes*
      - *Stay on top of studying for tests/quizzes and completing long-term projects*
      - *May lead to better grades – getting all assignments completed, studying for upcoming tests, and completing long-term projects*
      - *May lead to more free time – getting things done more quickly and efficiently.*

    - *What is a "Have to Do" Task?*

      - *These are assignments that need to be completed and are typically due the next day.*

    - *What is a "Want to Do" Task?*

      - *These are assignments that you may want to do but are not due the following day. When doing your homework at home, other "Want To Do" tasks might be things like watching television, playing video games, hanging out with friends, etc.*

- **Goals for Session 7 (1 min)**

  - *Our goals for today are the following:*

    - *Learn about different study strategies and determine which study strategies are most effective for you*
    - *Learn how the concepts of the 4–7 rule and the stickiness factor relate to studying.*
    - *Learn and practice the steps for making an AIMS Study Card.*

- **Why Study? (6 mins)**

  - Ask the teens the following questions and briefly discuss their responses:

    - *Why do you study?*
    - *How do you study for tests and quizzes?*
    - *When someone says, "Go study," what does that mean to you?*
    - *Do you study enough?*

- Ask 2–3 caregivers the following questions and briefly discuss their responses:

  - *What is the most effective way for your teen to study for tests and quizzes?*
  - *When you tell your teen to "Go study," what does that mean to you?*
  - *Do you feel that your teen studies enough?*

- Leaders should summarize the teen and caregiver responses and also point out any similarities or differences. For example, caregivers and teens often have very different expectations about what "Go study" truly means.
- Pass out and refer to <u>Effective Study Strategies and the Importance of Defining Studying</u> handout.

  - Leaders do not need to read the content on the handout because they will cover it as they review study strategies and define studying (see below).

- *Please feel free to jot down any notes on this handout as we discuss studying in more detail.*
- *Studying is important because teachers give tests and quizzes to determine if you remembered what you learned in class.*
- *Studying is also important because for knowledge to be useful, we must first be able to remember it, so that we can then apply it and use it. Studying effectively will help you get a good grade and do well in school.*
- *The good news is that there are very effective study strategies for teens in middle school and high school to help with studying for tests and quizzes.*
- *Study strategies are a set of techniques that help improve our ability to remember and apply information for tests and quizzes. Study strategies do the following*:

  - *Break larger amounts of information into smaller units*
  - *Identify similarities or patterns that can be recalled or learned*
  - *Organize the information into manageable amounts so that they can be memorized.*

- Ask: *Any questions so far about studying?*

- **Defining Studying (4 mins)**

  - *Caregivers and teens often argue about studying. When teens are told to "go study" or when teens tell caregivers "I already studied," there is often arguing over what "studying" is or what "studying" should look like.*
  - *Teens often spend large (or small) amounts of time looking at, reading, or reviewing book chapters, study guides, notes, or PowerPoints as part of studying, but this may not (and often does not) lead to being able to remember the information that is needed to get a good grade on a test or quiz.*
  - *It is helpful to define what it means to "go study" so that it is specific, observable, and measurable.*

    - *For example, saying "I will study for history" is not as clear or specific as "I will review my study guide for 30 minutes and then have my mom quiz me."*

- Check-in: *Teens – How many of you feel like you define what you are going to study in a clear and specific way?*
- Check-in: *Caregivers – How many of you feel like your teen may need some help with defining how to study?*
- *Caregivers can help to define and "grade" the studying that their teen is doing to increase their ability to retain and apply information on tests and quizzes and also get better grades.*
- *In order to define studying, caregivers and teens need to:*

  - *Identify the study skills that work for the teen*
  - *Determine the school subjects they need to study for*
  - *Define the study "solution"*
  - *Incentivize and reward the teen for studying.*

- *Clearly defining studying may have benefits including:*

  - *Reducing stress and conflict between caregivers and teens*
  - *Making studying useful for the teen*
  - *Reducing the time the teen spends on studying*
  - *Improving teen's performance/grade on tests/quizzes.*

- *We are going to focus on reviewing effective study strategies to help with defining studying.*
- Ask: *Any questions about defining studying?*

- **Using Effective Study Strategies (8 mins)**

  - Pass out and refer to the <u>My Study Strategies</u> handout.
  - *We would like you to take a few minutes to complete the My Study Strategies handout with your caregiver. This handout contains many effective study strategies, and it is helpful to think about what study strategies work for you in different classes.*
  - Give caregivers and teens 2–3 mins to complete the handout.

    - It may be helpful for Leaders to set a timer for this activity.

  - Ask the teens the following questions and briefly discuss their responses:

    - *What study strategies are most helpful?*
    - *What study strategies are not helpful?*
    - *Do you use certain strategies for different subjects such as using study cards to learn vocabulary words?*

  - *It can take some time to figure out what study strategies work best for you. While we do not have time to review all of the study strategies that can be used to study for tests/ quizzes across different school subjects, it will be important for you to determine what strategies are most effective for you. This is also something your caregiver can help you with. You want to figure out how to spend just enough time studying what is important so that you can learn and remember the information in order to get a good grade on your test.*

- **4–7 Rule (5 mins)**

  - *The key to the majority of effective study strategies is breaking information into smaller "chunks." The average brain can recall 4–7 things or chunks of information at a time.*
  - *I need one teen to volunteer to help me show how the 4–7 Rule works.*
  - Identify or select a teen to volunteer and tell them the following:

    - *I am going to say some numbers and I want you to say them back to me. Keep your eyes focused on me and don't write down what I say. I just want you to do your best to listen to the numbers and say them back. Any questions?*

  - Tell the other teens and caregivers:

    - *While [teen] volunteers, the rest of you can participate by listening to the numbers and then remembering them in your head.*

  - Begin 4–7 Rule Activity with participating teen:

    - *Alright [teen], ready? I'm going to start saying the numbers and then I'm going to give you a chance to say them back to me. Here we go!*
  - Say the following sets of numbers at a rate of about 1 number per second:

    - Easy (3 numbers): *9 - 7 - 4*

      ❏ Wait for and write down the teen's response.

    - Medium (5 numbers): *8 2 - 5 - 1 - 9*

      ❏ Wait for and write down the teen's response.

    - Hard (10 numbers): *1 - 6 - 4 - 0 - 3 - 1 - 9 - 2 - 5 - 8*

      ❏ Wait for and write down the teen's response.

    - Easy (10 numbers as a phone number): *513 - 298 - 3439*

      ❏ Wait for and write down the teen's response.

- Briefly discuss the teen's ability to remember the numbers and also ask about their experience (i.e., "Which number sets were the easiest to remember?" and "Which number sets were the hardest to remember?").
- *You can see that it got more difficult as you had to remember more numbers. It was hardest to remember ten numbers, but easier when you had to remember a phone number, which is also ten numbers, but consists of three separate chunks – 513-298-3439.*
- *It is helpful to 'chunk' information such as locker combinations, phone numbers, social security numbers, and account numbers so that we are able to remember them more effectively. The human brain is typically able to remember 4–7 chunks of information. This is called the 4–7 rule.*
- *We are going to be using the 4–7 rule to help us study effectively for tests so that we learn and remember the information in order to get a good grade. For example, you are more*

likely to remember the 4–7 keywords of the definition of photosynthesis than a 35 word definition of photosynthesis.
- Ask: *Any questions about the 4–7 rule?*

- **Study Cards (9 mins)**

  - Ask and briefly discuss the following questions with teens:

    - *How many of you have used flashcards to study in the past?*
    - *How did you make those flashcards?*
    - *Did you feel that the flashcards were effective at helping you to remember information for a test or quiz?*

  - *We are going to watch a video about a new study strategy that may remind you of flash cards, but this new strategy helps make important information stick inside of our brains – which is very helpful for tests and quizzes!*
  - Show AIMS Study Cards video (2m 55s).

    - NOTE: If the teens are having difficulty paying attention or staying engaged, the video can be paused and the Leader can ask questions (e.g., *What are the steps for creating study cards? What vocabulary word was used on the study card?*) to increase the likelihood that they will understand the concepts.

  - *As you can see in the video, there is a difference between flash cards and study cards, which we will be teaching you how to make and use today.*
  - *Flash cards often have a lot of words on them such that you may have to memorize a 15–20 word definition – which is hard! On the other hand, study cards have 4–7 key words or "chunks" of information.*
  - *Flash cards also go against the idea that our brain can only hold 4–7 chunks of information. When making study cards, you identify and memorize 4–7 key words or concepts – which is more doable for your brain, but it takes some time and effort to make the study cards.*
  - *Let's look at another example of how different a flash card and a study card look.*
  - Pass out and refer to <u>Study Card vs. Flashcard</u> handout.
  - Ask teens the following questions:

    - *Which card are you going to be able to memorize easier?*
    - *Which card are you going to be able to memorize faster?*
    - *Which card is more likely to "stick" in your brain such that you are going to remember it for a test or quiz?*

  - *Study cards are really helpful for tests and quizzes that require you to know vocabulary words, definitions of key concepts – such as the Bill of Rights – and details about key concepts – such as specific Constitutional Amendments.*
  - Ask: *Any questions about study cards?*

- **Stickiness Factor (5 mins)**

  - Write the word "bicycle" on a large post-it or whiteboard.

- *The process of creating study cards increases the "stickiness" of concepts in the brain so that you are less likely to forget them. We are going to show you how the "Stickiness Factor" works!*
- *As a group, we are going to create a study card for the word "bicycle." We are going to brainstorm keywords for the word bicycle and will then choose 4–7 keywords to put on our study card.*
- Keywords are typically the most important or critical words or short phrases for a definition. As we come up with keywordswe will talk about how important they are and if they should be included on our study card

- Ask the teens: *What is a keyword for bicycle?*
- Leaders should write down the keywords under the term "bicycle" on the whiteboard or large post-it. Once a list has been generated, the Leader can help teens identify the 4–7 most important keywords to the definition.
- The following points may be important for Leaders to address with teens as needed:

  - Keywords can be combined (e.g. "transportation" may represent the keywords of traveling, getting from place to place)
  - Keywords need to be specific (e.g. two-wheeled transportation could be included in the definition of a motorcycle and a bicycle)
  - Keywords such as "colorful," "seat," and "basket" may not be the most critical keywords
  - Teens may want to list off several parts of the bicycle, so it would be helpful to discuss which parts are most important for the definition of a bicycle (e.g., handlebars, gears).

- Once 4–7 keywords have been identified, have 2–3 teens volunteer to use the keywords (and any additional words) by asking: "*What is a bicycle?*"

  - As an example, if the keywords included (1) transportation, (2) two wheels, (3) pedals, (4) handlebars, (5) energy, and (6) steer, a good definition might be: "A bicycle is a type of transportation that uses energy from pedals to move the two wheels and is steered with handlebars."
  - Discuss that teens can always add in information that they know already (e.g., different sizes, different types of bikes such as mountain vs. road), but it may not be critical information to include on the study card if they already know it.

- After several teens have given a definition of a bicycle, ask the following questions:

  - *Did you just study?*
  - *Did you try to study?*
  - *How did you remember the definition?*

- *By identifying 4–7 keywords for bicycle and then using those keywords to create a definition, you made it stick in your brain. This is the stickiness factor in action. When we use the same process to study, we make the concepts and definitions stick in our brain so that we are more likely to remember them when we take a test.*

- **Steps for Creating Study Cards (4 mins)**

  - Pass out and refer to the <u>Steps for Creating Study Cards</u> handout.

- *Both the stickiness factor and the 4–7 rule apply to making study cards. By identifying the 4–7 keywords and then using them to create a longer definition or remember the details about a key concept, the information sticks in your brain and you are more likely to remember it when taking a test.*
- *There are 5 steps for creating study cards. It is often helpful to make study cards using index cards.*
- Have teens take turns reading each step from the <u>Steps for Creating Study Cards</u> handout.

  1. *Read and reread the content (e.g., notes, textbook).*
  2. *Underline or highlight keywords after you have read the content.*

     - *You can underline more than 4–7 keywords, but then you will have to narrow it down to the most critical and relevant keywords.*

  3. *On one side of the study card, write the word or term to be defined.*
  4. *On the other side of the study card, write a brief definition of 4–7 keywords.*

- *You do not want to include information that you already know. For example, if you are defining the "Constitution," you do not need to include the "United States" in your keywords because this is something you likely already know.*
- *You do not need to include words such as "the" or "and" because your brain can fill these words in when you create a definition out of the 4–7 keywords.*
- *If more than 7 keywords are needed, you can separate the definition into 2 study cards.*

  5. *Review study cards on your own or with a parent/caregiver or friend.*

- *Creating a study card using the 5 steps is actually when a lot of studying happens. By the time the study card is written, you have already learned and reviewed the information 3 times in 3 different ways by reading and re-reading, underlining/highlighting, and writing the 4–7 keywords on the study card. Then, you will study even more as you review the study cards on your own. All of these steps make it more likely that the key information will "stick" in your brain!*

- **Practice Making Study Cards (7 mins)**

  - Pass out and refer to the <u>Teleport Study Card</u> handout.
  - For this activity, Leaders should write down the word "teleport" on the whiteboard or large post-it. Leaders should then write down the keywords under the term "teleport" on the whiteboard or large post-it.
  - *Let's practice making a study card! The definition of teleport is at the top of this handout. As you can see, this is a long definition and would be hard to memorize. Let's take a look at it together and make a study card that has 4–7 keywords.*
  - *First, let's take out any words that we do not need or that mean the same thing. You can cross off these words on the handout.*

    - *3 "Transport" and "be transported" mean the thing, so we can keep "transport."*
    - *Shorten "across space and distance" to just "across space."*
    - *We can also cut out words like "to", "and", and "or."*

- *Next, let's choose the 4–7 keywords that seem to be most important to the definition of teleport. Take a moment to circle these words on the handout.*
- *What are the keywords that you circled?*
- Leaders should discuss teen responses. The main keywords are:

  - Transport
  - Across space
  - Instantly
  - Special technology
  - Imaginary power.

- *Lastly, let's create a study card. In the "One Side" box on the handout, write the word/term to be defined. In this case, we will all write "Teleport".*
- *In the "Other Side" box on the handout, we will write the 4–7 keywords that we circled and discussed.*
- Ask: *Who can give me the definition of the word teleport by just using the 4–7 keywords?*
- Provide explicit feedback and answer any questions that teens may have about making a study card.
- *By reviewing the study cards that you create from 4–7 keywords, it is more likely that the information will stick in your brain and that you will remember it when you take a test!*
- Ask: *Any questions before we break into our separate teen and caregiver groups?*
- Leaders should have caregivers and teens split into separate groups.

  - Remind teens to file handouts in their AIMS binder and provide assistance as needed.

Teen Group (15 mins)

- **Modifying Your Problem Solving Plan (5 mins)**

  - In order to facilitate a smooth and quick transition from the large group to the teen group, Leaders can ask teens to write down one thing that worked or was successful about using the Problem Solving Plan over the last week. Leaders can have the teens read their responses and briefly discuss.
  - Leaders can briefly go over the activities that are listed on the <u>Session 7 Schedule</u> handout for the Teen Group. State that teens can cross off activities on the schedule as they are completed.

  - *We discussed the Problem Solving Plan that you worked on with your caregiver over the last week at the beginning of today's session in detail.*
  - Ask: *Are there any questions or comments that you have about continuing to try out solutions to your problems by using a Problem Solving Plan?*
  - Pass out and refer to <u>Problem Solving Plan Examples for Using Effective Study Strategies</u> handout.
  - *On this handout, there are additional examples of how to use effective study strategies including making study cards using a Problem Solving Plan.*
  - The Leader should have teens read the problem, solution, EFs being targeted, plan and expectations for earning the reward, and identified reward for the first two examples on the <u>Problem Solving Plan Examples for Using Effective Study Strategies</u> handout.

- Ask: *Any questions about using a Problem Solving Plan to study effectively?*

- *For your Real World Practice assignment this week, you may be changing or adding to your current Problem Solving Plan by working on a solution that is related to using effective study strategies.*

  - *For example, if you struggle with knowing how to effectively study for History, you could make 5 study cards each day as a way to study a week before the test.*

- Ask and discuss the following questions with 2–3 teens:

  - *Would it be helpful to use study cards to study for tests or quizzes?*
  - *Which subjects might study cards be most helpful for?*
  - *What EF challenge would this solution address?*
  - *What reward could you earn for working on the solution?*

- *When we rejoin your caregivers, we will discuss your Real World Practice assignment. You will work together with your caregiver to continue using a Problem Solving Plan to continue targeting the solution from last week but will also add in a solution related to using a study strategy.*

- **More Practice Making Study Cards (10 mins)**

  - Pass out and refer to the <u>Study Cards Practice</u> handout and provide several blank index cards to each teen.
  - For this activity, Leaders should write down the words "supernova" and "asteroid" on the whiteboard or large post-it. Leaders should then write down the keywords as they are discussed under the words that are being defined on the whiteboard or large post-it.
  - *We are now going to work together as a large group to make study cards for the definitions of the terms "Supernova" and "Asteroid".*
  - *Let's start with "Supernova." Are there any words from the definition on the handout that we do not need or mean the same thing?*

    - *We can remove "supernova" since that is the word we are defining.*
    - *We can also cut out words like "a", "and", and "the."*

  - *Next, let's choose the 4–7 keywords that seem to be most important to the definition of supernova. Take a moment to circle these words on the handout.*
  - *What are the keywords that you circled?*
  - Leaders should discuss teen responses. The main keywords are:

    - Large explosion
    - Change in core
    - Too much matter
    - End of Life cycle
    - Bright.

  - *Lastly, let's create a study card. In the "One Side" box on the handout, write the word/term to be defined. In this case, we will all write "Supernova". In the "Other Side" box on the handout, we will write the 4–7 keywords that we circled and discussed.*

- Ask: *Who can give me the definition of the word supernova by just using the 4–7 keywords?*

- If time allows, repeat the same process for making a study card for the term "asteroid." The main keywords for "asteroid" are:

  - Rocky
  - Metal object
  - Orbits earth or sun
  - Mars and Jupiter
  - Minor planets.

- Remind teens to file handouts in their AIMS binder and provide assistance as needed.
- The Leader should pass out tickets to the teens as they participate in this activity.
- The teens should rejoin their caregivers for the reunification with the Large Group.

Caregiver Group (15 mins)

- **Discussion of Problem Solving Plan (5 mins)**

  - *We discussed the Problem Solving Plan that you worked on with your teen over the last week at the beginning of today's session in great detail. I am going to pass out a blank Problem Solving Plan so that you can jot down any notes about things you may want to add or edit for the upcoming week. Also, it can be helpful to review the <u>Tips for a Successful Problem Solving Plan</u> handout that we discussed a few weeks ago.*
  - Pass out <u>Problem Solving Plan</u> handout.

  - Ask: *Are there any questions or comments that you have about continuing to try out solutions to your teen's problems by using a Problem Solving Plan?*
  - *You and your teen may be changing or adding to the current Problem Solving Plan by working on a solution that is related to using effective study strategies.*

    - *For example, they may benefit from creating 5 study cards each evening as a way to study for an upcoming test.*

  - Pass out and refer to <u>Problem Solving Plan Examples for Using Effective Study Strategies</u>.
  - *On this handout, there are additional examples of how to target the use of effective study strategies using a Problem Solving Plan.*
  - Ask: *What solution related to using effective study strategies might be helpful for your teen?*

    - Leaders should write caregivers' responses on the whiteboard or large post-it.

- **Collaborating with Teens to Create a Problem Solving Plan (10 mins)**

  - *Your teen is practicing creating study cards so that they can start using this as a study strategy.*
  - *We do have less time this week to discuss the Problem Solving Plan for the upcoming week because we spent so much time discussing effective study strategies.*
  - *When the teens rejoin, we will discuss this week's Real World Practice assignment. You will work together with your teen to continue using a Problem Solving Plan to target the*

solution or solutions from last week, but also add in a solution related to studying for tests and quizzes.

- *For the remainder of our time together, let's each briefly discuss what you think your teen's Problem, Solution, EFs being Targeted, Plan and Expectations for Earning the Reward, and Reward will be on the Problem Solving Plan. Keep in mind that you also want to make sure that your teen feels heard and involved in this process – so it is likely that what you are planning may change slightly.*

  - *We also want to make sure that the teen's solution and plan for earning the reward is specific and doable so that they are set up for success as they build effective strategies for addressing their EF challenges.*
  - *We also want to make sure that it is feasible for you to implement the solution this week.*

- *We would like to add in a goal related to using effective study strategies. We understand that it can feel like a lot to be working on 3–5 solutions on the Problem Solving Plan, but we are here to provide support and figure out how to make this work for you and your teen.*

  - *For example, it may only be doable to make 3 study cards for an upcoming test. However, getting practice making study cards now will likely make it easier for your teen to use this study strategy in the future.*

- As each caregiver discusses their teen's Problem Solving Plan, the Leader should write the Problem Solving Plan components (i.e., problem, solution, EFs being targeted plan and expectations for earning reward, and reward) on the whiteboard or a large post-it.

  - Leaders should allow each caregiver to briefly discuss their thoughts for what solutions they would like to implement on their teen's Problem Solving Plan. They may keep the solution the same, modify a solution, and/or add a solution to a target problem.

Reunification – Large Group (7 mins)

- **Discussion of Teen Session Material (1 min)**

  - *In their session, the teens discussed their thoughts on using a Problem Solving Plan and also discussed what solution they may want to address for any challenges they have with studying for tests and quizzes. The teens also practiced making study cards.*
  - The Teen Leaders can share any additional details about the discussion and activities in the Teen Group.

- **Take Home Points (2 mins)**

  - *Let's go over our take home points.*
  - Ask the following questions (if time allows) and discuss as needed:

    - *How many chunks of information can the average brain hold?*

      - *4–7.*

- *In order, what are the steps to make a study card?*

  - *Read and re-read the content.*
  - *Underline or highlight the keywords.*
  - *On one side of the study card, write the vocabulary word/term to be defined.*
  - *On the other side of the study card, write a brief definition of 4–7 keywords.*
  - *Review study cards on your own or with parents/caregivers, siblings, or friends.*

- **Real World Practice Assignment (3 mins)**

  - Pass out and refer to <u>Real World Practice – Session 7</u> handout.
  - *For your Real World Practice Assignment this week, you will work with your caregiver on creating your Problem Solving Plan and start working on the solutions that you identify for your problems. Many of you will be working on 4–5 solutions – the 3–4 solutions from last week and a new solution addressing using effective study strategies.*

    - *After our discussion today, it is possible that you may want to make your solution more specific, clear, and doable and you can also outline this in the plan and expectations for earning the reward section of the Problem Solving Plan.*

  - Ask: *Any questions about your Real World Practice assignment?*
  - *You and your caregiver should set aside time either tonight or tomorrow to create the new Problem Solving Plan so that you have some time to work on it over the next week and get a chance to earn a reward. Take a minute to discuss when you can complete your Problem Solving Plan with your caregiver.*

    - *In your AIMS binder, take a moment to file your Real World Practice assignment now in the "To Do" side of the folder. You should also take a moment to file all of your other handouts behind the Session 7 divider.*
  - Ask: *Any final questions before we get ready to trade in your tickets for prizes?*

- **Trade in Tickets (1 min)**

  - The Leader should give all teens who earned a ticket an opportunity to trade them in for prizes using the Prize Menu.
  - Leaders should record the number of remaining tickets on the Ticket Tracker (if used).

Session 7 Schedule

Large Group

❏ Review Group Rules and Prize Menu

❏ Review Real World Practice Assignment

❏ Review of Material from Last Session

❏ Goals for Session 7

❏ Why Study?

❏ Defining Studying

❏ Using Effective Study Strategies

❏ Study Cards

❏ Stickiness Factor

❏ Steps for Creating a Study Card

❏ Practice Making Study Cards

Teen Group

❏ Modifying Your Problem Solving Plan

❏ More Practice Making Study Cards

Reunification – Large Group

❏ Discussion of Teen Session Material

❏ Take Home Points

❏ Real World Practice Assignment

❏ Trade in Tickets

Effective Study Strategies and the Importance of Defining Studying

Study strategies are a set of techniques that help improve our ability to remember and apply information for tests and quizzes.

Effective study strategies:

- Break larger amounts of information into smaller units.
- Identify similarities or patterns that can be recalled or learned.
- Organize the information into manageable amounts so that it can be memorized.

It is helpful to define what it means to "go study" so that it is specific, observable, and measurable.

- For example, saying "I will study for history" is not as clear or specific as saying "I will review my study guide for 30 minutes and then have my mom quiz me."

Caregivers can help to define and "grade" the studying that their teen is doing to increase their ability to retain and apply information on tests and quizzes, and also get better grades.

In order to <u>define studying</u>, caregivers and teens need to:

- Identify the study skills that work for the teen.
- Determine the school subjects they need to study for.
- Define the study "solution".
- Incentivize and reward the teen for studying.

Clearly defining studying may have <u>benefits</u> including:

- Reducing stress and conflict between parents and teens.
- Making studying useful for the teen.
- Reducing the time the teen spends on studying.
- Improving teen's performance/grade on tests/quizzes.

My Study Strategies

Directions: For each study strategy, indicate whether you have learned or used it before, if it is a successful strategy for studying, and what subjects the study strategy works best for. If there are other study strategies that you use, add them to "Other Strategy."

Strategy	Learned/ Used before?	Is this a successful strategy for me?	If YES, what subject(s) does this strategy work best for?
Reread/highlight information from a textbook	YES NO	YES NO DK	
Outline information in a textbook	YES NO	YES NO DK	
Reread notes	YES NO	YES NO DK	
Rewrite or outline notes	YES NO	YES NO DK	
Organize notes	YES NO	YES NO DK	
Complete and/or review study guide	YES NO	YES NO DK	
Take a practice test	YES NO	YES NO DK	
Make or review study cards	YES NO	YES NO DK	
Online study cards or online study games	YES NO	YES NO DK	
Acronyms or acrostics	YES NO	YES NO DK	
Songs	YES NO	YES NO DK	
Summaries (5 Ws, Star Graphic Organizer)	YES NO	YES NO DK	
Plot diagram and/or storyboard	YES NO	YES NO DK	
Quiz yourself	YES NO	YES NO DK	
Have someone else quiz you	YES NO	YES NO DK	
Study with others (e.g., friend)	YES NO	YES NO DK	
Study with parent	YES NO	YES NO DK	
Ask for help (e.g., from teacher, tutor)	YES NO	YES NO DK	
Other Strategy:	YES NO	YES NO DK	
Other Strategy:	YES NO	YES NO DK	

Study Cards vs. Flash Cards

Term to Learn for Test: Photosynthesis

Study Card	Flash Card

Study Card:

Process
Chlorophyll
Traps light energy
Produces food

Flash Card:

A process by which plants and other organisms use chlorophyll to capture the light energy in sunlight and use it to produce food.

Which one will stick in your brain more?

Steps for Creating Study Cards

1. Read and reread the content (e.g., notes, textbook).
2. Underline or highlight keywords after you have read the content.

   - You can initially underline many keywords, but then you will have to narrow it down to the most important 4–7 keywords.

3. On one side of the study card, write the word or term to be defined.
4. On the other side of the study card, write a brief definition of 4–7 keywords.

   - You do not want to include information that you already know. For example, if you are defining the "Constitution," you do not need to include the "United States" in your keywords because this is something you likely already know.
   - You do not need to include words such as "the" or "and" because your brain can fill these words in when you create a definition out of the 4–7 keywords.
   - If more than 7 keywords are needed, you can separate the definition into 2 study cards.

5. Review study cards on your own or with a parent/friend.

Study Card Practice

Teleport: To transport or be transported across space and distance instantly by using special technology or power.

One Side (Write ONLY the word/term to be defined)

The Other Side (Write the 4–7 keywords)

Study Cards Practice

Supernova

A supernova is a large explosion of a star. The star experiences a change in its core, which causes it to explode. Supernovas can happen in two ways: 1) when a star collects too much matter, or 2) when a star is at the end of its life cycle. From Earth, the star becomes suddenly very bright. It is the biggest explosion that happens in space and often takes place in other galaxies.

Asteroid

An asteroid is a rocky or metal object in space that orbits the Earth. Their size can range from a few feet wide to several hundred miles wide. There are thousands of asteroids orbiting the sun currently. However, most asteroids are between Mars and Jupiter. They are often referred to as minor planets.

Problem Solving Plan

Date: _____

Problem Who, What, Where, When, & Why	Solution	EF(s) Being Targeted	Plan and Expectations for Earning Reward	Reward	Reward Earned?
		Getting Started Planning Prioritizing Organizing Working Memory			☐ Monday ☐ Tuesday ☐ Wednesday ☐ Thursday ☐ Friday ☐ Saturday ☐ Sunday
		Getting Started Planning Prioritizing Organizing Working Memory			☐ Monday ☐ Tuesday ☐ Wednesday ☐ Thursday ☐ Friday ☐ Saturday ☐ Sunday

This agreement begins on _____ and we will review the agreement again on _____.

_____
Teen

_____
Parent/Caregiver

Problem Solving Plan Examples for Using Effective Study Strategies

Date: 9/1 – 9/5

Problem Who, What, Where, When, & Why	Solution	EF(s) Being Targeted	Plan and Expectations for Earning Reward	Reward	Reward Earned?
I have trouble memorizing the vocabulary words for my Language Arts quizzes on Friday.	I will make 5 study cards for my vocabulary words each day and study them until the quiz on Friday.	Getting Started <u>Planning</u> Prioritizing Organizing <u>Working Memory</u>	Make 5 study cards on Monday – Thursday by 8pm. My dad will quiz me each night using the study cards.	30 minutes of extra video game time from 8:15–8:45pm.	❑ Monday ❑ Tuesday ❑ Wednesday ❑ Thursday ❑ Friday ❑ Saturday ❑ Sunday
I do not know how to study for my tests and quizzes.	My mom will help me define how to study for a test. I will write what I need to do to study in my planner.	<u>Getting Started</u> <u>Planning</u> Prioritizing Organizing Working Memory	After school, my mom will help me define how to study for any upcoming tests or quizzes. I will use study guides, rewrite my notes, or make study cards. I will write down what I need to do to study in my planner.	$1 towards a new video game.	❑ Monday ❑ Tuesday ❑ Wednesday ❑ Thursday ❑ Friday ❑ Saturday ❑ Sunday

This agreement begins on 9/1 _____ and we will review the agreement again on 9/7 _____.

_____
Teen

_____
Parent/Caregiver

© 2026 Amie Duncan and Leanne Tamm, *Improving Academic Executive Functioning for Autistic Middle Schoolers*

Real World Practice – Session 7

- Work with your caregiver to modify your Problem Solving Plan and start working on the solutions that you identify for the problems. After our discussion today, it is possible that you may want to make your solution more specific, clear, and doable and you can also outline this in the Plan and Expectations for Earning the Reward section of the Problem Solving Plan. Over the next week, you should do the following:

  - Add on a solution to target studying more effectively (e.g., make study cards, define what you will be doing when you study for a test/quiz).
  - Continue working on any solutions from your previous Problem Solving Plan.

Problem Solving Plan

Date: _____

Problem Who, What, Where, When, & Why	Solution	EF(s) Being Targeted	Plan and Expectations for Earning Reward	Reward	Reward Earned?
		Getting Started Planning Prioritizing Organizing Working Memory			☐ Monday ☐ Tuesday ☐ Wednesday ☐ Thursday ☐ Friday ☐ Saturday ☐ Sunday
		Getting Started Planning Prioritizing Organizing Working Memory			☐ Monday ☐ Tuesday ☐ Wednesday ☐ Thursday ☐ Friday ☐ Saturday ☐ Sunday

This agreement begins on _____ and we will review the agreement again on _____.

_____
Teen

_____
Parent/Caregiver

© 2026 Amie Duncan and Leanne Tamm, *Improving Academic Executive Functioning for Autistic Middle Schoolers*

Problem Solving Plan

Date: _____

Problem Who, What, Where, When, & Why	Solution	EF(s) Being Targeted	Plan and Expectations for Earning Reward	Reward	Reward Earned?
		Getting Started Planning Prioritizing Organizing Working Memory			❏ Monday ❏ Tuesday ❏ Wednesday ❏ Thursday ❏ Friday ❏ Saturday ❏ Sunday
		Getting Started Planning Prioritizing Organizing Working Memory			❏ Monday ❏ Tuesday ❏ Wednesday ❏ Thursday ❏ Friday ❏ Saturday ❏ Sunday

This agreement begins on _____ and we will review the agreement again on _____.

_____
Teen

_____
Parent/Caregiver

Problem Solving Plan

Date: _____

Problem Who, What, Where, When, & Why	Solution	EF(s) Being Targeted	Plan and Expectations for Earning Reward	Reward	Reward Earned?
		Getting Started Planning Prioritizing Organizing Working Memory			☐ Monday ☐ Tuesday ☐ Wednesday ☐ Thursday ☐ Friday ☐ Saturday ☐ Sunday
		Getting Started Planning Prioritizing Organizing Working Memory			☐ Monday ☐ Tuesday ☐ Wednesday ☐ Thursday ☐ Friday ☐ Saturday ☐ Sunday

This agreement begins on _____ and we will review the agreement again on _____.

_____
Teen

_____
Parent/Caregiver

Session 8   Moving Forward After AIMS

Session 8 Preparation

Session Specific Supplies

- Projector/computer for Trivia Game
- AIMS Trivia Instructions (from Leader Materials)
- Personalized AIMS Graduation Certificate (from Leader Materials)

General AIMS Supplies

- AIMS Rules Poster
- Prize Menu and Prize Box
- Ticket Tracker and tickets
- Real World Practice Tracker
- Whiteboard and dry erase markers OR large Post-It easel pad and markers
- Pens/Pencils
- Game/Activity for Teen Group

Handouts Needed

- Large Group

  - Session 8 Schedule

- Teen Group

  - None

- Caregiver Group

  - Problem Solving Plan
  - Problem Solving Plan Examples for Additional AIMS Strategies
  - Computer Organization System
  - Rules for Naming Files
  - Organizing Email – Tips and Tricks

DOI: 10.4324/9781003500209-9

- Long Term Assignment Plan
- Long Term Assignment Plan – English Paper Example
- Study Plan
- Study Plan – Science Test Example
- 5 Ws
- Star Graphic Organizer
- Plot Diagram
- Storyboard
- School Communication Tips
- Moving Forward After AIMS

- Large Group

  - Real World Practice – Session 8

Important Points for Session 8

- **General Session Notes**

  - The focus of this session is providing support to the caregivers so that they feel like they are able to continue utilizing the various strategies that have been presented in AIMS as solutions to EF challenges on the Problem Solving Plan for their teen. The Leader will provide a brief overview of several additional strategies related to organization, planning, prioritizing, and studying for tests and quizzes that may be helpful both now and in the future.
  - Leaders should encourage caregivers to continue to utilize the Problem Solving Plan to solve academic problems that their teens may be having. It can be highly beneficial for caregivers and teens to continue to use the Problem Solving Plans even after AIMS ends so that the solutions being implemented become mastered and integrated into their daily life.
  - Leaders should ensure that they are addressing any questions that caregivers and teens have about using the Problem Solving Plan over the last week. There is time in the large group, the teen group, and the caregiver group to address any issues, questions, or concerns.
  - As the Leader discusses each teen's Problem Solving Plan, they should provide feedback on each component (e.g., solution, plan/expectations, reward) and also provide suggestions to increase the likelihood of success (e.g., specific, doable, realistic, appropriate amount of detail, motivating reward).
  - Consider rewarding teens who participate by passing out tickets when they:

    - Answer questions during the review
    - Discuss how their Problem Solving Plan went from the Real World Practice assignment
    - Participate in Trivia and EF games
    - Answer the Take Home Points questions.

- **Real World Practice**

  - During the large group, caregivers and teens will all have the opportunity to discuss the Real World Practice task of completing the Problem Solving Plan in detail, including discussion of any challenges, successes, or questions. It is likely that most teens' Problem Solving Plan will need to be modified, and time should be devoted to refining the solution, plan/expectations, and reward.

    - Leaders are encouraged to use a whiteboard or large post-it to write down each teen's identified problem, chosen solution, EFs being targeted, plan and expectations for earning the reward, and the reward. It is helpful for teens and caregivers to see the different problems, solutions, plans/expectations, and rewards on the Problem Solving Plans of other teens. This may also keep other caregivers and teens engaged as each teen discusses their Problem Solving Plan.
    - It may be helpful to have the Caregiver Leader facilitate the discussion with the teens and for another Leader to write down the details of the Problem Solving Plan on the whiteboard or a large post-it.

  - Caregivers will also have the opportunity to discuss the Problem Solving Plan away from the teens, and it can be helpful to remind caregivers about this if they start to express frustration or negativity towards or about their teen.

- **Teen Group**

  - The Leader should make the final session positive, fun, and engaging by playing an AIMS Trivia game, which reviews key concepts discussed in the AIMS intervention.

    - Leaders can utilize the pre-set questions and answers for the AIMS Trivia game and have teens compete against each other or in small groups to earn "money" or tickets for correctly answering questions (see Leader Materials for additional instructions and pre-set questions and answers).

      - Alternatively, Leaders can create a PowerPoint using a trivia template and enter the pre-set questions and answers into the template.

    - Leaders are encouraged to have teens take turns choosing a category and denomination (e.g., "EFs for $100") so that all teens get a chance to participate.

      - If the teen answers correctly, they "earn" the money and another teen then takes a turn at choosing a category and denomination.
      - If the teen answers incorrectly, other teens can steal by raising their hand. Leaders will need to set rules around how they judge which teen raises their hand first (e.g., have the Teen Therapist be the one who decides who raised their hand first). Once the question has been answered, the next teen in line takes a turn at choosing a category and denomination.

- Leaders can allow teens to look up answers in their AIMS binder when "stealing" a question.
- Leaders can provide tickets at the end of AIMS Trivia to reward teens for both participating and for answering questions correctly.

- Other EF games can also be played including Stack Attack, Penny Stack, Connect Four, Uno, etc. (see Leader Materials).

- Leaders may want to use a timer so that teens clearly know when the games will end.

- **Caregiver Group**

  - The Supplemental Materials contains additional terms that can be used to practice summarizing strategies, plot diagrams, and storyboards. This may be helpful for caregivers who want to increase their understanding of how to utilize these strategies with their teen.
  - The Leader will revisit any questions or challenges that the caregivers had as they worked with their teen to implement the Problem Solving Plan at home.

    - It can be helpful for Leaders to refer to the whiteboard or large post-it notes that document each teen's Problem Solving Plan.
    - Leaders can encourage caregivers to jot down notes of things that they may want to modify or discuss on a blank Problem Solving Plan.

  - The Leader will also discuss if each caregiver wants to modify their current Problem Solving Plan by modifying the solution from last week and also adding a solution that is focused on organizing the backpack or binder.
  - Teens will have different goals depending on their challenges and also how quickly they are able to implement new solutions.
  - Leaders should encourage caregivers and teens to continue to try out 4–5 solutions on the Problem Solving Plan and emphasize that even small changes (e.g., making 3 study cards to study for the Spanish test) can lead to big improvements (e.g., learning Spanish vocabulary, performing better on upcoming quizzes and tests).
  - While passing out handouts on various other effective strategies that could be implemented to address EF problems in the areas of organization, planning, prioritizing, and working memory, the Leader should briefly review each strategy and answer any questions about how they could be implemented for their teen.

    - The <u>Problem Solving Plan Examples for Additional AIMS Strategies</u> handout also provides several examples of incorporating these new strategies into a Problem Solving Plan. The goal of introducing these strategies is to provide caregivers with strategies that can be used now or in the future (e.g., high school, college).

  - Leaders are encouraged to provide examples of how teens could utilize the additional strategies discussed (e.g., organizing email using folders and subfolders with a caregiver's help, making a plot diagram before starting a book report, breaking down the steps of a long-term assignment or project, etc.).

- Leaders can also note that these are strategies that may be beneficial to implement as teens get older and may need to build their organization, planning, prioritizing, and study strategies.

- The Leader can also use the <u>School Communication Tips</u> handout to discuss how caregivers may discuss implementation of specific EF strategies at school (e.g., signing the teen's planner at the end of the day, reminding the teen to get completed assignments out of their HW folder).
- Leaders should try to review any questions that caregivers have about continuing to use the Problem Solving Plan now and in the future to build teens' strategies for improving their academic EF challenges. The <u>Moving Forward After AIMS</u> handout discusses the most common questions and issues that caregivers have and it may be helpful to review and have caregivers reflect on anything that is relevant for them and their teen.

- **Large Group**

  - Graduation

    - Leaders should have personalized AIMS Graduation Certificates for each teen to hand to them.
    - Leaders should also prepare brief comments about each teen (e.g., any progress or gains that they have made over the last 8 weeks, funny stories, etc.) that can be shared when giving them their AIMS Graduation Certificate.

Get Ready Checklist for Leaders

❑ Prep the handouts to be passed out
❑ Hang up AIMS Rules Poster
❑ Hang up Prize Menu
❑ Check that Prize Box has range of prizes to be earned
❑ Hang up the Real World Practice Assignment Tracker (if used)
❑ Hang up Ticket Tracker (if used)
❑ Set up projector and/or computer for the AIMS Trivia game in the Teen Group
❑ Get any supplies for the games to be played in the Teen Group
❑ Print out AIMS Graduation Certificates for each teen
❑ Discuss what Leaders will say about each teen prior to giving them their AIMS Graduation Certificate

Session 8 Manual

Large Group – Caregivers and Teens (30 mins)

- **Session Schedule (1 min)**

  - Pass out and refer to <u>Session 8 Schedule</u> handout.
  - *Let's make sure to get started the right way so that we can fully focus on what you will be learning today. Put all materials away except for your AIMS binder and a pen or pencil.*
  - Briefly go over the activities that are listed on the <u>Session 8 Schedule</u> handout. State that teens can cross off activities on the schedule as they are completed.

- **Review Group Rules and Prize Menu (1 min)**

  - Refer to the AIMS Rules Poster and briefly review each of the rules.
  - Remind teens that they will earn tickets that can be traded in for prizes at the end of each session when they:

    - Follow the group rules
    - Participate in the session
    - Complete activities in session
    - Complete Real World Practice Assignments.

  - Briefly review that the Prize Menu shows how many tickets are needed to earn various prizes.
  - Remind teens that this will be the last week for teens to trade in their tickets at the end of the session.

- **Review Real World Practice Assignment (25 mins)**

  - Instruct teens to get out their Real World Practice Assignment from their AIMS binder.
  - Ask: *Who completed the Real World Practice Assignment?*

    - If utilizing the Real World Practice Assignment Tracker, Leaders should indicate which teens completed their Real World Practice Assignment. This can be done by asking teens to raise their hands if they completed the assignment and/or walking around the room to check on whether the teens completed it.
    - Check that teens filed their Real World Practice Assignment in the "Completed" section of their Real World Practice folder in their AIMS binder.

  - *Your Real World Practice from the last session was to work with your caregiver to modify your Problem Solving Plan and start working on the solution that you identified for the problem. Last week, we talked about effective study strategies and learned how to make study cards, so we encouraged you to choose a solution to address any problems you were having with studying for tests and quizzes. You can earn a ticket for completing your Real World Practice.*

- To assess what caregivers and teens thought about using the Problem Solving Plan, poll the large group by asking the following questions:

  - *Was it easy to set up the Problem Solving Plan?*
  - *Was it doable to work on the solution you chose on your Problem Solving Plan?*
  - *Teens – were you able to negotiate the reward that you wanted?*
  - *Teens – did you earn a reward?*
  - *Teens – did your caregiver give you the reward if you earned it?*
  - *Teens – did you make progress towards becoming independent with your schoolwork?*
  - *Teens – did you have more free time to do the things you wanted to do?*

- Ask each caregiver/teen dyad to share their Problem Solving Plan. Specifically, first have each teen share the details of their Problem Solving Plan (i.e., problem, solution, EFs being targeted, plan and expectations for earning reward, and reward).

  - Due to time constraints, teens should share 1–2 of the solutions that they are targeting. If applicable, Leaders should encourage teens to discuss the use of a solution for backpack or binder organization systems.

- Leaders should write each teen's Problem Solving Plan components (i.e., problem, solution, EFs being targeted plan and expectations for earning reward, and reward) on the whiteboard or a large post-it.
- The following questions can be asked of each teen when reviewing their Problem Solving Plan and writing it on the whiteboard or large post-it:

  - *What was the target problem?*
  - *What was the solution?*
  - *What was the plan and expectations for earning the reward?*
  - *What was the reward?*
  - *How did it go trying out the solution?*

    - *Did it address your problem?*
    - *Was it worth it?*

  - *Did you earn a reward?*
  - *Did you feel you had more independence?*
  - *What worked well or what was successful about your Problem Solving Plan?*
  - *What did not work or what was challenging about your Problem Solving Plan?*

- While the caregiver can weigh in, they will have time to discuss their thoughts and experiences in the caregiver group session. Ask the caregiver the following questions (if time allows):

  - *How did it go trying out the solution?*

    - *Did they make progress towards addressing the problem?*

- *Did you feel that your teen showed more independence?*

- *This is our last week to discuss the Problem Solving Plan, but we encourage you to continue using these to address any problems that you are having. It can often take several weeks or months for a new solution to a problem to really start working and to see the results. However, the strategies that you have learned over the last several weeks can be used to increase the likelihood of success in middle school and high school, and also college and in the workplace.*
- Briefly ask each teen and caregiver dyad the following questions:

  - *Do you feel like the Problem Solving Plan helped with some of the problems you have related to organization, planning, prioritizing, getting started, and working memory?*
  - *What solutions on your Problem Solving Plan were particularly helpful?*
  - *How can you make sure you keep making progress on using the solutions on your Problem Solving Plan?*

- Remind teens to file their completed Real World Practice Assignment in their folder.
- If teens completed the Real World Practice Assignment, they should be rewarded with 1 ticket.

- **Review of Material from Last Session (2 mins)**

  - Ask the following questions (if time allows) and discuss as needed:

    - *How many chunks of information can the average brain hold?*

      - *4–7.*

    - *In order, what are the steps to make a study card?*

      - *Read and re-read the content.*
      - *Underline or highlight the keywords.*
      - *On one side of the study card, write the vocabulary word/term to be defined.*
      - *On the other side of the study card, write a brief definition of 4–7 keywords.*
      - *Review study cards on your own or with parents/caregivers, siblings, or friends.*

- **Goals for Session 8 (1 min)**

  - *Our goals for today are the following*:

    - *Review the different strategies you have learned throughout AIMS to address any EF challenges with planning, prioritizing, organization, getting started on tasks, and working memory.*
    - *Discuss how to continue to use your Problem Solving Plan to help with any problems you are having related to school or homework and studying.*
    - *Celebrate the successes you have had over the last 8 weeks.*

  - Ask: *Any questions before we break into our separate teen and caregiver groups?*
  - Leaders should have caregivers and teens split into separate groups.

    - Remind teens to file handouts in their AIMS binder and provide assistance as needed.

Teen Group (45 mins)

- **Modifying Your Problem Solving Plan (5 mins)**

  - In order to facilitate a smooth and quick transition from the large group to the teen group, Leaders can ask teens to write down one thing that worked or was successful about using the Problem Solving Plan over the last week. Leaders can have the teens read their responses and briefly discuss.
  - Leaders can briefly go over the activities that are listed on the Session 8 Schedule hand-out for the Teen Group. State that teens can cross off activities on the schedule as they are completed.
  - *We discussed the Problem Solving Plan that you worked on with your caregiver over the last week at the beginning of today's session in detail.*
  - *As a reminder, we are encouraging you to continue using a Problem Solving Plan even after AIMS ends, so this is the last time to address any questions you have within our teen group.*
  - Ask: *Are there any questions or comments that you have about continuing to try out solutions to your problems by using a Problem Solving Plan?*
  - *For your Real World Practice assignment this week, you may be changing or adding to your current Problem Solving Plan by modifying the solutions or the plan and expectations for earning your reward.*
  - *When we rejoin your caregivers, we will discuss your Real World Practice assignment. You will work together with your caregiver to keep using a Problem Solving Plan to continue targeting the solutions that you have been working on over the last several weeks!*

- **AIMS Trivia Game (30 mins)**

  - Use the pre-set questions and answers in the AIMS Trivia Game Instructions for Leaders handout (see Leader Materials) to review the core concepts discussed in AIMS over the last 7 sessions.

    - Alternatively, Leaders can choose to create a trivia game with a PowerPoint template.
    - The instructions, questions, and answer key are included in the AIMS Trivia Game Instructions for Leaders handout (see Leader Materials). Leaders can also edit the AIMS Trivia game as needed to personalize material to their particular group of teens.

  - Leaders should make this activity fun and engaging.

    - Tickets can be passed out throughout the game or at the end of the game (e.g., for participating, for correctly answering questions, for having the most points, for having the most steals, etc.).

- **EF Game (10 mins)**

  - If time allows, the Leader can allow the teens to play a short game that utilizes EF skills. Possible games to play include Stack Attack, Penny Stack, Connect 4, or Uno (see Leader Materials for additional information including instructions and materials needed for games).
  - Remind teens to file handouts in their AIMS binder and provide assistance as needed.

- The Leader should pass out tickets to the teens as they participate in this activity.
- The teens should rejoin their caregivers for the reunification with the Large Group.

Caregiver Group (45 mins)

- **Discussion of Problem Solving Plan (9 mins)**

  - *We discussed the Problem Solving Plan that you worked on with your teen over the last week at the beginning of today's session in great detail. I am going to pass out a blank Problem Solving Plan so that you can jot down any notes about things you may want to add or edit for the upcoming week. Also, it can be helpful to review the <u>Tips for a Successful Problem Solving Plan</u> handout that we discussed a few weeks ago.*
  - Pass out <u>Problem Solving Plan</u> handout.

  - Ask: *Are there any questions or comments that you have about continuing to try out solutions to your teen's problems by using a Problem Solving Plan?*
  - *Though the AIMS intervention is ended, we encourage you to continue to use a Problem Solving Plan to work on solutions that address your teen's problems in the areas of organization, planning, prioritizing, getting started, and working memory. The Problem Solving Plan is a way to continue to build your teen's ability to use these solutions now, but also in the future.*
  - *It can take several weeks and months for these solutions to become part of your teen's routine and to see progress. You will also likely need to continue to modify the Problem Solving Plan over time as you push your teen to learn more skills and become more independent.*
  - *Let's talk about some additional strategies that we did not cover during AIMS, but could be beneficial to teach to your teen in the future.*

- **Additional AIMS Strategies (12 mins)**

  - Pass out and refer to <u>Problem Solving Plan Examples for Additional AIMS Strategies</u> handout.
  - *We are going to talk about several additional strategies that may be helpful as you work to address EF challenges with your teen. We will pass out several handouts and briefly discuss strategies for organization, planning, prioritizing, and studying. We also have examples of how you can utilize these strategies in the <u>Problem Solving Plan Examples for Additional AIMS Strategies</u> handout.*

  - Organization Strategies

    - Pass out and refer to the <u>Computer Organization System, Rules for Naming Files,</u> and <u>Organizing Email – Tips and Tricks</u> handouts.

      - Leaders may want to hold up each handout as they are describing the new strategy.

    - *These handouts refer to strategies to help teens who are frequently using a computer or tablet for assignments either at school or for homework.*

- *The <u>Computer Organization</u> handout discusses how to organize files on one's computer to use folders and subfolders. For example, if teens have a Language Arts folder, the subfolders may include Study Guides, Essays, Homework Assignments, and Notes.*
- *It is also helpful for teens to learn how to name files in a clear and consistent way, and the <u>Rules for Naming Files</u> handout outlines simple guidelines for doing this.*
- *Lastly, teens may need assistance organizing email, especially if they are frequently using it for school to turn in assignments or communicate with teachers. The <u>Organizing Email – Tips and Tricks</u> handout reviews strategies for organizing their email inbox. In the same way it is helpful to create folders and subfolders on your computer, it can be helpful also set up folders in the teen's email inbox.*
- *It can be helpful for teens to implement an organization system before they are utilizing their computer for most classes and most assignments, which increases in high school and again in college.*
- Ask: *Any questions about you might use any of these organization strategies with your teen?*

- Planning and Prioritizing Strategies

  - Pass out and refer to the <u>Long Term Assignment Plan, Long Term Assignment Plan – English Paper Example, Study Plan</u>, and <u>Study Plan – Science Test Example</u> handouts.
  - *The <u>Long Term Assignment Plan</u> handout addresses planning and prioritizing challenges that teens may experience when breaking down the steps for a project or essay. It is meant to break down the steps so that teens can work on the project or essay a little at a time and write down each step separately in their planner. The <u>Long Term Assignment Plan – English Paper Example</u> illustrates how this could be used to break down the steps for writing a 5-paragraph essay.*
  - *The <u>Study Plan</u> is similar in that it is meant to help teens break down how to study for tests over several days. As you can see on the <u>Study Plan – Science Test Example</u>, studying is broken down into steps that can then be written down in the teen's planner.*
  - Ask: *Any questions about how you might use any of these planning and prioritizing strategies with your teen?*

- Study Strategies

  - Pass out and refer to the <u>5 W's, Star Graphic Organizer, Plot Diagram</u>, and <u>Storyboard</u> handouts.
  - *Summaries can be an extremely beneficial study strategy to teach as a way to not only comprehend material, but also study. Summaries restate the information by identifying the main point and key supporting details of a paragraph, chapter, or novel. By taking the time to create a summary, it makes it more likely that the teen will remember the information. Most summary strategies also very purposely reduce large amounts of information into 4–7 key points or chunks of information.*
  - *The <u>5 W's</u> and <u>Star Graphic Organizer</u> handouts break down information into Who, What, Where, When, and Why and may be particularly helpful for learning and studying subjects such as History and Language Arts.*

- *The <u>Plot Diagram</u> and <u>Storyboard</u> handouts break down the main components of a story or novel.*
- *As a reminder, it may take some time to figure out how your teen studies best. You can use the <u>My Study Strategies</u> handout that we passed out in Session 7 to refer back to as teens get older and as they are taking different classes.*

  - *For example, while a study guide may be effective for Biology, they may want to make study cards for History and may want to do a plot diagram before writing a book report in Language Arts.*

- Ask: *Any questions about how you might use any of these study strategies with your teen?*

- **Tips and Recommendations for Communication with School Personnel (8 mins)**

  - Pass out and refer to <u>School Communication Tips</u> handout.
  - *This handout provides guidance on how to communicate with school personnel about addressing your teen's EF challenges in the school setting.*
  - If time allows, briefly read and discuss each tip and recommendation on the handout. Caregivers should be encouraged to reflect and ask questions throughout.
  - Ask: *Any questions about communicating with school personnel – specifically about how to address your teen's EF challenges at school?*

- **Moving Forward after AIMS (7 mins)**

  - Pass out and refer to <u>Moving Forward After AIMS</u> handout.
  - *We understand that it can feel like a lot to be working on 3–5 solutions on the Problem Solving Plan, but you have likely seen success and growth in your teen as they implement solutions that target their EF challenges. It is important to think about how to continue this forward momentum after AIMS ends.*
  - *While we are building your teen's ability to use strategies to plan, prioritize, organize materials, do their homework, and study for tests, you can purposely and slowly increase the expectations you have for your teen as they demonstrate mastery and independence.*
  - Ask: Any questions about continuing to use a Problem Solving Plan to build effective strategies for your teen's EF challenges?

    - Leaders should address any questions or concerns (e.g., how to continue a weekly check-in for the Problem Solving Plan, how to fade back the use of rewards for specific solutions).

  - If time allows, ask and discuss the following questions about moving forward after the AIMS intervention is over:

    - *What questions do you have about the strategies and skills we've discussed over the past 8 weeks?*
    - *Do you feel that you will be able to sustain the current Problem Solving Plans? Why or why not?*

- *What are 2–3 challenges that you would like to address in the next several weeks or months?*
- *Do you have any questions about how to set up a Problem Solving Plan for these challenges?*

- **Collaborating with Teens to Create a Problem Solving Plan (9 mins)**

  - *When the teens rejoin, we will discuss this week's Real World Practice assignment. You will work together with your teen to continue using a Problem Solving Plan to target the solution or solutions from last week and can also add in any others. Again, we highly encourage you to continue using the Problem Solving Plan so that your teen masters these skills to help them become independent with organizing their materials, completing homework, and studying for tests.*
  - *For the remainder of our time together, let's each briefly discuss what you think your teen's Problem, Solution, EFs being Targeted, Plan and Expectations for Earning the Reward, and Reward will be on the Problem Solving Plan. Keep in mind that you also want to make sure that your teen feels heard and involved in this process – so it is likely that what you are planning may change slightly.*

    - *We also want to make sure that the teen's solution and plan for earning the reward is specific and doable so that they are set up for success as they build effective strategies for addressing their EF challenges.*
    - *We also want to make sure that it is feasible for you to implement the solution this week.*

  - As each caregiver discusses their teen's Problem Solving Plan going forward, the Leader should write the Problem Solving Plan components (i.e., problem, solution, EFs being targeted plan and expectations for earning reward, and reward) on the whiteboard or a large post-it.

    - Leaders should allow each caregiver to briefly discuss their thoughts for what solutions they would like to implement on their teen's Problem Solving Plan. They may keep the solution the same, modify a solution, and/or add a solution to a target problem.

Reunification – Large Group (15 mins)

- **Discussion of Teen Session Material (1 min)**

  - *In their session, the teens reviewed the strategies we have learned over the last 8 weeks by playing an AIMS Trivia game and were able to earn more tickets that they can trade in shortly.*
  - The Teen Leaders can share any additional details about the discussion and activities in the Teen Group.

- **Graduation Ceremony (8 mins)**

  - *Let's take a moment to celebrate all of the hard work that the teens, with support and guidance from their caregivers, have put in over the last 8 weeks.*

- Leaders should pass out each teen's personalized <u>AIMS Graduation Certificate</u> handout after reflecting on their hard work. Leaders can also share any funny stories or moments from working with the teen.

- **Real World Practice Assignment (4 mins)**

  - Pass out and refer to <u>Real World Practice – Session 8</u> handout.
  - *For your Real World Practice Assignment this week and going forward, you will work with your caregiver on creating your Problem Solving Plan and start working on the solutions that you identify for your problems. Many of you will be working on 3–4 solutions to address EF challenges that affect how you are doing at school or with doing homework and studying for tests.*

    - *After our discussion today, it is possible that you may want to make your solution more specific, clear, and doable and you can also outline this in the plan and expectations for earning the reward section of the Problem Solving Plan.*

  - Ask: *Any questions about your Real World Practice assignment?*
  - *You and your caregiver should set aside time either tonight or tomorrow to create the new Problem Solving Plan so that you have some time to work on it over the next week and get a chance to earn a reward.*

    - *Since you no longer have AIMS sessions, we encourage you to pick a consistent day and time that may work to talk about the Problem Solving Plan and make any changes. Take a minute to discuss when you can complete your Problem Solving Plan with your caregiver.*

  - *In your AIMS binder, take a moment to file your Real World Practice assignment now in the "To Do" side of the folder. You should also take a moment to file all of your other handouts behind the Session 8 divider.*
  - Ask: *Any final questions before we get ready to trade in your tickets for prizes?*

- **Trade in Tickets (2 mins)**

  - The Leader should give all teens who earned a ticket an opportunity to trade them in for prizes using the Prize Menu. This is the last opportunity for teens to use their tickets so they should be encouraged to trade them all in.

AIMS

Session 8 Schedule

Large Group

❏ Review Group Rules and Prize Menu

❏ Review Real World Practice Assignment

❏ Review of Material from Last Session

❏ Goals for Session 8

Teen Group

❏ Modifying Your Problem Solving Plan

❏ Jeopardy Game

Reunification – Large Group

❏ Discussion of Teen Session Material

❏ Graduation Ceremony

❏ Real World Practice Assignment

❏ Trade in Tickets

Problem Solving Plan

Date: _____

Problem Who, What, Where, When, & Why	Solution	EF(s) Being Targeted	Plan and Expectations for Earning Reward	Reward	Reward Earned?
		Getting Started Planning Prioritizing Organizing Working Memory			☐ Monday ☐ Tuesday ☐ Wednesday ☐ Thursday ☐ Friday ☐ Saturday ☐ Sunday
		Getting Started Planning Prioritizing Organizing Working Memory			☐ Monday ☐ Tuesday ☐ Wednesday ☐ Thursday ☐ Friday ☐ Saturday ☐ Sunday

This agreement begins on _____ and we will review the agreement again on _____.

_____
Teen

_____
Parent/Caregiver

Session 8 – Handout 2 – p. 1 of 1

Problem Solving Plan Examples for Using Additional AIMS Strategies

Date: 11/23 – 11/27

Problem Who, What, When, & Why	Solution	EF(s) Being Targeted	Plan and Expectations for Earning Reward	Reward	Reward Earned?
I get overwhelmed by writing essays for language arts and then procrastinate and do it the night before.	Break down my 5-paragraph essay assignment using the Long-Term Assignment Plan.	<u>Getting Started</u> <u>Planning</u> <u>Prioritizing</u> Organizing Working Memory	When an essay is assigned, I will break it down into steps using the Long-Term Assignment Plan with my dad. I will do each step in my planner on that day.	30 minutes of extra screen time each time I complete one step. Choice of ice cream if I complete all of the steps on the Long Term Assignment Plan.	☐ Monday ☐ Tuesday ☐ Wednesday ☐ Thursday ☐ Friday ☐ Saturday ☐ Sunday
I wait until the night before a test to study and then I am not able to study as much as I would like.	Break down the steps for studying 5 days before the test and write each step in my planner.	<u>Getting Started</u> <u>Planning</u> <u>Prioritizing</u> Organizing Working Memory	When a test is announced I will break it down into steps using the Study Plan with my grandma. I will do each study in my planner on that day.	$1 towards a new video game. $3 towards a new video game if I complete all of the steps on the Study Plan.	☐ Monday ☐ Tuesday ☐ Wednesday ☐ Thursday ☐ Friday ☐ Saturday ☐ Sunday

This agreement begins on 11/23 _____ and we will review the agreement again on 11/27 _____.

_____
Teen

_____
Parent/Caregiver

Session 8 – Handout 3 – p. 1 of 2

© 2026 Amie Duncan and Leanne Tamm, *Improving Academic Executive Functioning for Autistic Middle Schoolers*

Problem Solving Plan Examples for Using Additional AIMS Strategies

Date: 11/23 – 11/27

Problem Who, What, Where, When, & Why	Solution	EF(s) Being Targeted	Plan and Expectations for Earning Reward	Reward	Reward Earned?
I have files all over my desktop and I can never find what I need when I need it.	Create a computer organization system with folders and subfolders for each of my classes.	Getting Started _Planning_ Prioritizing _Organizing_ Working Memory	My mom will help me create the folders and then organize all files that are on my desktop. Going forward, I will organize my files into the correct folder. My mom will check my desktop and computer organization system each Sunday at 5pm.	Choice of dinner on Sunday night.	☐ Monday ☐ Tuesday ☐ Wednesday ☐ Thursday ☐ Friday ☐ Saturday ☐ Sunday
I have trouble with book reports and studying for tests and quizzes on books that we have to read for Language Arts.	Use summarizing strategies for book chapters and plot diagrams for entire books.	_Getting Started_ _Planning_ Prioritizing Organizing _Working Memory_	When a book is assigned in Language Arts, I will do a Star Graphic Organizer for each chapter. I will do a plot diagram for the entire book after I have read it. My mom will check it after I complete it.	30 minutes of TV time.	☐ Monday ☐ Tuesday ☐ Wednesday ☐ Thursday ☐ Friday ☐ Saturday ☐ Sunday

This agreement begins on 11/23 _____ and we will review the agreement again on 11/27 _____.

_____
Teen

_____
Parent/Caregiver

Session 8 – Handout 3 – p. 2 of 2

© 2026 Amie Duncan and Leanne Tamm, *Improving Academic Executive Functioning for Autistic Middle Schoolers*

Computer Organization System

How to create folders and subfolders:

1. Make a folder for each of your classes (e.g., "American History" or "Science").

2. Make subfolders for each of your classes. A rule is that you only want 4–6 subfolders. Subfolders might include:

   - Assignments
   - Notes
   - Tests and Quizzes
   - Class Materials (e.g., articles, handouts, study guide)
   - Group Projects
   - Essays.

3. File any files (i.e., documents or class materials) in the appropriate subfolder.

   - Only delete a file if you are absolutely 100% certain that you will not need it in the future.
   - One way to organize files that you do not use anymore is to create a folder titled "Old Files" and put all of the files that you no longer need in this folder.

4. Only keep items on your desktop that you use regularly. Everything else should be filed away.

Rules for Naming Files

- **Use this formula when naming files**:
  Keyword **+** Type of Assignment **+** Date **=** File Name

- Use keywords **for naming files so that you can easily find it in the right folders or when you type in keywords in the search bar!** Keywords **might include the name of a book, the title of a textbook chapter, or the concept that you are learning about.**

- **Abbreviations can be used when creating** keywords, **but it is important that you use abbreviations that you know and will easily remember:**
  - Mockingbird – stands for *To Kill a Mockingbird* book
  - WWII – stands for World War II
  - VocabChap12 – stands for Vocabulary Words in Chapter 12.

- **Put the** type of assignment **after the** keyword.
  - Type of assignments might include a book report, study guide, class notes, essay, presentation, speech, etc.
  - Try to be consistent in labeling the types of assignments!

- **Put the** date **at the end of the file**.
  - When writing the date you want to choose a consistent format such as MMDD, MMDDYY, or MonthYear.

- It can be helpful to put a space or a _ between the keyword, type of assignment, and date.

- **Examples of how to name files**:
  - Mockingbird Book Report 0424
  - Photosynthesis_Study Guide_0315
  - WWII Class Notes Nov13
  - Constitution_Essay_1019

Organizing Email: Tips and Tricks

- **After you read an email, make a plan to (1) reply, (2) file it, or (3) respond at a later time.**

  - Tip: Move emails to their folder or label after you have read them.

- **Create folders or labels to organize your email that are simple and easy to understand.**

  - Tip: Create a folder for each of your classes.
  - Tip: Create folders for your interests or hobbies (e.g., video games, anime, music).

- **Set aside blocks of time (e.g., before and after school) for checking and responding to emails.**

  - Tip: Respond to emails within one day of receiving it (especially if it is from a teacher!).

- **Do not leave junk email sitting in your inbox. Just delete it!**

  - Tip: Unsubscribe from emails that you do not read or do not want!

Long Term Assignment Plan

Assignment: _____

Materials needed: _____

Due Date: _____

Steps (*Be specific and detailed!*)	When will I do it? (*Write this in my planner!*)
1.	
2.	
3.	
4.	
5.	
6.	
7.	
8.	

Session 8 – Handout 7 – p. 1 of 1

Long Term Assignment Plan

Assignment: <u>Complete book report on *To Kill a Mockingbird*</u>

Due Date: <u>Next Friday 2/28</u>   Materials needed: <u>book, laptop, notebook, pencil</u>

Steps *(Be specific and detailed!)*	When will I do it? *(Write this in my planner!)*
1. Finish reading *To Kill a Mockingbird*	Tuesday 2/18
2. Complete a book report outline by writing my ideas for the (1) Introduction, (2) Summary, (3) Characters, (4) Plot, and (5) Conclusion.	Wed 2/19
3. Write Introduction paragraph.	Thursday 2/20
4. Write the Summary paragraph.	Friday 2/21
5. Write the Characters paragraph.	Monday 2/24
6. Write the Plot paragraph.	Tuesday 2/25
7. Write the Conclusion paragraph.	Wed 2/26
8. Revise and edit book report. Print it out and check for spelling and grammar issues.	Thursday 2/27

Study Plan

Test/Quiz: _____ **Date of Test/Quiz:** _____

Possible Study Strategies to Use: _____

	What will I study? (Be specific and detailed!)	What strategies will I use?	When will I do it? (Write this in my planner!)
5 days before			
4 days before			
3 days before			
2 days before			
1 day before			

Session 8 – Handout 9 – p. 1 of 1

Study Plan

Test/Quiz: <u>Science Test on the Water Cycle</u>   **Date of Test/Quiz**: <u>3/19</u>

Possible Study Strategies to Use: study cards, study guide, notes from class, textbook

	What will I study? (*Be specific and detailed!*)	*What strategies will I use?*	*When will I do it?* (*Write this in my planner!*)
5 days before	The process of evaporation, precipitation, condensation, and transportation in the ocean.	Notes from class and my textbook, make 5 study cards	Sun 3/14
4 days before	The process of evaporation, precipitation, condensation, and transportation in and from the mountains.	Notes from class and my textbook, make 5 study cards	Mon 3/15
3 days before	The process of evaporation, precipitation, condensation, and transportation in the lakes and soil.	Notes from class and my textbook, make 5 study cards	Tue 3/16
2 days before	All the water cycle processes.	The study guide from my teacher and make 5 study cards	Wed 3/17
1 daybefore	The complete water cycle.	Study guide and review my 20 study cards	Thur 3/18

Session 8 – Handout 10 – p. 1 of 1

5 Ws

Directions: Read (and re-read if needed!) the paragraph, chapter, or book. After you have underlined 4–7 important words or phrases, create a summary restating the main point that answers the 5 Ws of (1) Who, (2) What, (3) When, (4) Where, and (5) Why.

(1) **Who** was there?

_____

(2) **What** happened?

_____

(3) **When** did it happen?

_____

(4) **Where** did it happen?

_____

(5) **Why** did it happen?

_____

AIMS

Star Graphic Organizer

Directions: Read (and re-read) the paragraph, chapter, or book. After you have underlined 4–7 keywords or phrases, fill in the section on the star for the 5 Ws of (1) Who, (2), What, (3) Where, (4) When, and (5) Why. Any additional information can be placed in the center.

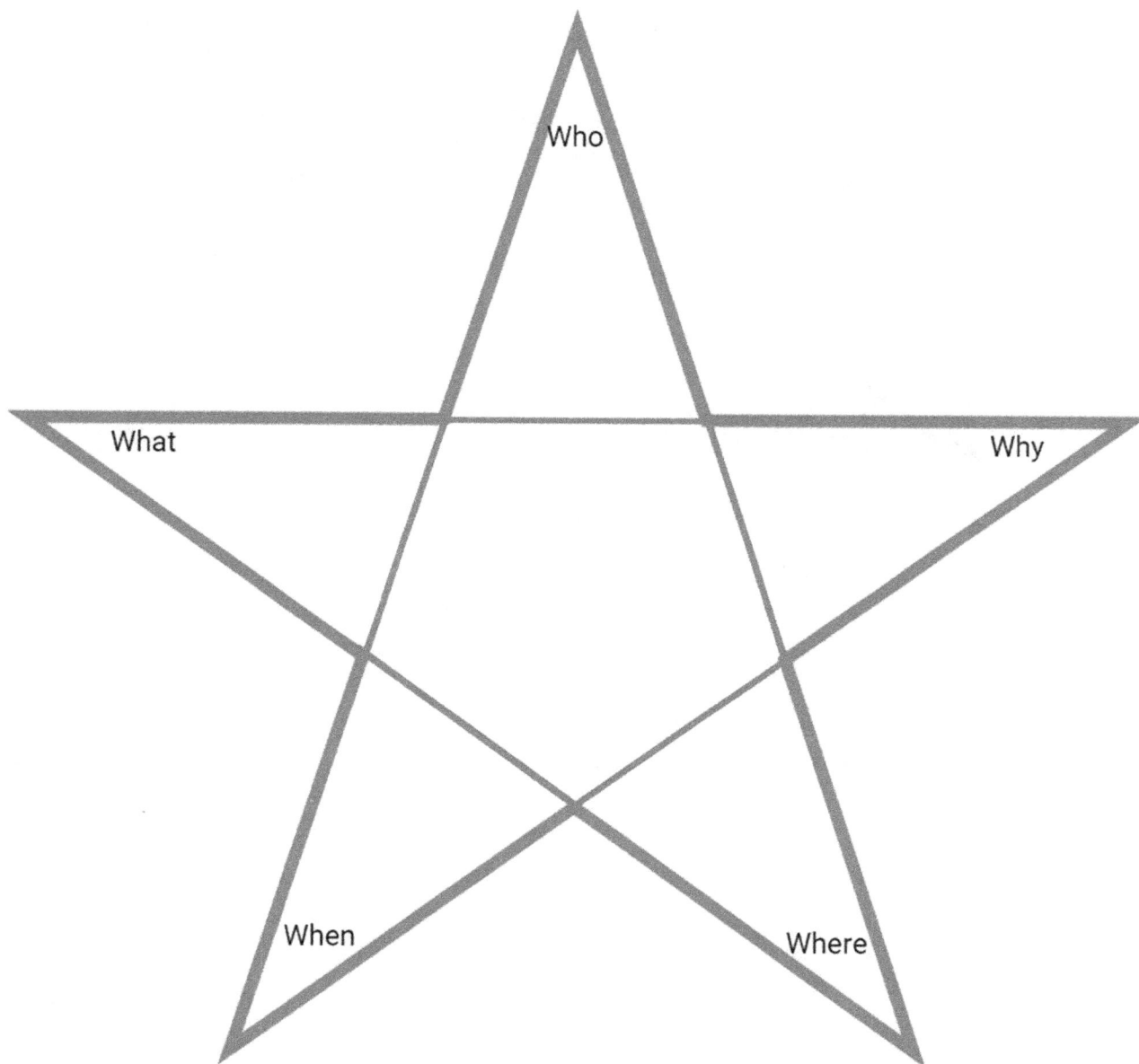

Who

What

Why

When

Where

AIMS

Plot Diagram

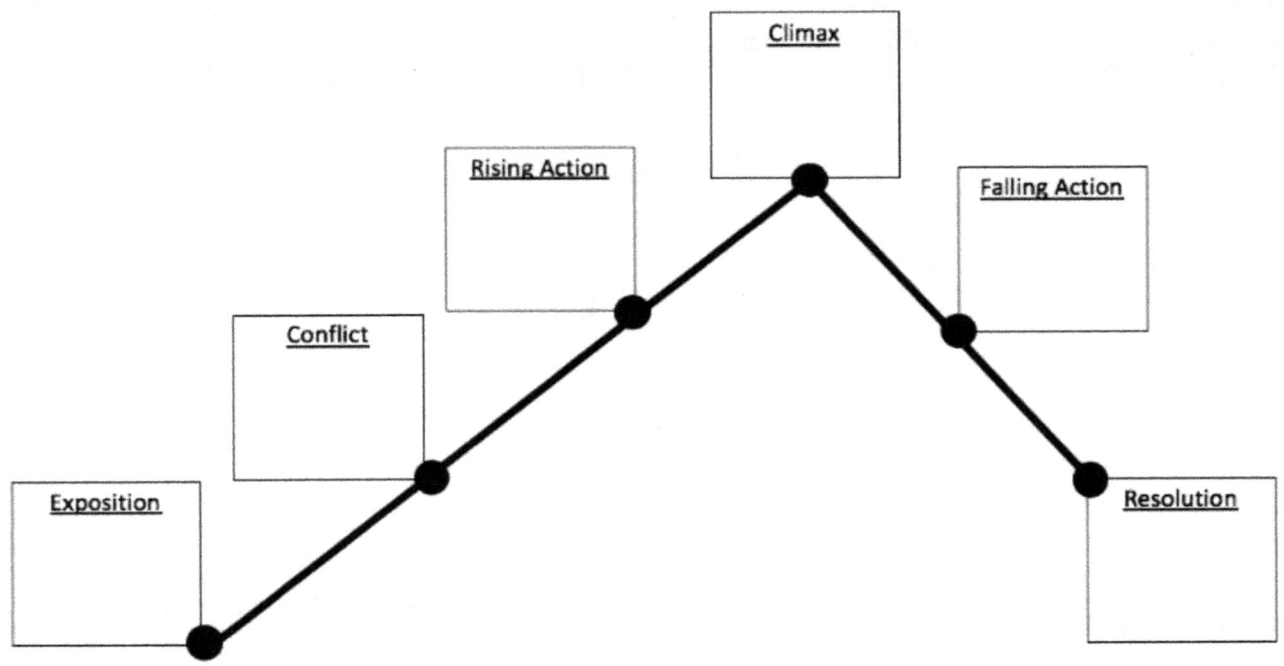

Climax

Rising Action

Falling Action

Conflict

Exposition

Resolution

Storyboard

Exposition

Conflict

Rising Action

Climax

Falling Action

Resolution

School Communication Tips

Below are some tips and recommendations for caregivers to cultivate positive interactions with school personnel (e.g., teachers, special education staff, intervention specialists, etc.).

- **Be purposefully positive in your interactions.**
  - This includes times when interactions with school staff have been frustrating.
  - Try not to focus on blame for why the difficulties are happening. Rather, focus on steps to take to address them and build your teen's independence.

- **Think about the Teachers(s).**
  - Recognize that some of your teen's difficulties may pose challenges for the teacher.
  - The teacher may already be doing things to support your teen in the classroom.
  - Middle school teachers who have been teaching for several years typically report that they have observed an increase in student behavioral challenges.
  - Keep in mind that teachers may not have received much training in their education programs regarding how to address difficulties that autistic youth may have, or how to address executive functioning difficulties in the classroom.

- **Collaborate.**
  - Find ways to partner with the teacher and show that you want to help the teacher, rather than focusing on asking the teacher to help your teen.
    - "I'd like to find ways to build my teens independence so we can help you spend more time with the other students in the classroom and less time with my teen."
    - "We are hoping that signing Nina's planner at the end of class will ultimately allow you to spend less time managing the issues related to her missing assignments and more time with all the other students in the classroom."
  - Present your knowledge about and experience with your teen in a manner that is helpful and productive rather than only to demonstrate that you know what you are talking about.

- **Be patient, but persistent.**
  - Check with the teacher to determine their preferred method of follow-up conversation (e.g., in-person, phone, email).

- **Highlight what steps you are doing at home.**
  - Highlight for the teacher the steps you are taking at home to support what they are doing at school so the teacher understands your level of investment.
    - "We have setup a home reward system where Sam can earn time on the computer for each social studies study card she makes."
    - "We have setup a home reward system where Leo can earn time playing video games for each teacher signature he receives in his planner."

- **Make your teen part of the solution**.
- If you are asking the teacher to do something (e.g., sign the student's planner), explicitly discuss how the student will also take responsibility (e.g., the student brings the planner to the teacher to be signed).

- **Show your gratitude**.
  - Find ways to let the teacher know you value the extra effort (e.g., thank you note, email to express appreciation, gift card, etc.).

Moving Forward After AIMS

1. Continue to Use the Problem Solving Plan.

- The Problem Solving Plan is meant to be a tool that you can continue to use after AIMS to monitor and modify solutions to address a teen's EF challenges.
- It takes a long time for a solution to become a habit. Keep a Problem Solving Plan in place for 2–3 months so that the solution can become a consistent routine that the teen can independently do.
- Teens should be able to state the details of their Problem Solving Plan because this ensures that they know what they are supposed to do.

  - If teens are not aware that they agreed to do something, then they are much less likely to do it or be successful.

- The teen's solution and plan for earning the reward should be specific, detailed, and doable.
- Continue to reward teens as they work on implementing solutions.

  - Rewards should be tangible (e.g., put money into an electronic bank account that they can check, give a paper IOU if you cannot give a physical reward, have a visual chart that shows a long-term reward that they are working towards).
  - Provide verbal praise and encouragement as teens work towards using strategies and skills for their academic and EF challenges.

- Have weekly check-ins (similar to what you have been doing) to:

  - Discuss overall progress with solutions
  - Discuss any obstacles and brainstorm how to address them (e.g., increase check-ins, modify plan)
  - Discuss whether any rewards need to be changed
  - Celebrate successes.

2. **Modify Solutions and/or Add New Solution(s) to the Problem Solving Plan**.

- Think about adding a new solution to the Problem Solving Plan when:

  - Teen has been successful with a solution and is consistently following the specified plan for earning a reward.

    - Depending on frequency of the solution (daily vs. weekly) it could take weeks or months for a solution to be mastered.

  - Caregiver and teen have the time and energy to commit to working on another solution that targets a challenge.

- Prioritize new solutions that will have a lasting impact by improving academic performance and independence with homework and studying.

- Consider modifying current solutions by targeting teen's accuracy.

  - Must follow the plans and expectations exactly to earn a reward (e.g., start homework by 4pm and not 4:45pm).

  - Require accuracy of at least 80% to earn a reward (e.g., correctly write down 80% of assignments in planner).

3. Fade Rewards

- You should not remove or decrease any rewards your teen has been earning <u>until they have truly mastered using a solution on the Problem Solving Plan.</u>
- When your teen has mastered a solution and you feel it is time to start fading a reward, here are some helpful steps:

  - Schedule a specific time to have a conversation about the solution and reward (e.g., during the weekly check-in).
  - Remain calm and neutral during the discussion with your teen – it is a big deal that they have mastered a solution!
  - Allow the teen to ask questions (especially if this is the first time a reward has been faded!).
  - State that they seem like they are now ready to start doing the solution on their own without earning a reward.
  - Note that it is still expected that the teen do the solution even though they are not being rewarded.

    - Provide examples of skills the teen (e.g., brushing teeth, feeding the dog, taking vitamins) or caregiver (e.g., cooking meals, paying bills, mopping, cutting grass) does without being rewarded.
    - Discuss that as they get older and become more independent the teen will be expected to do things that they do not receive a reward for.

  - Discuss how to make sure the teen continues to be successful with mastered solution they are not being rewarded for (e.g., discuss mastered solutions in weekly check-ins, continue to track mastered goals on Problem Solving Plan).
  - Discuss any additional incentives for mastered solutions (e.g., can earn a weekly bonus if teen does all the solutions (including mastered solutions) on their Problem Solving Plan.

Real World Practice – Session 8

- Work with your caregiver to modify your Problem Solving Plan and continue working on the solutions that you identify for the problems. After our discussion today, it is possible that you may want to make your solution more specific, clear, and doable, and you can also outline this in the Plan and Expectations for Earning the Reward section of the Problem Solving Plan. Over the next week, you should do the following:

  - Add on any solutions that would help you with any of your problems related to organization of materials, planning and prioritizing assignments and tests, studying for tests, and getting started on schoolwork.
  - Continue working on any solutions from your previous Problem Solving Plan.

Problem Solving Plan

Date: _____

Problem Who, What, Where, When, & Why	Solution	EF(s) Being Targeted	Plan and Expectations for Earning Reward	Reward	Reward Earned?
		☐ Getting Started ☐ Planning ☐ Prioritizing ☐ Organizing ☐ Working Memory			☐ Monday ☐ Tuesday ☐ Wednesday ☐ Thursday ☐ Friday ☐ Saturday ☐ Sunday
		☐ Getting Started ☐ Planning ☐ Prioritizing ☐ Organizing ☐ Working Memory			☐ Monday ☐ Tuesday ☐ Wednesday ☐ Thursday ☐ Friday ☐ Saturday ☐ Sunday

This agreement begins on _____ and we will review the agreement again on _____

_____
Parent/Caregiver

_____
Teen

Problem Solving Plan

Date: _____

Problem Who, What, Where, When, & Why	Solution	EF(s) Being Targeted	Plan and Expectations for Earning Reward	Reward	Reward Earned?
		Getting Started Planning Prioritizing Organizing Working Memory			☐ Monday ☐ Tuesday ☐ Wednesday ☐ Thursday ☐ Friday ☐ Saturday ☐ Sunday
		Getting Started Planning Prioritizing Organizing Working Memory			☐ Monday ☐ Tuesday ☐ Wednesday ☐ Thursday ☐ Friday ☐ Saturday ☐ Sunday

This agreement begins on _____ and we will review the agreement again on _____.

_____
Teen

_____
Parent/Caregiver

Problem Solving Plan

Date: _____

Problem Who, What, Where, When, & Why	Solution	EF(s) Being Targeted	Plan and Expectations for Earning Reward	Reward	Reward Earned?
		Getting Started Planning Prioritizing Organizing Working Memory			☐ Monday ☐ Tuesday ☐ Wednesday ☐ Thursday ☐ Friday ☐ Saturday ☐ Sunday
		Getting Started Planning Prioritizing Organizing Working Memory			☐ Monday ☐ Tuesday ☐ Wednesday ☐ Thursday ☐ Friday ☐ Saturday ☐ Sunday

This agreement begins on _____ and we will review the agreement again on _____ .

_____
Teen

_____
Parent/Caregiver

References

Cannon, L., Kenworthy, L., Alexander, K., Werner, M., & Anthony, L. G. (2021). *Unstuck and On Target!: An Executive Function Curriculum to Improve Flexibility, Planning, and Organization* (2nd ed.). Brookes Publishing.

Duncan, A., Evans, A., Vaughn, A. & Tamm, L. (2025). An in-depth examination of learning behaviors in autistic middle-schoolers without intellectual disability. *Psychology in the Schools*, 62(5), 1383–1396. doi: 10.1002/pits.23406

Duncan, A., Risley, S., Combs, A., Lacey, H.M., Hamik, E., Fershtman, C., Kneeskern, E., Patel, M., Crosby, L., Hood, A., Zoromski, A.K., Tamm, L. (2023). School challenges and services related to executive functioning for fully included middle schoolers with autism. *Focus on Autism and Other Developmental Disabilities*, 38(2), 90–100. doi: 10.1177/10883576221110167

Laugeson, E. A. (2013). *The PEERS Curriculum for School-Based Professionals: Social Skills Training for Adolescents with Autism Spectrum Disorder*. Routledge.

Tamm, L., Duncan, A., Vaughn, A.J., McDade, R., Estell, N., Birnschein, A., & Crosby, L. (2020a). Academic needs in middle school: Perspectives of parents and youth with Autism. *Journal of Autism and Developmental Disorders*, 50(9), 3126–3139. doi:10.1007/s10803-019-03995-1

Tamm, L., Hamik, E., Yeung, T.S., Zoromski, A.K., Mara, C.A., & Duncan, A. (2023). Achieving Independence & Mastery in School: A school-based executive function group intervention for autistic middle schoolers. *Journal of Autism and Developmental Disorders*, 54, 4357–4368. doi: 10.1007/s10803-023-06164-7

Tamm, L., Hamik, E.M., Zoromski, A.K., & Duncan, A. (2024a). Use of the Weekly Calendar Planning Activity to assess executive functioning in autistic adolescents. *American Journal of Occupational Therapy*, 78(1), 7801205040. doi: 10.5014/ajot.2024.050295

Tamm, L., Risley, S.M., Hamik, E., Combs, A., Jones, L.B., Patronick, J., Yeung, T.S., Zoromski, A.K., & Duncan, A. (2024b). Improving academic performance through a school-based intervention targeting academic executive functions – A pilot study. *International Journal of Developmental Disabilities*, 70(3), 549–557. doi: 10.1080/20473869.2022.2095690

Tamm, L., Zoromski, A.K., Kneeskern, E.E., Patel, M.D., Lacey, H.M., Vaughn, A.J., Ciesielski, H.A., Weadick, H.K., & Duncan, A. (2020b). Achieving Independence and Mastery in School: An open trial in the outpatient setting. *Journal of Autism and Developmental Disorders*, 51(5), 1705–1718. doi: 10.1007/s10803-020-04652-8

Leader Materials

- Prize Menu
- Prize Menu Example
- Ticket Savings Tracker
- Real World Practice Tracker
- Blank handouts from AIMS Sessions

  - Problem Solving Plan
  - Long Term Assignment Plan
  - Study Plan
  - 5 Ws
  - Star Graphic Organizer
  - Plot Diagram
  - Storyboard

- AIMS Evaluation Form
- AIMS Trivia Game Instructions for Leaders
- Graduation Certificate
- Games for AIMS sessions

  - Stack Attack
  - Penny Stack
  - Suck it Up

AIMS	Prize Menu
Tickets	Prize(s)

Prize Menu Example

AIMS	Prize Menu
Tickets	Prize(s)
2	small snack/treat eraser
6	mechanical pencil notepad
10	small sketchpad post-it notes
16	pencil case highlighter
24	set of colored pencils Rubik's cube DOS card game

Ticket Savings Tracker

Session Number

Teen	1	2	3	4	5	6	7	8

Real World Practice Tracker

Session Number

Teen	1	2	3	4	5	6	7	8

Problem Solving Plan

Date: _____

Problem Who, What, Where, When, & Why	Solution	EF(s) Being Targeted	Plan and Expectations for Earning Reward	Reward	Reward Earned?
		Getting Started Planning Prioritizing Organizing Working Memory			☐ Monday ☐ Tuesday ☐ Wednesday ☐ Thursday ☐ Friday ☐ Saturday ☐ Sunday
		Getting Started Planning Prioritizing Organizing Working Memory			☐ Monday ☐ Tuesday ☐ Wednesday ☐ Thursday ☐ Friday ☐ Saturday ☐ Sunday

This agreement begins on _____ and we will review the agreement again on _____.

Teen _____

Parent/Caregiver _____

Long Term Assignment Plan

Assignment: _____

Due Date: _____

Steps (Be detailed and specific!)	How much time will it take?	When will you do it?
1.		
2.		
3.		
4.		
5.		
6.		
7.		
8.		

Study Plan

Test/Quiz: _____   **Date of Test/Quiz:** _____

Possible Strategies to Use: _____

Day	What will you study? (Be specific and detailed!)	What strategies will you use?	How long will you study for?
5 days before			
4 days before			
3 days before			
2 days before			
1 day before			

5 Ws

Directions: Read (and re-read if needed!) the paragraph, chapter, or book. After you have underlined 4–7 important words or phrases, create a summary restating the main point that answers the 5 Ws of (1) Who, (2) What, (3) When, (4) Where, and (5) Why.

1 Who was there?

_____

2 What happened?

_____

3 When did it happen?

_____

4 Where did it happen?

_____

5 Why did it happen?

_____

Star Graphic Organizer

Directions: Read (and re-read) the paragraph, chapter, or book. After you have underlined 4-7 keywords or phrases, fill in the section on the star for the 5 Ws of (1) Who, (2), What, (3) Where, (4) When, and (5) Why. Any additional information can be placed in the

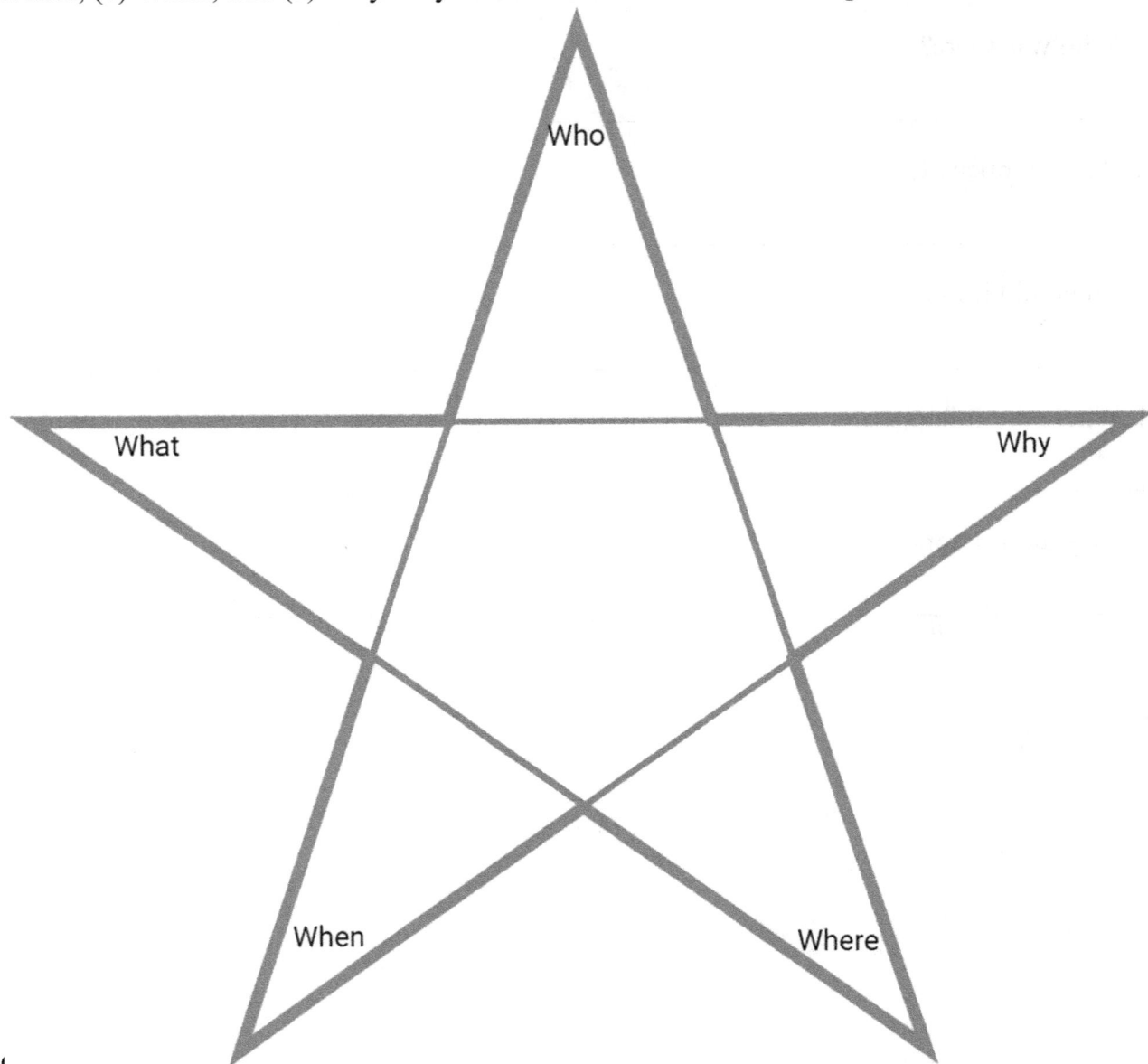

Who

What

Why

When

Where

Plot Diagram

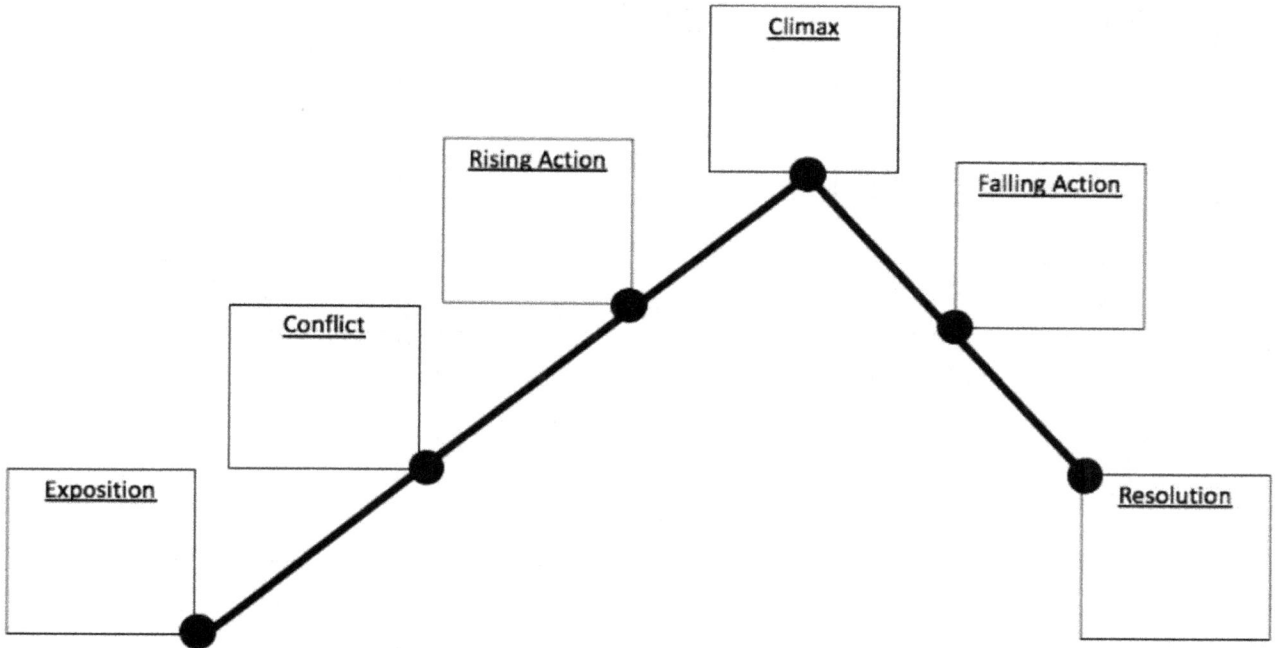

Storyboard

Exposition

Conflict

Rising Action

Climax

Falling Action

Resolution

AIMS Evaluation Form

Name: _____

Date:_____

1. How helpful do you think the information you learned in AIMS will be?

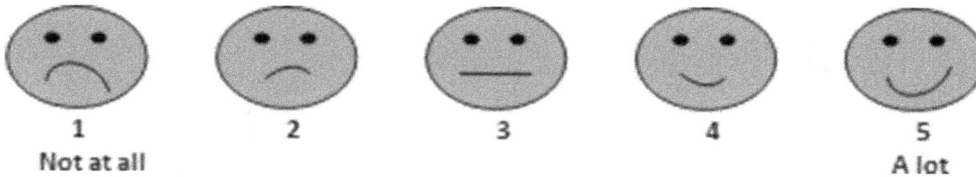

1	2	3	4	5
Not at all				A lot

2. How well do you understand that organization, planning, prioritizing, working memory, and getting started can cause problems with school and homework?

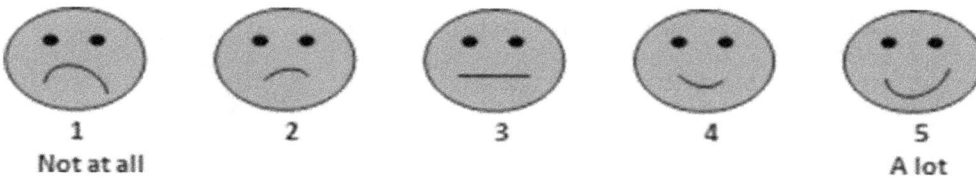

1	2	3	4	5
Not at all				A lot

3. How well do you understand what an executive function (EF) is?

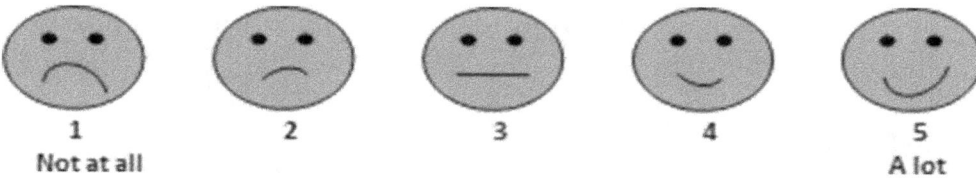

1	2	3	4	5
Not at all				A lot

4. How well do you understand what your academic strengths and challenges are?

1	2	3	4	5
Not at all				A lot

5. How well do you understand how to solve problems?

1	2	3	4	5
Not at all				A lot

6. How well do you understand how to set up a homework system (e.g., consistent space with your supplies, distraction free)?

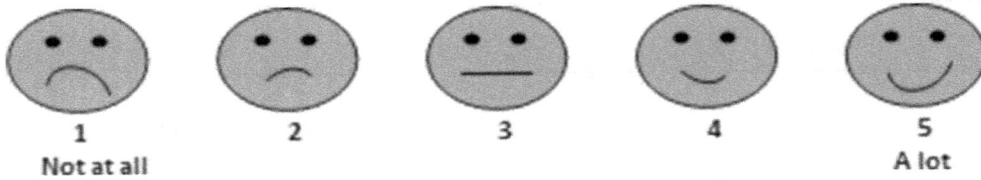

1	2	3	4	5
Not at all				A lot

7. How well do you understand how to organize your binder?

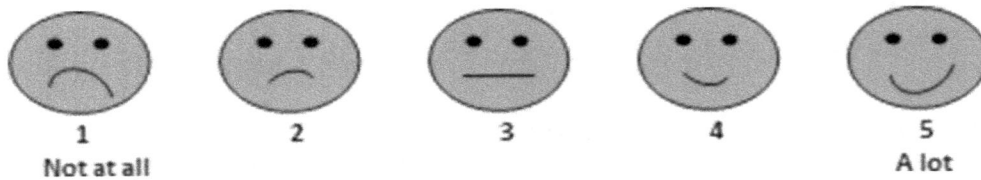

1	2	3	4	5
Not at all				A lot

8. How well do you understand how to organize your backpack?

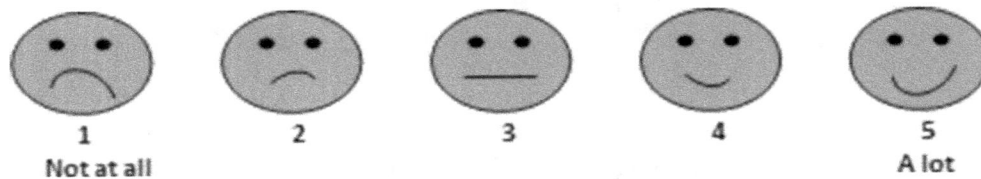

1	2	3	4	5
Not at all				A lot

9. How well do you understand how to write down your assignments using a planner?

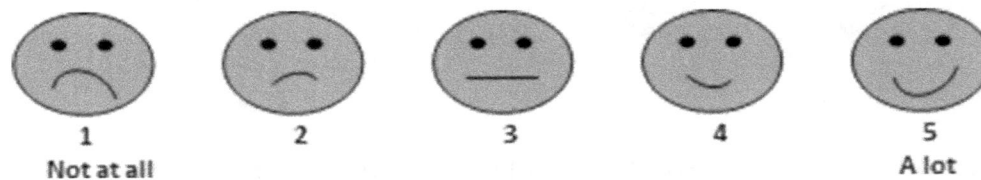

1	2	3	4	5
Not at all				A lot

10. How well do you understand how to prioritize your assignments using a planner?

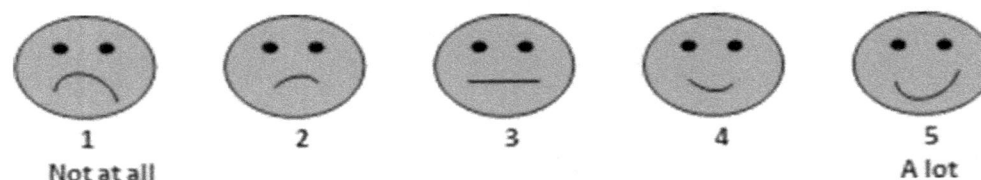

1	2	3	4	5
Not at all				A lot

11. How well do you understand that there are many effective study strategies you can utilize to do well on tests and quizzes?

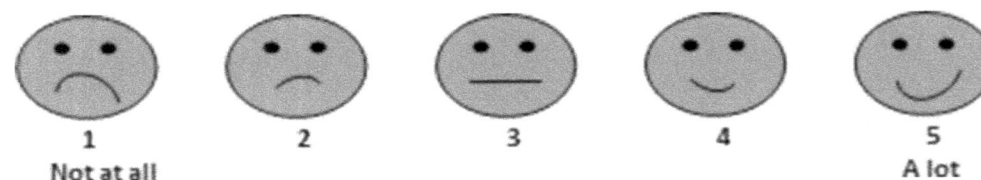

1	2	3	4	5
Not at all				A lot

12. How well do you understand how to make study cards?

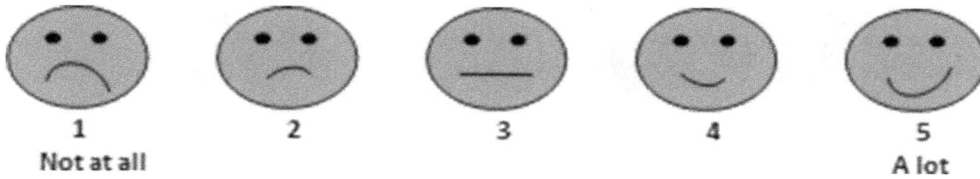

1	2	3	4	5
Not at all				A lot

13. How well do you understand how to make and use a Problem Solving Plan?

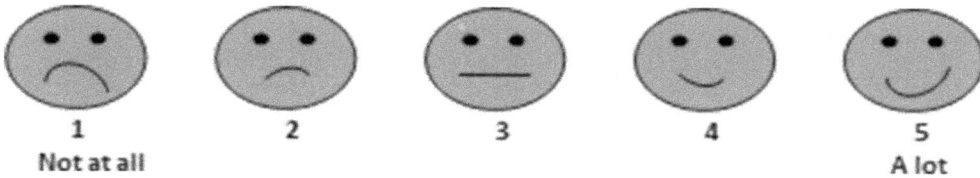

1	2	3	4	5
Not at all				A lot

14. How much did you like the handouts?

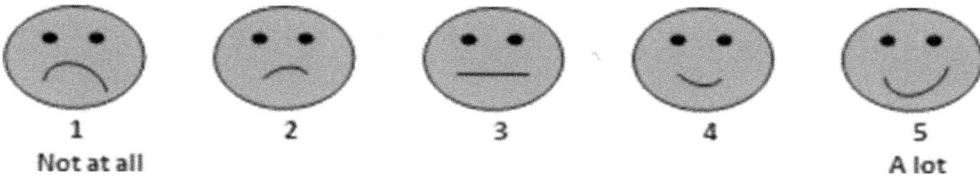

1	2	3	4	5
Not at all				A lot

15. How much did you like the videos?

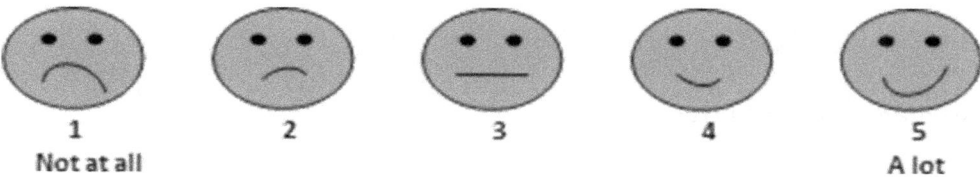

1	2	3	4	5
Not at all				A lot

16. How much did you like the activities/games?

1	2	3	4	5
Not at all				A lot

17. How much do you think you will use the information you learned in AIMS in the future?

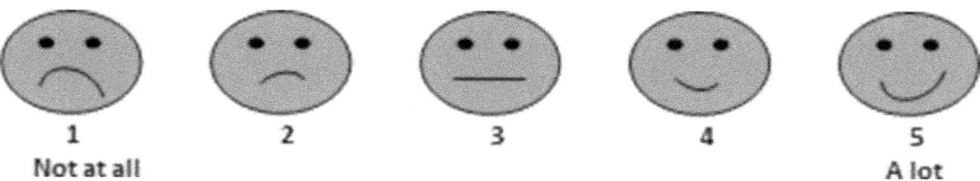

1	2	3	4	5
Not at all				A lot

18. How confident do you feel about using a Problem Solving Plan after AIMS is over?

1	2	3	4	5
Not at all				A lot

What was your favorite part of AIMS?

What was your least favorite part of AIMS?

What did you learn from AIMS?

What could we do to make AIMS better?

AIMS Trivia Instructions for Leaders

Instructions: Use the categories with pre-set questions and answers to create a trivia game for the teens in Session 8. AIMS Leaders have several different options for facilitating the AIMS Trivia game including: (1) putting the categories and monetary value on a white board or large post-it and then taking turns asking each teen to choose and then answer a question; (2) having the teens work in small groups to choose and then answer a question; and (3) using a PowerPoint template to create an interactive trivia game that can be displaying using the projector for teens to play individually or in small groups. Leaders can reward teens with tickets at the end of the game (e.g., the winner of AIMS Trivia gets 5 tickets and everyone else gets 2–3 tickets). Leaders should be flexible and should aim to make the AIMS Trivia game fun and enjoyable for teens as they review key AIMS concepts.

	Executive Functions	Study Strategies	ABCs of Problem Solving	Planning, Prioritizing, & Organization	Problem Solving Plan
$100	Q: Examples of these are planning, prioritizing, working memory, getting started, and organization. A: What are Executive Functions (EF)?	Q: This is the number of chunks of information that the average brain can recall at one time. A: What is 4–7?	Q: Think of as many solutions to a problem as you can – more is better! A: What is B: Brainstorm Solutions?	Q: This is how you prioritize assignments in your planner. A: What is numbering the assignments?	Q: Problem, Solution, Plan and Expectations for Earning the Reward, EFs being targeted, Reward, Checklist for earning reward, When it begins and ends, and Signatures A: What are the parts of the Problem Solving Plan?
$200	Q: This is the EF that helps you stop procrastinating before beginning a task. A: What is getting started?	Q: Better than using flashcards, this study strategy helps information to stick in your brain so that you can memorize terms faster by writing down 4–7 keywords on a notecard. A: What are Study Cards?	Q: Identify the pros and cons to a list of solutions and select one or two to try. A: What is the C: Choose Solution step?	Q: These are 3 things you should write down and prioritize in your planner. A: What are: 1. Homework? 2. Projects? 3. Tests? 4. Quizzes? 5. Long-term assignments? (any three)	Q: Helps you identify solutions to help target a problem; Allows you to earn a reward; May increase independence; May lead to better grades. A: What are the benefits of using a Problem Solving Plan?
$300	Q: This is the EF that helps make sure that you can find materials in your binder and backpack. A: What is organization?	Q: This is the name of your favorite study strategy. A: What is (any study strategy)? – Textbooks – Notes – Study guides – Practice tests – Songs – Acronyms – Acrostics – Study cards – WH-questions – Star graphic organizers – Plot diagrams – Storyboards	Q: Ask whether the solution worked. A: What is E: Evaluate?	Q: This is one thing you can do to keep your binder organized. A: What is (any part of binder organization system)? - Pencil case - Homework folder - Subject dividers - Notebooks - Class schedule - Class folders	Q: Screen time, staying up 30 minutes later, extra dessert, money, and game night. A: What are examples of rewards that can be earned on a Problem Solving Plan?

$400	Q: This is the EF where you choose and then order the most important information over less important information. A: What is prioritizing?	Q: This is the name of the process where you create study cards that increases the likelihood the concepts will stick in your brain. A: What is the "Stickiness Factor?"	Q: The questions Who?, What?, When?, Where?, and Why? can be helpful to ask at this step. A: What is A: Aim Identify the Problem?	Q: Name 2 factors you consider when prioritizing assignments. A: What are: 1. Easiness? 2. Difficulty? 3. Length? 4. Favorite subjects? 5. Least favorite subjects? 6. Have to do vs. Want to do? (any two)	Q: May include a binder organization system, using a planner, or setting up a homework system. A: What is the solution on a Problem Solving Plan?
$500	Q: This is the EF where you keep things in mind while you need to use them. A: What is working memory?	Q: These are 3 out of the 5 steps of making a study card. A: What are: 1. Read and reread? 2. Underline or highlight keywords? 3. Write the term you want to study on the front? 4. Write the 4–7 keywords on the back? 5. Review study cards? (any three)	Q: A Problem Solving Plan can be used for this step. A: What is D: Do It?	Q: These are 2 reasons why it is important to use a binder organization system. A: What are: 1. Keeping all classroom materials organized? 2. Finding classroom materials for each class more easily? 3. Having access to your planner/assignment notebook in each class to write down assignments/tests/quizzes? 4. Having a consistent place to put homework (to do & to turn in)? (any two)	Q: May come from the Aim: Identify the Problem from the ABCs of Problem Solving. A: What is the problem on the Problem Solving Plan?

Final Question: These are the 5 Executive Functions that were discussed during the AIMS intervention.
Final Answer: What is Planning, Prioritizing, Organization, Getting Started, and Working Memory?

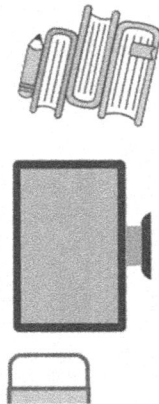

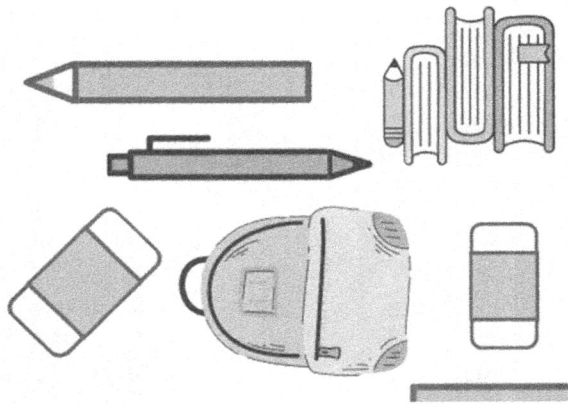

CERTIFICATE OF ACHIEVEMENT

This acknowledges that

_____

Has successfully completed the

Achieving Independence and Mastery in School Program

AIMS

ACHIEVING INDEPENDENCE
and MASTERY *in* SCHOOL
Academic Success is for Everyone

Stack Attack Instructions

- Each person will be given **28 cups**.
- Make a pyramid with:

  - 7 cups on the bottom row
  - 6 in the next row
  - 5 cups on the next row
  - 4 in the row after that
  - 3 cups in the row after that
  - 2 in the next row, until
  - 1 cup left at the top.

Make a pyramid and then unstack the pyramid **in under one minute with only one hand (one hand needs to remain behind your back at all times!).** Whoever completes the pyramid, unstacks the pyramid, and then stacks the cups back into the original position first (and within one minute) wins the game!

Penny Stack Instructions

You will have 60 seconds to create a stack of pennies **using only one hand!**

Whoever has the biggest stack of pennies wins!

Suck it Up Instructions

The goal is to move the candy from one plate to the other using only a straw.

- You each will be given 1 straw and some Smarties.
- There will be two different plates on the table.

Whoever can move the most smarties from one plate to the other plate in one minute wins!

Index

For Product Safety Concerns and Information please contact our EU
representative GPSR@taylorandfrancis.com
Taylor & Francis Verlag GmbH, Kaufingerstraße 24, 80331 München, Germany

www.ingramcontent.com/pod-product-compliance
Lightning Source LLC
Chambersburg PA
CBHW081737270326
41932CB00020B/3300